PENGUIN CLASSICS

THE ROOSEVELT I KNEW

FRANCES PERKINS began her career in social work at Hull House and continued on this path, leading to a master's degree in social work from Columbia University in 1910. Before President Roosevelt chose her as secretary of labor in 1933, she had worked with him for many years in Albany and had served in various public capacities, including executive secretary of the National Consumers League, 1910–12; lecturer in sociology, Adelphi College, 1911–12; director of investigations, New York State Factory Commission, 1912–13; commissioner, New York State Industrial Commission, 1919–21; member of the New York State Industrial Board, 1923–29, becoming the board's chairwoman in 1926; and then industrial commissioner of the State of New York, 1929–32. In 1933 she was awarded the medal "for eminent achievement" by the American Women's Association. From 1933 until she resigned as secretary of labor in May 1945, she served the president on many industrial and economic agencies. In October 1945, she went to Paris as a member of the U.S. delegation to the International Labor Organization Conference. She was the author of several books in the labor field, including *People at Work* and *A Social Experiment under the Workmen's Compensation Jurisdiction.*

ADAM COHEN, the author of *Nothing to Fear: FDR's Inner Circle and the Hundred Days That Created Modern America,* teaches at Yale Law School.

FRANCES PERKINS

The Roosevelt
I Knew

Introduction by
ADAM COHEN

PENGUIN BOOKS

PENGUIN BOOKS
Published by the Penguin Group
Penguin Group (USA) Inc., 375 Hudson Street, New York, New York 10014, U.S.A.
Penguin Group (Canada), 90 Eglinton Avenue East, Suite 700, Toronto, Ontario, Canada
M4P 2Y3 (a division of Pearson Penguin Canada Inc.)
Penguin Books Ltd, 80 Strand, London WC2R 0RL, England
Penguin Ireland, 25 St Stephen's Green, Dublin 2, Ireland (a division of Penguin Books Ltd)
Penguin Group (Australia), 250 Camberwell Road, Camberwell, Victoria 3124, Australia
(a division of Pearson Australia Group Pty Ltd)
Penguin Books India Pvt Ltd, 11 Community Centre, Panchsheel Park, New Delhi - 110 017, India
Penguin Group (NZ), 67 Apollo Drive, Rosedale, Auckland 0632, New Zealand (a division of Pearson
New Zealand Ltd)
Penguin Books (South Africa) (Pty) Ltd, 24 Sturdee Avenue, Rosebank, Johannesburg 2196,
South Africa

Penguin Books Ltd, Registered Offices:
80 Strand, London WC2R 0RL, England

First published in the United States of America by The Viking Press 1946
This edition with an introduction by Adam Cohen published in Penguin Books 2011

A portion of this book appeared serially in *Collier's*.

For editorial and critical assistance in the preparation of this book the author acknowledges a deep
debt to Mr. Howard Taubman of *The New York Times*.

LIBRARY OF CONGRESS CATALOGING-IN-PUBLICATION DATA
Perkins, Frances, 1880–1965.
The Roosevelt I knew / Frances Perkins ; introduction by Adam Cohen.
p. cm.
Includes index.
Originally published: New York : Viking Press, 1946. With new introd.
ISBN 978-0-14-310641-8
1. Roosevelt, Franklin D. (Franklin Delano), 1882–1945. 2. Roosevelt, Franklin D. (Franklin
Delano), 1882–1945—Friends and associates. 3. United States—Politics and government—1933–1945.
4. Presidents—United States—Biography. 5. Perkins, Frances, 1880–1965. I. Cohen, Adam (Adam
Seth) II. Title.
E807.P4 2011
973.917092—dc22
[B] 2011007576

Set in Sabon

Contents

PART FOUR:
THE WORLD

Introduction

If American history textbooks accurately reflected the past, Frances Perkins would be recognized as one of the nation's greatest heroes—as iconic as Benjamin Franklin or Thomas Paine. Like Franklin, Perkins was a brilliant self-creation: There had not been anyone like her before and there has not been anyone like her since. Like Paine, Perkins helped to start a revolution.

Francis Perkins was Franklin Delano Roosevelt's secretary of labor, and the first woman ever to serve in a presidential cabinet. She was also one of the key architects of the New Deal, the ambitious series of programs initiated by the federal government in the 1930s. The New Deal was Perkins's revolution, and it did nothing less than create modern America.

When Perkins arrived in the capital in 1933, the Great Depression was at its darkest. The stock market had fallen 85 percent, and one quarter of the workforce was unemployed. Every state had declared a "bank holiday," officially closing the banks. President Herbert Hoover had largely stood by, allowing the free market and private charity to respond to the economic cataclysm.

The federal government had historically done little more than defend the country and deliver the mail. That changed dramatically during the Roosevelt years. A large and dynamic federal government emerged—one that helped the jobless provide for themselves and their families, ensured that the elderly had enough to live on, ran programs that allowed struggling farmers and homeowners to stay on their property, and generally intervened when people could not make it on their own.

This extraordinary national transformation arose in large

part out of the unique partnership between Roosevelt and Perkins. They were, in many ways, an unlikely pair. Roosevelt was a Harvard-educated patrician who had coasted to political success on personal charm, inherited wealth, and his familial connection to Theodore Roosevelt. Perkins had been born into more modest circumstances and earned her success by hard work and perseverance. Roosevelt was a shrewd politician, adept at the art of the practical. Perkins was an idealist who fought for broad principles and was prone to talk, as one profile of her observed, "like an editorial in *The Survey*," the national social-work magazine.

Perkins was born into a conservative middle-class family in Worcester, Massachusetts. She was a talented student with a curious mind. At a time when few girls pursued higher education, Perkins left home to attend nearby Mount Holyoke College. She had been raised to believe that poor people were largely responsible for their troubles, but a favorite college professor gave her a different perspective. The professor's influence, and a visit from the founder of the National Consumers League, helped persuade Perkins to become a social reformer.

Perkins's father believed the only acceptable career for a proper young woman was teaching. To placate him, Perkins took a job at a private school in Lake Forest, Illinois. Once she was out from under her parents' watchful gaze, she began spending her free time at Hull House, the settlement house Jane Addams ran in a poor immigrant neighborhood of Chicago. Perkins was introduced to tenement living conditions, labor organizing, and a cadre of people who were dedicated to improving the lives of the poor.

Perkins had found her calling. She took a job in Philadelphia with a reform group that studied the poor and provided aid to them. One of her duties was assisting with one of the group's grittier services—meeting immigrant women who arrived by boat and helping to ensure that they were not lured into prostitution by the unsavory men who waited at the docks.

From Philadelphia, Perkins moved to New York. She earned a master's degree in social work from Columbia University and took a job with the National Consumers League, a leading reform group fighting for the rights of working people. Perkins spent much of her time in Albany trying to persuade a largely hostile state legislature to adopt pro-worker legislation, including a maximum-hours law for women. She also became one of the nation's leading experts on factory safety.

On March 25, 1911, Perkins was having tea with a friend on Washington Square when a butler announced that there was a fire. Perkins rushed to a nearby factory building and witnessed the Triangle Shirtwaist fire as it happened. She watched as factory girls, unable to escape or to stand the heat of the flames, jumped to their deaths.

With the city grieving for 146 workers who lost their lives, the causes Perkins had been fighting for had a new urgency. The Triangle Shirtwaist fire was "a torch that lighted up the whole industrial scene," Perkins would later say. Two blue-ribbon commissions were established to investigate factory safety, and Perkins worked with both of them. The outrage stirred by the fire helped Perkins win passage of the main bill she had been fighting for, a law limiting women's workweeks to fifty-four hours.

On her visits to Albany, Perkins had been able to persuade many legislators to back her cause. One new state senator, however, resisted her appeals. Franklin Roosevelt, who had just been elected from rural upstate New York, voted for the bill in the end, but he would not publicly support it or help lobby his colleagues. Perkins was not all that surprised. They had traveled in the same social circles in Manhattan, and Roosevelt had struck her as something of a spoiled aristocrat who lacked compassion for those who were less well off.

As a young woman in New York City, Perkins struck a remarkably modern figure. She socialized with bohemians in Greenwich Village and got to know many notable figures, from the novelist Sinclair Lewis to young Winston Churchill. Perkins freely told friends that she did not intend to marry. When she changed her mind and accepted a proposal from Paul Wilson, a promising young municipal reformer from an affluent family, they married in a small ceremony with no family present, and she insisted on keeping her name.

Perkins's career took a sharp turn in 1919, when Al Smith became governor of New York. Smith had gotten to know Perkins when he served as vice chairman of one of the commissions investigating the Triangle Shirtwaist fire, and he had been impressed by her knowledge and passion for working people. Smith appointed Perkins to a seat on the state Industrial Commission. It marked the end of her career as an outside lobbyist and the beginning of her life as a government official.

The appointment was a breakthrough for women, who had only just won the right to vote. It was also a bold choice because Perkins was so clearly identified with the battle for workers' rights. Perkins's focus as commissioner was workers' compensation, and she fought to make sure that working people who were injured on the job had a fair chance to make their case and get the money they were entitled to.

Al Smith was the Democratic nominee for president in 1928, and Perkins hit the campaign trail for him. Smith lost to Hoover, but in the same election, Roosevelt was narrowly elected to succeed Smith as governor. Roosevelt offered Perkins a newly configured position of industrial commissioner, which would make her not merely one of several members of a commission, but the top labor administrator in the state.

Perkins accepted the new position. The Roosevelt she agreed to work for was a different person from the callow young man she had once known. The main reason, she believed, was that he had been stricken with polio in the interim. Roosevelt's disability had stripped away his privileged self-satisfaction. Polio led him to have a "total change of heart," Perkins later said. "Nobody was dull. Nobody was a great nuisance. Nobody made no sense. Nobody was good for nothing. Because they were human beings who could walk, and run, and exercise, they were all superior to him."

Perkins supervised 1,800 employees in the largest labor department in the nation. No less important, she advised Roosevelt on industrial and labor policy. In his first year as governor, the Crash of 1929 sent stock prices plunging, and the Great Depression was underway. Millions of Americans were thrown out of work, and many were struggling to find food and shelter.

Perkins was a resolute voice within Roosevelt's inner circle pushing for New York State to take an active role in helping victims of the hard economic times.

At her urging, Roosevelt established a committee to explore ways to address the Depression. Perkins selected the governor's appointees to the Committee for Stabilization of Industry, which met out of her offices. In its final report, the committee called for the state to begin a major public-works program to put jobless New Yorkers to work. It also recommended the creation of an unemployment insurance system to tide people over between jobs.

In 1932, Roosevelt ran for president, calling for a more aggressive response to the economic turmoil than President Hoover was providing. In his speech accepting the Democratic nomination, he promised the nation a "new deal," though the details were sketchy.

Roosevelt won in a landslide and quickly got to work assembling a cabinet. Perkins was an obvious choice for secretary of labor. Roosevelt knew her and her work well, but she was no mere local functionary. Perkins's two decades of advocacy on behalf of workers had won her a sterling national reputation. Perkins had one more thing in her favor: Democratic women who had worked to elect Roosevelt were also pressing him to choose the nation's first woman cabinet member, and many of them were asking for Perkins in particular. Her selection would not be well received by organized labor, which had gotten used to having the labor secretary be a union official, but Roosevelt seemed prepared to disappoint them.

One of the few people, it seemed, who were not persuaded that Perkins should be the next secretary of labor was Perkins herself. She liked her life in New York, where she lived with her fourteen-year-old daughter, and she was nervous about starting her life over in Washington. She also had a more personal concern. Paul Wilson had begun showing signs of manic depression soon after their marriage and was now confined to an institution. There was considerable stigma to mental illness at the time, and Perkins worried that if she joined the cabinet, her husband would be thrust into the limelight. After giving it considerable thought, she wrote to the president-elect and told him she did not wish to be considered.

Ignoring the plea, Roosevelt called Perkins in for a meeting at his Manhattan town house. Suspecting what the subject would be, Perkins brought along a list of the causes she had been fighting for and told Roosevelt she would take the job only if he agreed to back all of them.

The agenda she came armed with was an ambitious one. Perkins wanted the Roosevelt administration to establish a federal relief system and large-scale public-works programs to help people who had been thrown out of work. She wanted federal unemployment insurance and old-age pensions. She also wanted the government to adopt minimum-wage and maximum-hour laws and a ban on child labor.

Perkins's causes could be counted on to attract fierce political opposition. Roosevelt himself was ambivalent about some of the items, notably unemployment insurance. It was still a fairly novel idea, and Roosevelt worried that it would amount to "the dole"—paying people not to work in a way that would sap their work ethic. In exchange for Perkins's agreement to join the cabinet, however, Roosevelt endorsed her full list.

When Perkins took over the federal Department of Labor, it was a backwater. Labor was the most recently created cabinet department, and its portfolio was narrow. The biggest part of its work was tracking down illegal aliens, hardly the most pressing issue for a nation wracked by economic crisis. It was also riddled with corruption, including systematic efforts to shake down immigrants by threatening them with deportation.

Perkins ousted the corrupt officials and then got to work refocusing the department on the needs of workers. She became the strongest voice in the cabinet for public works and emergency relief for the unemployed. She continually brought them up at cabinet meetings and squared off against Lewis Douglas, Roosevelt's fiscally conservative budget director, who kept insisting that the nation could not afford big social programs.

Roosevelt asked Perkins to bring him a plan for a federal emergency relief program. The proposal she brought him was one prepared by Harry Hopkins, the young social worker who was running the nation's first state emergency relief program in New York. Roosevelt liked the plan and asked Democratic leaders in Congress to draft a bill to make it law. He then asked Hopkins to run the program.

Toward the end of the first hundred days, the administration's focus was on drafting a sweeping National Industrial Recovery Act to try to jump-start American business. Members of Roosevelt's inner circle had different priorities for what to include in the bill. Many were pushing for an elaborate system of government-industrial partnership. Perkins attended the drafting meetings, but she went with a single goal: making sure that the bill contained a major public-works provision. In the end, she persuaded Roosevelt to allocate $3.3 billion for public works. Just before the bill was introduced in Congress, Douglas persuaded Roosevelt to take the money out, but Perkins swooped in at the last minute and, in her own private meeting with Roosevelt, got it restored.

Perkins was one of only two cabinet members who remained with Roosevelt for all four terms. (Interior secretary Harold Ickes was the other.) Over the next twelve years, Perkins accomplished a great deal more. Roosevelt appointed her to head a committee to explore old-age pensions. The committee issued a report that called for creating a broad federal safety net, including pensions for older Americans, unemployment insurance for those who were temporarily out of work, and programs of aid for the needy and the disabled. These recommendations laid the groundwork for the Social Security Act, which Roosevelt signed into law in the summer of 1935. In 1938, another major bill that Perkins drew up, the Fair Labor Standards Act, became law. That act achieved her lifelong goal of establishing federal minimum-wage and maximum-hour standards.

For all of her triumphs, Perkins's time as labor secretary had many low moments. Some of her difficulties arose in her private life. Perkins regularly shuttled back and forth to New York City to look after her husband and her daughter, who remained in school there. Paul Wilson's mental health remained a source of constant concern. On the same August morning in 1935 that

Roosevelt signed the Social Security Act, Perkins got a call telling her that Wilson was missing. She went to the White House for the signing, to avoid calling attention to her husband's disappearance, and then rushed to New York to help find him.

Perkins also had considerable difficulty on the job. She made no secret of her dislike of reporters and their constant attempts to invade her privacy. The Washington press corps returned the frosty feelings, giving her generally negative coverage and, at one point, electing her the "most useless" of Washington officials. Perkins was also unpopular in Congress, in large part due to her firm resistance to allowing political patronage in the programs she supervised.

Many of Roosevelt's critics focused on Perkins as a symbol of all that was wrong with his administration and the New Deal. Her enemies spread rumors that she was not from an old New England family but rather was a Jewish immigrant. To appease the Daughters of the American Revolution, she provided evidence that she was born in Boston to a Christian family—though she said that if she had been born a Jew she would have been proud of it. The most controversial chapter of her career was the Harry Bridges case. Perkins refused to deport Bridges, a foreign-born union leader with communist sympathies, because she could find no legal basis for doing so. Her refusal created an uproar on the right, and Republican senators responded by introducing a resolution to impeach her.

It was hard, however, even for Perkins's critics to deny how much she had managed to get done in her twelve years as secretary of labor. There were emergency relief for the unemployed and large-scale public works, old-age pensions and unemployment insurance, minimum-wage laws and maximum-hour restrictions—by the end of Roosevelt's presidency in April 1945, the whole agenda that she had asked him to sign off on in 1933 had been enacted into law.

In the final days, *Collier's* magazine published a profile of Perkins that was largely negative. Amid the barbs about her failings and wonderment that she was still in office, however, it had to acknowledge just how much substantive legislation she had gotten enacted. It could be said, the profile conceded, that what the past twelve years had produced was "not so much the Roosevelt New Deal as it is the Perkins New Deal."

When Roosevelt died, Perkins was suddenly adrift. Things would have been different if Henry Wallace, the previous vice president and a good friend of Perkins's, had succeeded Roosevelt. But the 1944 Democratic Convention had removed Wallace from the ticket and replaced him with Harry Truman, whom she did not know well. It was clear when Truman became president that Perkins would not be in his inner circle. What was not clear was what she would do next.

Perkins's old friend George Bye, who was a literary agent, urged her to write a biography of Roosevelt. With the nation in grief over his death, the time was right for a portrait of the late president written by one of his most trusted aides. Perkins declined, insisting that she was not a great writer and did not have the time. Bye persisted, however, and by the fall of 1945, he had persuaded her.

Viking Press wanted the book within months, to beat out any other Roosevelt biographies that might be in the works. When Perkins despaired of meeting the deadline, Bye urged her to collaborate with Howard Taubman, a music critic for the *New York Times.* Perkins and Taubman settled into her Washington, D.C., home, Perkins supplying the reminiscences and Taubman turning them into a narrative. Within weeks, they had completed a manuscript. The writing was mostly Taubman's, but the memories, insights, and conclusions in *The Roosevelt I Knew* were all Perkins's.

During the presidency and after, so many of Roosevelt advisers wrote books that the New Deal memoir became something of a literary subgenre. Many of these books were reverential; a few were harshly critical. *The Roosevelt I Knew* falls between those extremes. It is unambiguously admiring of Roosevelt as a man and a president—as Perkins says at the outset, her book is "biased in his favor," in part because she was "bound to him by ties of affection, common purpose, and joint undertakings." Perkins was also, however, forthright about what she saw as his flaws.

The Roosevelt I Knew got a mixed reception. A pair of reviews in the *New York Times* reflected the division of opinion. A reviewer in the daily newspaper criticized its writing and organization and complained that it was "almost, but not quite, a blanket endorsement of everything Roosevelt did as Governor and President." A critic writing in the Sunday edition of the paper praised its "penetrating yet generous" portrait of Roosevelt and predicted that it would be a valuable resource for future historians. I can vouch for this final observation. When I wrote a book about Roosevelt's inner circle during his first hundred days in office, I drew heavily on Perkins's assessment of her boss.

There is no denying that *The Roosevelt I Knew* is a largely sympathetic portrait—just as Perkins bills it at the outset. It describes a president who was deeply involved in substantive policy matters. Roosevelt was initially pulled in several directions on a public-works program—Perkins and Harry Hopkins pulling him toward it, Lewis Douglas away from it. Roosevelt was always very engaged with the issue and eventually became a fierce advocate for public works. Under his leadership, the programs expanded greatly, putting millions of jobless Americans to work.

Perkins recounts how adept Roosevelt was at moving the levers of government. She describes his skill at arbitrating among the various proposals that his cabinet members brought to him and his ability to see which made good sense and which were politically achievable. In her chapter on Social Security, she presents Roosevelt as a masterful technician, stage-managing the development of a bill to ensure that it moved forward while remaining under his control.

Perkins presents Roosevelt as fundamentally principled. At the height of the Harry Bridges affair, she went to meet with Roosevelt to tell him that pressure was building to deport Bridges. Roosevelt asked if Bridges had done anything to overthrow the government. When Perkins said that he had not, Roosevelt responded that punishing a man for what he believes was "against the Constitution." Later, when she told him that there was a movement afoot to impeach her over the matter, Roosevelt told her, "Don't worry."

In *The Roosevelt I Knew*, Perkins talks about how unimpressed she was with Roosevelt when she first met him. She remembers the youthful Franklin as "unpromising." She recalls, more than three decades after the fact, her disappointment at his refusal to publicly back her fifty-four-hour bill. "I took it hard," she writes, "that a young man who had so much spirit," would not support a bill that was "a measure of the progressive convictions of the politicians" of the time.

Her criticism is not limited to the early years. Perkins writes honestly about other shortcomings of Roosevelt, including his limited understanding of some of the matters he had to deal with as president. At one point, she relates how John Maynard Keynes, the great British economist, came to see Roosevelt in 1934. After the meeting, Roosevelt told her that Keynes had left him with a "rigmarole of figures." Keynes told Perkins that he had "supposed the President was more literate, economically speaking."

Overall, though, *The Roosevelt I Knew* is a frankly admiring portrait—and one presented with real affection. In life, Perkins did not often come off as sentimental. She was best known for her command of complex subject matter and her moral suasion—the qualities that had people likening her to an "editorial in *The Survey*." In this memoir, however, Perkins was heartfelt about Roosevelt and about what they were able to accomplish together.

In the final chapter of *The Roosevelt I Knew*, "Last Months," the author recalls the president's illness and death. In his waning days, he refused Perkins's repeated offers to resign, telling her at one point, "I can't think of anybody else, and I can't get used to anybody else." He then thanked her, in a voice "filled with exhaustion," telling her, "Frances, you have done awfully well. I know what you have been through. I know what you have accomplished." Perkins was deeply moved. They both, she recalled, had tears in their eyes.

The Roosevelt I Knew is a great book but not a perfect one. At some points, it reveals the rushed circumstances under which it was written. The organization can be loose and even a bit chaotic, and the writing style is at times uninspired. Perkins says at the outset that she does not intend to give an overview of Roosevelt's presidency, but even with that proviso, the book's subject matter is too telescoped, focusing on a few issues, notably working conditions and labor strife, issues that were close to Perkins's heart, but not always to Roosevelt's.

In the end, though, the book has two enormous strengths, which set it apart. The first is the wealth of personal experience that Perkins is able to draw on to create her portrait of Roosevelt and of the New Deal. It is remarkable, for example, to read that the genesis of the federal minimum-wage law lay in Roosevelt's wryly asking Perkins, shortly after he was reelected in 1936, "What happened to that nice unconstitutional bill you had tucked away?" It is perhaps even more striking to read how haphazardly it was that this same bill came to include, at the last minute, a nationwide ban on child labor.

The book's other great strength is Perkins's shrewd assessments of what made Roosevelt tick. The short chapter entitled "A Little Left of Center" conveys Roosevelt's political views better than many far lengthier and more formal biographies. It makes the case that Roosevelt was openly critical of big business but inherently sympathetic to it. He believed government should play a more active role in the economy but that it must not go too far. In explaining this, Perkins includes yet another telling anecdote, this one about a "superficial young reporter" who tries to pin Roosevelt down on whether he is a communist, a socialist, or a capitalist. Roosevelt answered no on all three scores, adding that he was "a Christian and a Democrat— that's all."

In *The Roosevelt I Knew*, Perkins never presents a grand theory of her longtime boss and friend. She does not reduce him, as some biographers have been apt to do, to a hero or a villain, to an idealistic reformer or a calculating politician, to capitalism's savior or its greatest enemy. Perkins describes Roosevelt as simply "the most complicated human being I ever knew." He had many qualities that were in tension, she says, and "he *was* all these things." Her admiring but unfailingly clear-eyed portrait is as good a guidebook as we are likely to get to Roosevelt's many complications.

ADAM COHEN

The Roosevelt
I Knew

PREAMBLE

Franklin Roosevelt was not a simple man. That quality of simplicity which we delight to think marks the great and noble was not his. He was the most complicated human being I ever knew; and out of this complicated nature there sprang much of the drive which brought achievement, much of the sympathy which made him like, and liked by, such oddly different types of people, much of the detachment which enabled him to forget his problems in play or rest, and much of the apparent contradiction which so exasperated those associates of his who expected "crystal clear" and unwavering decisions. But this very complication of his nature made it possible for him to have insight and imagination into the most varied human experiences, and this he applied to the physical, social, geographical, economic, and strategic circumstances thrust upon him as responsibilities by his times.

He was capable of almost childish vanity about his skill in catching fish, his seamanship in small boats, his exploits in teasing Winston Churchill and in making Stalin laugh and unbend; and at the same time he could be unself-consciously humble and ask the advice of a most casual visitor about some problem he could not solve. He enjoyed the gay, boisterous, and sometimes silly fellows with whom he went on fishing trips. The reason was not only "no mental strain," as a keen columnist discerned; he really liked the banter and teasing. He used the same coin of personal funmaking when he sat down to talk with a group of labor leaders. Some of them are deadly serious men, or humorless, and were bothered by it. Many loved it and felt warm and included by it.

Many books will be written about Franklin Roosevelt, but no two will give the same picture. For no two people saw the same thing in him. The variety and conflict of the pictures will be startling. It will be many years before a definitive biography and true appraisal of Franklin Roosevelt is written. People who knew him and lived in his times are too close to him, and too partisan about him, either for or against, to have the necessary objectivity. Those who knew him and his times will write what they knew, saw, felt, and understood about him. It will be source material for future historians. It will surely encourage people to continue their own efforts to overcome handicaps and to develop themselves as individuals; but even more important, it will encourage them to seek greater social justice and higher standards of living in the corporate life of our country.

This book about Roosevelt is not a biography. It is biased in his favor. I agreed with most of his positions and policies and worked for many years to help develop, spread, and establish them in action. I am bound to him by ties of affection, common purpose, and joint undertakings. All doubts have been resolved in his favor. Despite his shortcomings, I, on the whole, respect the methods he used to handle his problems and develop his strength.

He was many things—not clear, not simple, with drives and compulsions in a dozen different directions, with curiosity sending him from one field and experience to another, with imagination making it possible for him to identify himself, at least partly and temporarily, with widely different phenomena and people. There was undoubted conflict within him. He *was* all these things—the rich man's friend, the poor man's brother, the stern puritan conscience, the easygoing, indulgent, and forgiving friend of the irregulars. These conflicts, however, did not result in neurotic stagnation, but in life and movement in many directions; and shrewd planning kept them from ruining one another.

Without these conflicts in Roosevelt's thinking and feeling there would have been less action. He responded to one impulse, was checked by another. By diverting two conflicting impulses and starting something new, he compounded or made

compromises out of both. In this way opposition dropped off
and progress was made. This was never wholly conscious on
his part. Out of these impulses, interests, curiosities, and sympathies came the dynamic quality which made movement, action, and creative living possible for him.

The core of Roosevelt's character was viability—a capacity
for living and growing that remained to his dying day. It accounts for his rise from a rather unpromising young man to a
great man—not merely a President, but a man who so impressed
himself upon his time that he can never be forgotten and will be
loved as a symbol of hope and social justice long after his generation and his works have passed away.

One cannot predict what Roosevelt would have said or done
in the postwar world. It is unfortunate that already there may
be growing a rigid "Roosevelt legend." Some are expressing
quite personal ideas as if they were definitely what Roosevelt
wanted, and urging them as a guide for the present and future
in political and international action. I wonder if they know
what he would have done. He was essentially adaptable to new
circumstances, always quick to understand the changing needs
and hopes of the people and to vary his action to meet changing situations. Methods which he pursued in the past are not
necessarily what he would have used today.

He made an indelible impression on his own country and on
the world, changing the direction of political thought through
knowledge of human needs and suffering and emphasis upon
the provision of the good life for the common man. He grew to
greatness by a full utilization of all of his talent and personality; he began where he was and used what he had. He ignored
his handicaps, both physical and intellectual, and let nothing
hinder him from doing the work he had to do in the world. He
was not born great but he became great. The words most often
on his lips to describe what he regarded as the good democratic
society were: "free," "fair," and "decent." To his dying day he
held the philosophy that "If you treat people right they will
treat you right—ninety per cent of the time." He left no political system, no basis for a cult. Some of his personal rules of life
remain and they will offer guidance and inspiration to many.

Never let fear rise; take constructive action with whatever capacities are available; be flexible in all dealings with human
beings; overcome unnecessary discouragement and gloom by
laughter and by faith. "Move forward with a strong and active
faith," he wrote on his last day, as on his first day in office as
President he had said: "The only thing we have to fear is fear
itself."

He learned to love people, and they returned it. Seldom has
a man been so beloved within his own generation. On the night
he died, a young soldier stood in the silent group which clus-
tered for comfort around the White House where he had lived.
The young soldier sighed as I nodded to him and, still looking
at the house, he said: "I felt as if I knew him." (A pause.) "I felt
as if he knew me—and I felt as if he liked me."

This man cannot be made into the founder of a cult, the supporter of a group. He belonged to everyone. If this book can
help to establish the real rather than the legendary leader by
getting closer to the man himself, I shall feel that I have done
him some service.

PART ONE

THE MAN

I.

FIRST IMPRESSIONS

I first saw Franklin Roosevelt in 1910 at a tea dance in the house of Mrs. Walston Brown in Gramercy Park, New York City. I was studying at Columbia University for a Master's degree and working in a settlement house on a survey of the social conditions in the neighborhood.

Roosevelt had just entered politics with a Dutchess County campaign, which was not taken too seriously either by Roosevelt himself, his supporters, or his friends. The Republicans and farmers had voted for him as state senator largely because of his name. It was the era of Theodore Roosevelt, and we were all still under his spell.

Mrs. Brown was a pleasant lady who delighted to entertain serious-minded young people who were not too serious to dance and relax, strictly on tea, for such was the innocent habit of late afternoon parties of the pre–World War I period.

There was nothing particularly interesting about the tall, thin young man with the high collar and pince-nez; and I should not later have remembered this meeting except for the fact that in an interval between dances someone in the group I joined mentioned Theodore Roosevelt, speaking with some scorn of his "progressive" ideas. The tall young man named Roosevelt, I didn't catch his first name on introduction, made a spirited defense of Theodore Roosevelt, being careful to proclaim that he was not his kin except by marriage.

Like many young people, I was an ardent admirer of Theodore Roosevelt. He had been a vigorous and educative President. He had recommended to the people Jacob Riis's book *How the Other Half Lives*. I had read it, and Theodore Roose-

velt's inaugural address of 1905, and had straightaway felt that
the pursuit of social justice would be my vocation. Therefore
this tall young man who was one of Theodore Roosevelt's ad-
mirers made a slight impression on me. We did not become well
acquainted, but occasionally I saw him at purely social functions.

I did not give him a second thought until I went to Albany, as
a representative of the Consumers' League, to work for passage
of the fifty-four-hour bill for women, known as the Jackson-
McManus bill. I had already had a conviction, a "concern," as
the Quakers say, about social justice; and it was clear in my
own mind that the promotion of social justice could be made to
work practically. As a student and professional social worker, I
was taking an active part in proposals to use the legislative
authority of the state to correct social abuses—long hours, low
wages, bad housing, child labor, and unsanitary conditions.

This was a period of confusion. The ancient concept of the
rights of man was in conflict with the expansion and needs of
big business and mass production. None of us was clear in our
thinking, but our emotions were inevitably attracted by the
dynamic quality of Theodore Roosevelt (whose attachment to
the principles of social justice has never been sufficiently developed by his biographers) and by the qualities of leadership in
social reform, both in Great Britain and in our own country,
which were being demonstrated on the political plane by Lloyd
George and Woodrow Wilson.

Franklin Roosevelt was then a member of the state Senate, a
Democrat in an administration with a Democratic governor
and a Democratic majority in both houses. No one who saw
him in those years would have been likely to think of him as a
potential President of the U.S.A.

I believe that at that time Franklin Roosevelt had little, if any,
concern about specific social reforms. Nothing in his conversation or action would have indicated it. He was, of course, engaged in 1911 and 1912 in a violent controversy with the regular
Democratic party of the state over the election by the legislature
of William Sheehan as United States Senator from New York.
Roosevelt and many of the Democrats of the nonprofessional

type believed this appointment savored of "dirty politics."
There can be no question but that he sincerely felt he was doing
a great service in making a spectacular battle against the party
organization. He won the battle, but it did not leave him with
many friends in the Senate or Democratic party of the state.

I have a vivid picture of him operating on the floor of the
Senate: tall and slender, very active and alert, moving around
the floor, going in and out of committee rooms, rarely talking
with the members, who more or less avoided him, not particularly charming (that came later), artificially serious of face,
rarely smiling, with an unfortunate habit—so natural that he
was unaware of it—of throwing his head up. This, combined
with his pince-nez and great height, gave him the appearance
of looking down his nose at most people.

It is interesting that this habit of throwing his head up, which
when he was young and unchastened gave him a slightly supercilious appearance, later had a completely different effect. By
1933, and for the rest of his life, it was a gesture of courage and
hope, and people were responsive to it as such.

Many staunch old Tammany Democrats in those days felt
that he did look down his nose at them. I remember old Tim
Sullivan, himself the acme of personal amiability, saying after
a bout with Roosevelt, "Awful arrogant fellow, that Roosevelt."

I can see "that Roosevelt" now, standing back of the brass
rail with two or three Democratic senators arguing with him
to be "reasonable," as they called it, about something; his small
mouth pursed up and slightly open, his nostrils distended, his
head in the air, and his cool, remote voice saying, "No, no, I
won't hear of it!"

I think he started that way not because he was born with
a silver spoon in his mouth and had a good education at Harvard (which in itself constitutes a political handicap), but because he really didn't like people very much and because he had
a youthful lack of humility, a streak of self-righteousness, and
a deafness to the hopes, fears, and aspirations which are the
common lot.

The marvel is that these handicaps were washed out of him
by life, experience, punishment, and his capacity to grow. He

never wholly ignored these youthful traits himself. He once said to me when he was President, "You know, I was an awfully mean cuss when I first went into politics."

During this period he was, in his personal as distinguished from his public relations, gay and agreeable. He loved to laugh in 1911 as in 1945.

The regular Democrats in Albany, however, found him austere. Personally he got great fun out of his fight against Sheehan, although it was just a drastic application of the old-fashioned reform program of honesty and intelligence in government. A young and inexperienced person like myself could not fail to observe that it *was* fun to put "corruption," as Theodore Roosevelt called it, to rout. The regular Democrats of the Tammany Hall persuasion just gritted their teeth and endured him. They disliked him, and I include among them Robert Wagner, Alfred E. Smith, Jim Foley, Harvey Ferris, Hugh Frawley, Henry Grady, and many others who thought him impossible and said so privately.

I was tremendously interested and intrigued by politicians, like Tim Sullivan of the Bowery and his cousin Christy; Senator Grady, the great orator who was nearly always slightly intoxicated when he made his orations in the Senate of New York; The MacManus, called by a columnist of his day "the Devil's Deputy from Hell's Kitchen." The warm, human sympathies of these people, less than perfect as I examine their record, gave me insight into a whole stratum of American society I had not known. In contrast with these roughnecks, I don't hesitate to say now, Franklin Roosevelt seemed just an ordinary, respectable, intelligent, correct young man.

In the first Albany period of Franklin Roosevelt, I repeat, I was not much impressed by him. I knew innumerable young men who had been educated in private schools and had gone to Harvard. He did not seem different except that he had political rather than professional or scholarly interests. Many years later I realized that Franklin Roosevelt had learned from rough Tammany politicians like Tim Sullivan and The MacManus. In the spring of 1938 when I was trying to impress upon him the seriousness of a problem relating to immigration policy, he sud-

denly said, "Tim Sullivan used to say that the America of the
future would be made out of the people who had come over in
steerage and who knew in their own hearts and lives the difference between being despised and being accepted and liked."
Then he added, "Poor old Tim Sullivan never understood about
modern politics, but he was right about the human heart."

On the last night of the legislative session of the spring of 1912,
the fifty-four-hour bill for women came to a test vote, but the
forces in the New York state legislature at Albany were scattered. The Democrats had proclaimed for a number of years
that they favored this law. The strategy of those of us promoting it had been to force the bill to a vote. An acceptable bill had
gone through the Senate, but in the Assembly an amendment
had been attached by floor vote exempting women who worked
in the canneries. We had been very strongly on record as opposed to this exemption.

I later came to realize that this was part of a plan, and some
of our Democratic friends by indirection had agreed to it. It
was taken for granted that the friends of the bill would con-
demn it as amended and that it would be dropped without a
roll call in the Senate. I didn't figure this out for myself. Tim
Sullivan, the senator from the Bowery, told me. It was hard to
believe, for I hadn't yet learned about "practical politics."

When the bill arrived in the Senate as amended, I had to
decide whether to accept the amendment or see the bill die. I
decided to accept the amendment and to ask to have the bill put
through the Senate. Josiah Newcombe and Mayhew Wain-
wright, liberal Republicans, and Tim Sullivan and other Democrats really favorable to the bill advised me to do so and said
they would put it through. Here the test came.

Robert Wagner, the chairman of the Rules Committee, was in
the Chair. Tim Sullivan, the next ranking member, had boarded
the Hudson River boat in the belief that the bill was safe, as all
had agreed to the amendment. But it was still a critical moment,
as the opposition had planned not to let a vote be taken, and he
had to be called back.

When Tim Sullivan came puffing up the hill after being pulled off the Albany boat, he said to me, "It's all right, me gal, we is wid ya. De bosses thought they was going to kill your bill, but they forgot about Tim Sullivan. I'm a poor man meself. Me father and me mother were poor and struggling. I seen me sister go out to work when she was only fourteen and I know we ought to help these gals by giving 'em a law which will prevent 'em from being broken down while they're still young."

This was a simple emotional response with no sophisticated political consideration involved. Certainly Tim Sullivan never realized the extent to which this type of measure twenty years later would bring nation-wide support to Franklin Roosevelt.

Tim Sullivan got the bill passed. True, it was an amended bill, but it made possible shorter hours for hundreds of thousands of women in the factories and mills of New York State.

Franklin Roosevelt did not associate himself actively with this bill, which was a measure of the progressive convictions of the politicians of 1910. I remember it clearly because I took it hard that a young man who had so much spirit did not do so well in this, which I thought a test, as did Tim Sullivan and The MacManus, undoubtedly corrupt politicians.

2.

WILSON ERA

When Roosevelt first became interested in Wilson, or Wilson in him, I do not know, but certainly it was well before the Democratic national convention of 1912. I remember that Roosevelt's name was attached to the invitation to join a "New York Committee for Wilson for President" which was a preconvention activity. I have been told by others that Wilson was attracted to him by his opposition to the election of "Billy" Sheehan as United States Senator. It had been a vigorous fight, based on the principle of personal and political integrity as a prerequisite for public office.

I saw Roosevelt at the 1912 convention in Baltimore. He was energetic, high-minded, and still looking down his nose through the pince-nez. Because of his devotion to Wilson and his ideas, Roosevelt was learning to make adjustments in his personal position to satisfy the greater needs of the party and of society. Wilson's high intellectual quality and complete devotion to his program of the "New Freedom" evoked lasting admiration in young Franklin Roosevelt.

The influence of Wilson, both personally and objectively, upon young Franklin Roosevelt can be gathered from what Roosevelt once said to me as late as 1941 or 1942: "You know, Wilson had an uncanny understanding of the European problem. He understood the moral drives of modern man. He was a Presbyterian, you know, and a tough one, and he was perfectly sure that all men are sinful by nature. He figured it out that Western civilization would attempt to destroy itself through the natural sinful activities of modern man unless [and here F.D.R. paused to trace an exclamation point with his finger] by the

grace of God the decent people of Western civilization resolved
to support the doctrine of the Golden Rule."

This was the beginning of a new life for Franklin Roosevelt.
He had never before been associated with people who arrived
at convictions by intellectual rather than emotional processes.
His father had based his attitudes on tradition, his mother had
derived hers from love, his school and college associates had
derived theirs from respectability. Wilson was something new.
He derived not only from intellectual convictions, but also
from a new idealism and humanitarianism in which the economic and cultural aspirations of the common man were beginning to play a part in the political program.

These concepts began to come alive in this country in the
late nineties and early 1900's and found expression in literature, poetry, drama, and the graphic arts. The pity and terror
of the slums, mills, and work shops, with their low wages and
long hours, were used for artistic effect as in Greek tragedy.
The feelings and minds of people responded to the exposure of
degraded living and working conditions in *The Jungle* by Upton
Sinclair, *Experiences as a Factory Girl* by Mary Van Vorst,
How the Other Half Lives by Jacob Riis, and Ernest Poole's
novel of the working class, *The Harbor*. The muckraking magazine writers, like Will Irwin, Sam Merwin, Lincoln Steffens,
Ray Baker, startled the American people with documents of
American life that showed deep suffering, social injustice, and
indifference to it in large areas of our population. John Sloan
and George Bellows were painting the life and portraits of "the
poor" with beauty, pity, and passion.

These ideas crept into the political field. American sympathy
is quickly stirred, and, furthermore, we have the natural and
old American habit of using democratic and legislative processes to correct abuses and adversity. The town meeting system
of the seventeenth and eighteenth centuries used this method.
They put it simply: "It is the sense of the meeting that the select-
men should provide for the Widow Jones."

Proposals began to be made for laws to overcome social dis-
advantages. Societies and voluntary agencies, aiming to prevent
abuses and promote remedies, sprang up. There was a sincere

effort on the part of the American people to find the way of social justice. Shorter hours and better wages, removal of slums, new tenement house laws for sanitation, fire safety, and decency; reforms to prevent child labor, prevention of the use of hazardous chemicals in industry began to be mentioned in political speeches and legislation in some states. The phossy-jaw of the match industry, which so horrified the public, gave way before the pressure of public opinion in the Diamond Match Company's simple moral action making public property of its patents for effective matches without phosphorus.

The Bull Moose, or Progressive, party of Theodore Roosevelt, the Wilson wing of the Democratic party, the Republican party in Wisconsin, and the Democratic party in New York began to pledge specific bills to advance social justice where abuses had been shown by investigation and where there was a popular demand for a remedy. Political commitments lagged behind the literary and cultural concepts and moral implications, but the tide was turning.

Alfred E. Smith and Robert Wagner, who later became great leaders in the state and nation in social justice achieved by legislative techniques, got their education as members of the Factory Investigation Commission appointed by the state legislature after the terrible Triangle Factory fire in New York City, March 11, 1911. They got a firsthand look at industrial and labor conditions, and from that look they never recovered. They became firm and unshakable sponsors of political and legislative measures designed to overcome conditions unfavorable to human life.

Franklin Roosevelt had been called to Washington by President Wilson in 1913 and did not share in that educative experience. But the Wilson school embraced social justice as a part of political action, and Roosevelt became responsive to these ideas. Newton D. Baker, Secretary of War in the cabinet and very influential intellectually and politically, had considerable effect upon young Roosevelt. Baker had been president of the National Consumers' League and had been associated with Florence Kelley and John Graham Brooks in devising legislative measures to make the ethical gains of social justice a reality by legislation. Margaret Wilson was a professional social worker. Francis Sayre, who married into the Wilson family, had a record of commitment to similar purposes.

There was no broad legislative program along social lines. It was an ethical climate, and the friends Roosevelt made in the Wilson administration served to develop new standards of judgment in him. Foremost was the idea that poverty is preventable, that poverty is destructive, wasteful, demoralizing, and that poverty in the midst of potential plenty is morally unacceptable in a Christian and democratic society. One began to see the "poor" as people, with hopes, fears, virtues, and vices, as fellow citizens who were part of the fabric of American life instead of as a depressed class who would be always with us.

Before Roosevelt had been in Washington a year he had begun to show his capacity to grow and flourish under the infection of these ideas. His administrative duties brought him into direct contact with labor unions, and perhaps for the first time he got to know some labor leaders pretty well. They were labor leaders whose business with him was terms and conditions of work for the workers in the Navy yards. He liked and respected them. He found it not only easy, but agreeable, to be popular with them. Moreover, his wife had joined the Consumers' League and had associated herself in a modest way with some of its activities for industrial reform by education and persuasion as well as by law. Ethical principles and human sympathy led him also in that direction.

Wilson appointed him Assistant Secretary of the Navy with the hearty approval of Josephus Daniels, the Secretary. It is said that Wilson offered Roosevelt two other posts often thought of as more important and likely to be more rewarding financially in the future. Roosevelt's love of the sea prompted him to accept the Navy job without hesitation. "I'd rather have that place," he said, "than any other in public life."

It was March 1913 when the Roosevelts arrived in Washington. Although it was more than a year before World War I, Roosevelt could see the clouds gathering over Europe. With supervision over the Navy's civilian personnel and yards and docks, he set about to prepare for the worst. He worked out estimates of supplies needed in the event of war, gathered statistics on the productive capacity of plants, and placed contracts. Slashing red tape and eliminating middlemen, he stepped up the flow of supplies to naval plants. He did such a thorough job that Wilson called him to a conference one day with the Army Chief of Staff and said: "I'm very sorry, but you've cornered the market for supplies. You'll have to divide up with the Army."

By the time the United States entered the war, Roosevelt had naval plants and yards operating shipshape. He worked hard to keep the men contented and happy. As the war progressed, Roosevelt branched out into other activities. He carried out housing projects for naval workers. He campaigned for more 110-foot submarine chasers and helped to map plans for the battle of the North Sea which broke the effectiveness of German U-boat warfare.

During these years he made friends on all levels of capital life. The lights burned late in the house on R Street as people came and went. The Roosevelts were hospitable and had many visitors. They had friends not only among American officials but among the people attached to foreign embassies and legations.

From his Washington vantage point Roosevelt saw the seed of Wilson's idea for a League of Nations germinate and flower. And from its eventual failure he learned a lesson that shaped his own thinking and action in foreign policy in the years to come.

On the second day of 1919, less than two months after the war ended, Roosevelt sailed for Europe accompanied by Mrs. Roosevelt. On the same ship were members of the preparatory commission for the Versailles Peace Conference. Roosevelt's job was to liquidate American naval stations and stores in Europe. The European scene was familiar to him. In addition to earlier trips, he had visited the continent in July 1918, where he had talked with King Albert of Belgium, Lloyd George, Foch, Clemenceau, and others. On this second visit abroad in six months, Roosevelt found Versailles, and, indeed, all Europe, eager and excited over the coming of Wilson, who was being hailed in every land as the great liberator. Everywhere Roosevelt went he found great sympathy for Wilson's idea of nations being free, with the strong to protect the weak.

As a member of the Wilson administration, Roosevelt noted Wilson's personal difficulties with the politicians, his remoteness and isolation from them. Taking state committeemen to luncheons to listen to and mollify their grievances was one of the chores Roosevelt undertook. He gave up the notion of strictly formal and professional relations between political associates. He unbent, laughed with them, swapped yarns, and began to be as easy and natural as with old friends and neighbors.

In telling about it as a guide to me years later he said, "They'd rather have a nice jolly understanding of their problems than lots of patronage. A little patronage, a lot of pleasure, and public signs of friendship and prestige—that's what makes a political leader secure with his people and that is what he wants anyhow."

F.D.R. was good at this. He learned to be a politician. At least he thought he learned it during this period. He had a good time. He knew everybody, played hard, and worked as well. I saw him only a few times in those years and then only at official and social events. His habit of looking down his nose was greatly modified now—it was hardly noticeable. The toss of the head up and back was softened—it had become a gesture of cheerfulness, not arrogance. He smiled when he did it.

He learned the tough techniques of government. Assistant secretaries are responsible for departmental budgets, Civil Service procedures, purchase of supplies, the legal intricacies of government policy, accounting, and the like. It became his policy that what has to be done can be done somehow. "There's always a way to get through it," he would say when, as President, some high officer would tell him that the lawyers, or the Civil Service, or the budget, or a congressional committee prevented carrying out some project of merit or need.

The knowledge gained as a subordinate administrator was

invaluable to him as Governor of New York and as President. He had to think constantly about government as a system, and he gained a sense of its form and structure and of the reasons for its checks and balances which few people equaled.

He began to like people—just anybody—and to stimulate himself by new contacts with new people. Newton Baker, who liked him, once said to me, "Young Roosevelt is very promising, but I should think he'd wear himself out in the promiscuous and extended contacts he maintains with people. But as I have observed him, he seems to clarify his ideas and teach himself as he goes along by that very conversational method."

As one saw him do the same thing in later life, both as Governor and as President, one realized how important for him were these varied and manifold points of contact. An "audience" friend was just as stimulating and sometimes more helpful to him than the friend who came bearing well-established opinion and recommendation. If the caller was a good listener, he talked himself and his visitor into an understanding of the specific problem and the principles underlying it—an approach he certainly didn't have at the beginning of the conversation.

In this period investigation and inquiry into factory working conditions on contracts for the War Department were undertaken, probably the first time that such a matter had been thought important. Secretary of War Baker called on Florence Kelley of the Consumers' League to organize an inspection service for war contract factories and to recommend changes in working conditions in the interest of health, safety, and human comfort. The Women's Bureau, organized in the Department of Labor, set up standards for women workers in the war industries. Industrial accident prevention was inaugurated. The young Assistant Secretary of the Navy supported these ideas. Although he sometimes did not fully understand the social adversity to be remedied by the proposed measures, like the Women's Bureau rule about providing seats for women and exhaust fans to draw out fumes and gases from workrooms, he was in favor of anything that would make people more comfortable and happier at their work. He himself had not seen factory girls with silicosis and carbon monoxide poisoning or fallen arches and aching backs from long standing at work; but he believed the investigators' reports, and his vigorous imagination and warm sympathy filled in the realities. If he had remained in New York and been a member of the Factory Investigation Commission, he would have seen and learned more directly.

I was an investigator for the Factory Investigation Commission and we used to make it our business to take Al Smith, the East Side boy who later became New York's Governor and a presidential candidate, to see the women, thousands of them, coming off the ten-hour night-shift on the rope walks in Auburn. We made sure that Robert Wagner personally crawled through the tiny hole in the wall that gave egress to a steep iron ladder covered with ice and ending twelve feet from the ground, which was euphemistically labeled "Fire Escape" in many factories. We saw to it that the austere legislative members of the Commission got up at dawn and drove with us for an unannounced visit to a Cattaraugus County cannery and that they saw with their own eyes the little children, not adolescents, but five-, six-, and seven-year-olds, snipping beans and shelling peas. We made sure that they saw the machinery that would scalp a girl or cut off a man's arm. Hours so long that both men and women were depleted and exhausted became realities to them through seeing for themselves the dirty little factories. These men realized something could be done about it from discussions with New York State employers who had succeeded in remedying adverse working conditions and standards of pay. Such a man was Edmund Huyck, a blanket and wool textile manufacturer at Rensselaer; such businesses were the Carolyn Laundry in the Bronx and a concern in Rochester with the strange name of "Art in Buttons."

It was the experiments of these and other manufacturers (all successful moneymakers) that brought conviction to the members of the Commission that conditions in industry were frequently bad for the workers; that they were correctable by practical means; and that correction by lawful process would benefit industries as well as workers. Production and business would increase and the whole state would profit.

These principles the Commission recommended, and the legislature, over a period of three to five years, put into law the program of compulsory shorter work day and week for women, limitation of age of children at work, prohibition of night work for women, workmen's compensation for industrial accidents, measures to prevent industrial accidents, and elaborate requirements for the construction of factory and mercantile premises in the interests of the health and safety of the people who worked in them.

The extent to which this legislation in New York marked a change in American political attitudes and policies toward social responsibility can scarcely be overrated. It was, I am convinced, a turning point; it was not only successful in effecting practical remedies but, surprisingly, it proved to be successful also in vote-getting.

New York was a great industrial state. It had within its borders one huge city, the largest in the United States, and a number of other large cities. This differentiated the influence of this program of labor legislation in New York from that, for example, in the State of Wisconsin. Wisconsin was a small homogeneous community, more agricultural than industrial, with a few large industries and no large cities. The experimental development of legislation to remedy social adversity in Wisconsin was of great value and was quoted in support of the New York legislation, even though in Wisconsin it was of lesser scope. But New York! If it could be done there, it could be done anywhere. The fact that the Democratic party became dominant in New York for many years largely on the basis of this program of legislation (combined with competent, sympathetic administration), riveted in American life the conception that it was the duty and opportunity of people elected to office to develop programs for prevention of poverty and for improving the conditions of life and work of all the people.

As a young, relatively uninfluential social worker, with a beginning acquaintance of Albany politicians and political methods, I was able to have a hand in these programs. I am convinced that the pull of social forces rather than vote-getting considerations moved the politicians in this direction. It was not because

some of the Democrats were poor boys and many of the Republicans were well-to-do in their youth that the Democrats were
more responsive to social reform. I think it was purely chance
that the Democrats were in office when the opportunities and
necessities to move in this direction came. Thousands of people
became Democrats or voted that ticket when the Democrats
espoused these ideas.

There was nothing social minded about the upstate Democrats who boasted they were Jeffersonians, whatever that means.
In my experience it meant that they were for the farmers and the
canneries and regarded labor laws as interfering with the liberty
of individuals.

Certainly there was nothing social minded about the head of
Tammany Hall, Charles Murphy, whom I went to see when legislation on factory buildings was before the state legislature. I
went to enlist his support for this legislation. I climbed up the
stairs of old Tammany Hall on 14th Street in a good deal of
trepidation. Tammany Hall had a sinister reputation in New
York, and I hardly knew how I would be greeted, but, as I later
learned, a lady was invariably treated with respect and gallantry
and a poor old woman with infinite kindness and courtesy. Mr.
Murphy, solemn dignity itself, received me in a reserved but
courteous way. He listened to my story and arguments. Then,
leaning forward in his chair, he said quietly, "You are the young
lady, aren't you, who managed to get the fifty-four-hour bill
passed?"

I admitted I was.

"Well, young lady, I was opposed to that bill."

"Yes, I so gathered, Mr. Murphy."

"It is my observation," he went on, "that that bill made us
many votes. I will tell the boys to give all the help they can to
this new bill. Good-by."

As I went out of the door, saying "Thank you," he said, "Are
you one of these women suffragists?"

Torn between a fear of being faithless to my convictions and
losing the so recently gained support of a political boss, I stam-
mered, "Yes, I am."

"Well, I am not," he replied, "but if anybody ever gives them the vote, I hope you will remember that you would make a good Democrat."

All through this period a moral turmoil was going on. The twentieth century had witnessed a great change in American economy and culture. The frontier was conquered. Machinery was universally in use, with consequent increase in production. Transportation and communications were fast. The population was increasing (a million a year by immigration alone). The standard of living was rising. It was possible to conceive of production which would give the great majority of the people access to comfort, good wages, good living conditions, and opportunities for education.

We knew from our own experience, although we rarely said so, that a primitive society in which everybody must work all the time barely to keep alive is inevitably a deficit economy; and although many legislators and businessmen recalled sentimentally their days as barefoot boys, people generally understood that these days were not so good as the surplus economy which we were beginning to develop. Simon Patten of the Wharton School of Economics coined the phrases "surplus civilization" and "deficit civilization." Many who never heard his name as well as many of his students agree with him that a surplus civilization makes generosity and social progress possible; whereas a deficit civilization, although it may not always result in cannibalism and although it advances the virtues of thrift and mechanical invention, does not advance the social and economic satisfactions of the community.

The Democratic party in New York may not have been aware of these principles, but it understood political success. Democratic candidates were elected over and over again because they said that they were in favor of the measures proposed by the Factory Investigation Commission. Even upstate Democrats found themselves delivering similar speeches at campaign time, and although they sometimes may have wished that we reformers who had entered the party had been "reasonable," they went along. They gradually converted themselves, and ten years later were under the impression that they had originated these ideas and laws.

I have often wished that Roosevelt could have had the first-hand experience of the politicians who served on the Factory Investigation Commission of New York, but the miracle is that he understood it secondhand and that these ideas penetrated into his personality by a kind of intellectual and spiritual osmosis.

3.

THROUGH THE VALLEY

Early in August 1920 the Democrats held their convention at San Francisco. Franklin Roosevelt was in the thick of it. Tall, strong, handsome, and popular, he was one of the stars of the show. I recall how he displayed his athletic ability by vaulting over a row of chairs to get to the platform in a hurry. James M. Cox of Ohio was nominated to be the party's standard bearer, and word came out that Franklin Roosevelt, then only thirty-eight, had been selected by the steering committee as his running mate. His name was placed before the convention with Al Smith making a seconding speech. Al always thought of this as the beginning of his friendship with Roosevelt and often referred to it as Roosevelt's real start in important political life. And so it was. Roosevelt always agreed. His election as state senator had been an accident and a stunt. His service with Wilson, while it gave him prestige, did not put him in vote-getting politics in a big way.

Roosevelt won the nomination, and a new phase of his education began. His campaign was conducted to the limit of his great vitality. He stumped the country—north and south, east and west. He spoke in small towns and large cities and bore the strain of two or three meetings a day without slackening of pace. He talked with party leaders and the rank and file wherever he went. He established a wide personal friendship, and left new friends and old with a hearty "Come and see me some time" that in later years taxed the resources of the Executive Mansion at Albany and the White House. He became a good judge of people and learned to distinguish the sincere from the insincere. He learned the value of presenting programs and issues to the people themselves. His political education came as candidate and party spokesman, not as the ward worker who pushes doorbells, hands out party literature, and gets out the vote. It made a difference in his equipment and attitude as a politician.

He found that the interest of the people was in their jobs, families, security, and future rather than in political theories. Party platforms left them cold and puzzled. He learned a great deal about America too. As a farmer from a well-watered valley in New York, he learned that irrigation rights are life and death matters in the West and Southwest. He was a keen observer, asked hundreds of questions, and increased his knowledge of the land he was to serve one day as President. Out of the Cox campaign he brought a firm conviction that agricultural and industrial life could be made much better for the people by conscious government programs.

The campaign days whizzed by at breakneck speed. Roosevelt gained experience, but the Republicans got the votes. The Cox-Roosevelt ticket went down under an avalanche of ballots that swept Warren G. Harding into the White House and Roosevelt back into private life for the first time in ten years.

Back in New York, Roosevelt resumed law practice. His chief interest in politics for the moment was the progress of Governor Al Smith's new administration in New York. Mrs. Roosevelt also renewed old acquaintances after all the years in Washington. Through her work in the Consumers' League and the Women's Trade Union League she met new and active people in and out of politics.

During this period Roosevelt learned more about the labor movement and some of its problems in his assignment as counsel for the American Construction Council. This organization was interested in low-cost housing projects, and he got an inside view of the problems of wages and limitation practices in the building trades unions. He also got to know some of the building trades leaders. He plunged into other activities, among them chairmanship of a fund-raising committee for the Woodrow Wilson Foundation.

And then his own tragedy struck. In August 1921, while the family was at Campobello, New Brunswick, on a summer holiday, Roosevelt was stricken with infantile paralysis. He escaped death by a narrow margin and then, through the dynamic force of his realistic courage, he slowly began to fight his way back to health.

In this struggle he had the intelligent support of Mrs. Roosevelt and Louis Howe, his faithful aide of Navy Department days. Howe had a fixation about Roosevelt's future as a great political leader and worked for it unremittingly.

After the danger of death had passed, Roosevelt's illness and convalescence led into more years of liberal education. He and Mrs. Roosevelt made this period of disaster serve a constructive purpose in his life.

Franklin Roosevelt underwent a spiritual transformation during the years of his illness. I noticed when he came back that the years of pain and suffering had purged the slightly arrogant attitude he had displayed on occasion before he was stricken. The man emerged completely warmhearted, with humility of spirit and with a deeper philosophy. Having been to the depths of trouble, he understood the problems of people in trouble. Although he rarely, almost never, spoke of his illness in later years, he showed that he had developed faith in the capacity of troubled people to respond to help and encouragement. He learned in that period and began to express firm belief that the "only thing to fear is fear itself."

He never displayed the slightest bitterness over his misfortune. In occasional asides he revealed that he had also had a great strengthening of religious faith. He believed that Divine Providence had intervened to save him from total paralysis, despair, and death. His understanding of the spiritual laws of faith and of the association of man's feeble powers with God's great power must have come at this time. It was a solid basis for his future inner security in times of stress.

I saw Roosevelt only once between 1921 and 1924, and I was instantly struck by his growth. He was young, he was crippled, he was physically weak, but he had a firmer grip on life and on himself than ever before. He was serious, not playing now. Politics had become important to him as a means to a good life. He had become conscious of other people, of weak people, of human frailty. I remember thinking that he would never be so hard and harsh in judgment on stupid people—even on wrongdoers. His viability—his power to grow in response to experience—was beginning to show.

In the years of his illness Mrs. Roosevelt developed a remarkable reportorial quality. She had always been an observant woman. She learned to be more observant and to be able to repeat in detail what she saw and heard. This was of priceless help to him, handicapped as he was, longing to be in touch with the people, and having to learn to take vicarious instead of direct personal experience. The friends who became most useful to him were those who reported truthfully, colorfully, on what they saw and heard. His own sympathy and imagination built on these reports. Mrs. Roosevelt realized that in his invalid period he needed all the help and strengthening that could come to him through his mind. With great perspicacity she brought him people with whom he could share the things going on in his mind. She realized she could introduce new and stimulating ideas through people who were thoughtful, had had a variety of experience, and wanted to know what he thought. She began to take out to see him two friends in the Women's Trade Union League—Rose Schneiderman and Maude Schwartz. These intelligent trade unionists made a great many things clear to Franklin Roosevelt that he would hardly have known in any other way. These girls knew the theory and history of the trade union movement. They were not run-of-the-mill organizers making their way as best they could.

Maude Schwartz, an English-Irish woman, had been a member of a British trade union ever since she was a young girl. A printer by trade, she had had a good deal of experience in the trade union movement in England before she came to this country and was grounded in the high-mindedness of the British Labor movement. She was witty and amusing, and told a story well. Her descriptions of trade union meetings were vivid, realistic, lightened with humor. She knew labor men well. She did not think them angels. She knew them for the ordinary hard-working men they were. But she had ideals, and so did they.

So had Rose Schneiderman, an organizer in the garment and needle trades, who had been working at the sewing trade in New York City since she had been a little girl. She had grown up in a poor family, but had taken advantage of the free educational opportunities the city provided. She had studied the theory of trade unionism in the classes organized by the garment unions for their members. She had taken part in the effort to set up health and recreation centers. She had been an organizer of the shirtwaist workers, a branch of the garment workers. A fiery redhead, she had spoken with ardor at the Carnegie Hall meeting, on the Sunday after the Triangle fire of 1911, which had led to the Factory Investigation Commission.

Roosevelt's principal social talent lay in making people feel at ease in his society and in getting them to talk about the things they knew. He was soon learning from these girls a great deal about the trade union movement. He saw it in a new light. While he was well disposed toward it, he never had understood with real detail the purpose of the movement. He had neither seen the background of exploitation in industries from which the movement had grown in England and in this country, nor had he been a technical academic student of the movement itself. I doubt that he had ever read any of the standard works on trade unionism.

His attitude toward trade unionism might have been different if his first contacts with labor leaders had been with some of the hard-boiled men who ran the building trades unions. But through the eyes of these girls he saw the exploitation in the sweat shops, and how the tuberculosis rate had shot up in the printing industry before the union stepped in with regulation of hours and wages. He heard about the English co-operative movement which had sprung out of union activities. He heard about improvements in labor conditions in the textile industries where the unions had been organized for some years. He heard about the prevailing thirteen-hour day, with a longer day on Saturday because Sunday was to be a day off for "pious recreation." He heard about wages of four and five dollars a week and the theory that larger wages would lead to immorality. He heard about the efforts to organize the mass production industries and why they had failed. He heard how the trade unions had been the first to demand that little children under ten should not be employed.

He learned why labor leaders are sometimes rough—often quite rough. He learned that in the days of organizing against severe opposition the police and the hired thugs were often set upon trade union organizers. It took a "roughneck" to stand up to that kind of thing, and the sweet reasonableness which some think so much better than toughness had no chance to develop until a union was well established and could deal with its employers.

Later on he became acquainted with other labor leaders—even during the years of his illness he met a few. Mostly their conversations were vague because they had nothing to bargain about. Theoretical conversation was not as easy for most of them as it was for Rose and Maude. As Governor of New York he met a considerable number of state labor leaders. When he talked with them, relying upon the knowledge he had gained from these girls, he appeared to have a real understanding of the trade union movement. A labor leader once said to me, "You'd almost think he had participated in some strike or organizing campaign the way he knew and felt about it."

In other ways, too, the years of illness were constructive years for him. As he grew stronger he liked to read to his family. He once said to me, "You know, I like to read aloud—I would almost rather read to somebody than read to myself." Those words stuck in my mind because they illustrated his capacity to learn while he was taking part in an experience. Reading to others enabled him to absorb more from the writer than if he had been reading by himself. There was something incurably sociable about this man. His sociability was not only for purposes of pleasure and recreation. He was sociable in his intellectual as well as his playful moods.

He read a great deal of political history, political memoirs, books of travel. Naval history and naval technical works he had always read, and he continued to read them, but he read more general literature during those days. Other things he read during this period were farm and agricultural journals and, I suppose, a few books on agriculture. He was alert to developments in modern agriculture and was particularly interested in their application to the small farm which is so characteristic of the East. He also acquired a taste for the modern American soothing sirup—detective stories—and learned to read himself to sleep on them as so many other distinguished people have. I do not think he read much poetry or philosophy.

He had a first-rate knowledge of geography gained not only from studying his stamps, the usual explanation, but also from being an avid atlas reader. He had an amazing amount of information about the height of mountains and the depth of oceans, the rivers and their sources and the plains they watered. He read books of travel and exploration, from *Arabia Deserta* to Colonel Younghusband's brilliant story of the hazardous penetration into Tibet. Of American history he read a great deal, and he knew American history in a way which indicated a man who has talked with old people who had talked with older people who remembered many things: their own part in the War of the Revolution, the launching of sailing ships that went out to China, the driving of spikes in the railroad that crossed the continent, the fighting with Indians, and the driving of buffaloes out of the path of the engines.

The history and social life and organization of any community he visited or lived in absorbed him. The years of illness brought him more contacts with his neighbors at Hyde Park. He drove about the country as he got better and stopped to chat over the fence and learned how things were going in that particular little house. He knew the Hudson Valley, of course, as a native, as one who knows all the old stories and folklore of the Dutch settlements and of the English penetration. He knew the story of the passage of the American and British armies over that part of the country, as was natural for one who had listened eagerly to the tales of the old people in the neighborhood. His years at his mother's summer home on Campobello had awakened his interest in the history of those remote and hardy regions.

He was not a great student. I never was able to make out that even during the days of his illness he had read substantially in the field of economics. He rarely mentioned a book on economics.

He read Elsie Clews Parsons' book entitled *The Family* be-

cause he knew Elsie Parsons, and he used to refer to it laughingly as "a lot of words," saying that he knew what a family was
and didn't have to read a long book about it. But he thought it
amusing that a girl he knew could write such a heavy-weight
book, and he was particularly amused because it created such
consternation in conservative circles and shocked so many of
the clerics of the day.

In reading political handbooks, he discovered the handbook
of the Socialist party. He called it to my attention years afterward, saying, "You know, it's a funny thing—the Socialists
have what they call their immediate and long-term programs.
The immediate program, as you read it over, sounds almost
exactly like the Bull Moose party of Ted's day."

I think this was almost his only adventure into the reading
of the unorthodox political groups, and I doubt that he really
had full understanding of what the Socialists were driving at.
He was interested in political possibilities, and he didn't see
much political possibility for their point of view.

During this time Mrs. Roosevelt broadened her own social
and political contacts—she made a habit of keeping in touch
with party activities in the state. She entered into local campaign work. She made a broad political acquaintance; she was
anxious to keep her husband's interest in political affairs alive.
It had been his primary concern, and she saw in it something
he could build on as he began to recover. She was well aware
that if one is ill and out of things too long one is forgotten, and
she made, I think, a determined effort to keep alive Franklin
Roosevelt's name and good reputation within the party.

As he grew better he apparently kept up with the immediate
political situation, followed the platform and campaign speeches
of candidates in various states, the attitude of Democrats and
Republicans alike all over the country. He became well acquainted, just by reading the record, with the work of Al Smith
and his administration in New York, and he developed considerable enthusiasm for it.

Politics, I assume, were never out of his friend Louis Howe's
mind. His admiration for Roosevelt was based partly upon the
idea, which he conceived early, that he could make a great pol-

itician out of Roosevelt. Howe called attention to political movements developing and made a point of seeing that Roosevelt became acquainted with different politicians whom he brought in to see him.

Roosevelt's discovery of Warm Springs also helped broaden his horizon. Hydrotherapy treatment had been only slightly developed, but it was an old local tradition to go and bathe in the Warm Springs if you were ill of any disease. Somebody who had been lame had strengthened himself by learning to swim in the warm saline waters, and Roosevelt heard of it. At once he was stirred with enthusiasm to try it. His doctors thought it would help, and he started upon this program of getting back the use of his legs.

When Roosevelt took a little house in Warm Springs, he did not know that part of the country well and he immediately became interested in the people and the area in which they lived. He also became aware of the large number of people handicapped by partial or total paralysis, and became stirred with the idea that something could be done for them. He began to plan what could be done to make Warm Springs a center for the cure and relief of victims of paralysis.

The models of the European spas did not suit him. He knew they were for rich people. His plan was to keep the place simple and cheap, to make it possible for people to help themselves, to give them something to do if they were able, and to make the scale of living more like a camp than a hotel.

He put his own money into it, and he got some of his friends to put money into it, to build the place up and make it a practical, modern, and scientific therapeutic center. He also conceived the idea that some day there ought to be an endowment which not only would make this place available to the thousands who have paralysis, but would also make better medical and nursing care and better appliances available to victims of the disease everywhere. He thought that, above everything else, there should be medical research into the causes of paralysis and into methods of preventing it or curing it in the early stages.

His relations with the other patients at Warm Springs, after the place had been somewhat developed, were interesting and charming to see. He was one of them—he was a big brother— he had been through it—he was smiling—he was courageous— he was feeling fine—he encouraged you to try—he said you could do it. "I did it, you can do it" was the attitude.

He will go down in folklore as a man who could overcome terrible handicaps. In many households for many years the story will be told, and children and adults in the midst of a hard time will gain the faith and strength to bear a terrible disfigurement, or maiming, or loss in their fortunes or persons. They will say to themselves, "Roosevelt did it. If he did it, I can too."

He had an instinct for sharing his spiritual strength. During World War II he made a great effort to go to the hospitals where the badly injured were, the men who must face life handicapped. Even in the last year of his life, when the strain was beginning to tell on him, he continued to visit the hospital wards. There is no question that his hearty "You'll make it, brother" helped to keep up the morale of those men.

At Warm Springs, the daily baths in the warm waters, and the swimming, strengthened his muscles. Soon he recovered some strength in his paralyzed legs and could drive a specially designed, hand-operated automobile. By 1928 he could walk with the aid of braces and two canes.

During the long haul back to recovery he made one major political appearance—in 1924. He appeared at Madison Square Garden in New York City to make a nominating speech for Al Smith in the Democratic national convention that finally selected John W. Davis to head the party ticket. That was the memorable speech in which Roosevelt called Smith "the happy warrior." To those of us who remembered the strong, radiant, successful Roosevelt of the San Francisco convention of 1920, the man who appeared at Madison Square Garden in 1924 was deeply moving. He was thin and pale. He struggled along the platform on crutches, smiling only when he reached the security of the speaker's rostrum. When he smiled at last, his face had a warm friendliness that included everyone in the auditorium. He seemed to be sharing his personal victory.

His "happy warrior" speech rang out in a clear, ardent voice. The thunderous applause that followed was a tribute to him as well as to the candidate he placed in nomination.

By 1928 his cure had progressed so that he could get about more readily. He felt up to the long trip to Houston, Texas, for the Democratic national convention. It was a happy occasion for him. He met old friends who noted that here was a new Roosevelt. One heard comments that some day he might return to active politics.

PART TWO

THE STATE

4.

THE MAKING OF A
GOVERNOR

Alfred E. Smith was one of those deeply impressed by the new
Roosevelt who had captivated the delegates at Madison Square
Garden and again at Houston. Back in Albany to prepare for
the ill-fated presidential campaign of 1928, Smith looked over
the field for someone who could carry on his work as Chief
Executive of the State of New York and strengthen the national
ticket in New York State. By the time the Democratic state convention opened at Syracuse, Smith had conceived the idea that
Franklin Roosevelt was the essential man and that, though
handicapped, he could make the run.

Roosevelt was at Warm Springs. Mrs. Roosevelt was at the
convention. Governor Al approached her and asked if she
thought Roosevelt would consent to run.

"Why, that's absolutely impossible, Governor," Mrs. Roosevelt replied.

But Smith was determined. "I need him to carry the state for
me," he insisted. Finally he persuaded Mrs. Roosevelt to put
the question to her husband by long-distance telephone.

I was in the room at the Hotel Syracuse the night the call was
put through. I remember vividly the conversation that took
place. Mrs. Roosevelt wasted little time with preliminaries. She
told her husband that Smith wanted him to run for governor.
There was a pause as Roosevelt replied to her.

Then Mrs. Roosevelt spoke again, "Yes, I know, Franklin. I
told him that, but . . ."

Later we learned that Roosevelt had said, "I'm not well
enough to run. It's out of the question."

Mrs. Roosevelt turned around to the Governor. The look in her eyes told you that she thought it was hopeless to press the matter. Governor Smith took the phone.

"I need you, Frank," he said. "This is why. The progress which the Democratic party has made in this state must go on. We've got to carry on our program. You've got a great name. We believe you are the man to carry the state for the ticket. We need a big vote to swing New York. It all depends on you."

But Roosevelt refused to yield, and finally the Governor gave up. The word went out to the committee that Roosevelt would not consent to be drafted. And it came right back that he must be persuaded to run. The choice was—Roosevelt or defeat.

It was a most exciting time for those of us privileged to see this chapter of political history unfold. The hour was growing late, but it was decided to make one more try. They called Warm Springs again, but it was the same story.

"I need another year of treatment," Roosevelt said in substance, "and then I'll be as good as ever, ready to do whatever they ask of me. But if I leave now I'll not get my health and strength back. It means just that. My cure depends on it. It's now or never."

Mrs. Roosevelt replied, "I've told them all that, but the Governor is very insistent."

With that the conversation ended, but the next night Governor Smith was ready to try again with a new line of attack. The Governor made his plea personal, over and above politics. He was very persuasive.

"I need you," Smith said. "It's your duty to run. This is no broken-down administration you will inherit. It's a going concern. I'll help you. We'll all help you."

Roosevelt was weakening. He asked to speak to Mrs. Roosevelt. I had a hunch that he wanted to check his own half-persuaded mind.

"Do you think carrying New York depends on my running for governor?" Roosevelt asked his wife.

"I'm afraid it does," she replied.

"It appears," Roosevelt went on, "that they think I have an obligation to run. What do you think?"

"I know it's hard, but that's what they believe."

Roosevelt gave his assent. He was nominated by acclamation. In a few days he was back in New York, ready to start campaigning. Although doctors had pronounced him in "splendid physical health," party leaders planned that Roosevelt would make only a handful of speeches—a half-dozen at most—in the large, easily reached centers of population. But Roosevelt was interested now. He made the half-dozen speeches all right, and many more besides.

Roosevelt surprised all of his friends, and I think himself, by the vigor and drive he, just out of the sickroom, put into the whirlwind visits to the hundreds of districts that the gubernatorial campaign and the difficult presidential campaign for Smith seemed to make necessary. He took to the automobile as a method of getting around and spoke from the back of it at outdoor meetings. Prejudice in upstate communities against Smith was great. Roosevelt undoubtedly felt a deep desire to overcome it by a personal appearance, which emphasized that he, a farmer of the old stock and a Protestant, supported Smith, a city man of immigrant stock and a Catholic. He put his heart into the campaign.

Roosevelt had undertaken the campaign on the plea that he would strengthen the Smith national ticket in the state. He carried out the contract. Undoubtedly, however, he increased his own prestige enormously by these personal appearances. He proved to himself and the people that he was not too sick to assume responsibility, as his opponents claimed. He had that imponderable human quality which made people feel they were close to him. The rank-and-file politicians, the heads of little county and local committees, pulled up a seat and whispered their deepest hopes to him.

I remember watching him once in Utica. The people who ran things were Republicans in that town. Certainly some of the Democratic rank-and-file were pretty tiresome, with a lot of things to say that were of no consequence. However, he sat and nodded and smiled and said, "That's fine," when they reported some slight progress. I remembered, in contrast, how he had walked away from bores a few years earlier when he was in the state Senate.

Now he could not walk away when he was bored. He lis-

tened, and out of it learned what he later held with such conviction as a basis of action—that "everybody wants to have the
sense of belonging, of being on the inside," that "no one wants
to be left out," as he put it years later in a Columbus, Ohio,
speech. He learned that people are afraid of insecurity and that
they cling to small accustomed activities. He learned that only
a few are ambitious. He became thoroughly familiar with the
concept that good and evil, hope and fear, wisdom and ignorance, selfishness and sacrifice, are inseparably mixed in most
human beings.

I remember plainly the mixture of admiration and consternation I felt when I saw him speak in a small hall in New York
City's Yorkville district. The auditorium was crowded. The
only entrance was up the broad stairway from the street, then
down narrow aisles to the small stage. There was a direct emergency approach to the stage by way of the fire escape in the
rear. This was devoid of crowds and was subject to police control. The only possible way for any candidate to enter the stage
without being crushed by the throng was by the fire escape.

I stood in the wings backstage, being among the fifty-odd
people who were to sit upon the platform that night. I realized
with sudden horror that the only way he could get over that fire
escape was in the arms of strong men. That was how he arrived.

Those of us who saw this incident, with our hands on our
throats to hold down our emotion, realized that this man had
accepted the ultimate humility which comes from being helped
physically. He had accepted it smiling. He came up over that
perilous, uncomfortable, and humiliating "entrance," and his
manner was pleasant, courteous, enthusiastic. He got up on his
braces, adjusted them, straightened himself, smoothed his hair,
linked his arm in his son Jim's, and walked out on the platform
as if this were nothing unusual.

Then he launched into his speech. I don't recall the speech at
all. For me and for others who saw that episode his speech was
less important than his courage. That was creative. Before the
campaign was over I saw similar episodes a good many times,
and I began to see what the great teachers of religion meant
when they said that humility is the greatest of virtues, and that

if you can't learn it, God will teach it to you by humiliation. Only so can a man be really great, and it was in those accommodations to necessity that Franklin Roosevelt began to approach the stature of humility and inner integrity which made him truly great.

So he went on through this campaign, being carried up back stairs, speaking from the back of an automobile, holding a general reception in a hotel lobby or in a railroad station, speaking to hundreds of people and gaining with every contact a knowledge of the heart of the people. The politicians who had not seen Roosevelt since the San Francisco convention were struck by the contrast between this man and the handsome, gay, vigorous young athlete he had been then. He was physically weak but he asked for no quarter. He was politically inexperienced from the point of view of the old-time state politicians, but his heart was in the right place and his purposes were politically sound from the politicians' point of view. Their affection, based partly on a protective sense, began to develop. There was no question that his handicap made it possible for many of the old politicians to forgive old scores. It made it possible for the common people to trust him to understand what it is to be handicapped by poverty and ignorance, as well as by physical misfortunes.

During this campaign in the State of New York, in which the gubernatorial race was somewhat obscured by the presidential campaign, Eleanor Roosevelt became more acquainted with political figures and problems. A large part of my time was absorbed in the presidential campaign for Al Smith. I learned, as Eleanor Roosevelt did, the depths of prejudice and ignorance throughout the country. We learned also the depths of dissatisfaction with the old-line politicians and with reactionary attitudes in both parties.

Because I was a Protestant of old American stock I was sent out to the deep South, to the Middle West, and to the centers of greatest prejudice against Smith. Prejudice was profound because he was a Roman Catholic and a "city fellow," New York City at that! The story that I told, that Irene Gibson, Aileen Webb, and other speakers told, was that we had known this man, Al Smith, that we knew him well; that we knew him to be honest, high-minded, independent, competent, and intelligent; a man in the true pattern of American life and development. People broke down and cried in Ohio and Indiana audiences when I told that he was a true Christian and said his prayers—said the prayers that his mother had taught him. Many agreed that they would rather have a man in the White House who said his prayers than one who had a cynical disregard of the laws of God, but they were bothered by the sign of the Cross and the Rosary. The Democrats in many of those areas voted against him, but for the most part they never quite forgave themselves.

In New York it was not much different. People who had willingly voted for Al Smith as Governor time after time turned tail when it came to voting for him for President. No governor in New York State had commanded such respect and affection as Al Smith, but too many people were frightened of the idea, so hard to combat, so unreal in its conception, that the Church of Rome might take control of the United States if he were made President. In a reflective mood many years later, Al Smith said to me, "Well, the time just hasn't come when a man can say his beads in the White House."

But within the state Roosevelt inherited in that campaign the good will thousands bore to Al Smith. He represented also to many ignorant people a continuation of the name of Theodore Roosevelt. This sometimes irritated him. Politically he could not escape it. In many of the remoter upstate communities people did vote for him under the impression it was Theodore Roosevelt they were voting for. Franklin Roosevelt also inherited the garment of Wilson, and intelligent, thoughtful people, the large minority who thought of political responsibility in terms of international problems and the League of Nations, voted for him.

He made a brave, vigorous fight. He ran primarily to support Smith. It never crossed his mind that he could be elected if Smith did not carry the state. When the news came to headquarters that Smith had lost the state, Roosevelt went home convinced that it was all over. He was disappointed, as we all were, that Smith was not elected. That he himself would win was out of the question.

I have the clearest recollection of going back and forth that evening between state and national headquarters. Finally, I was convinced, against my ardent hope, that Smith had lost New York and the country. At Smith headquarters and at national headquarters feeling was intense. Affection and respect for Smith were sincere and omnipresent. He was gallant and self-possessed in defeat. Everybody took it for granted that, since the state had been lost for the presidential candidate, it was also lost for the gubernatorial candidate.

As a matter of courtesy and with lingering hope, I went back to the Roosevelt headquarters at the Biltmore Hotel. Most people had gone or were leaving gloomily, but the returns from the small upstate districts which I knew well were still coming in. Surprising numbers of small districts had gone for Roosevelt, but these were quickly blotted out by larger districts which had gone against him. The platform on which he had campaigned was a platform of social reform and labor legislation. It was a campaign for the continuance of an administration devoted to the idea that these things mattered in a modern state: the life of the people, the opportunity for a high standard of living based on a comfortable income, the opportunity to work, and protection in distress. I found it hard to believe that that idea could have been defeated. I had campaigned in the state many times on that platform. I knew the people believed in that platform. I could not believe that because they were giving up their beloved Governor Smith, they would also give up his program.

I made up my mind to sit out the night on the ridiculous theory that if I didn't give up somehow the result would be changed. Only one other person seemed to have that idea—Sara Delano Roosevelt. Almost everyone else went home, except the telephone operators and the tally men. Hoover's election was conceded before midnight and the Republican gubernatorial candidate's election was announced for the morning papers. About two o'clock in the morning surprising returns began to come in. Forty votes here, one hundred votes there, and seventy-five votes somewhere else. They mounted up.

About four o'clock in the morning the tally men agreed that Franklin Roosevelt had been elected Governor of New York by a narrow margin. The morning papers carried the contrary news because they had already been printed, but the evening papers announced his election, though Smith had lost the state and the nation. Mrs. Sara Roosevelt and I had a private if exhausted jubilation and I saw her home as dawn was breaking.

It was a strange situation. Roosevelt himself was confused by it. Smith was confused and deeply disturbed. He had been through a harassing campaign. It devastated his understanding of American life and politics, but that is another story. He came back from a brief rest more than ever devoted to the problems, hopes, and interests of the State of New York, which he loved deeply. He would help Roosevelt be a good governor. He himself had been a good governor; everybody admitted it. He would sublimate his disappointment in his own defeat and continue to serve the state, which he loved in a more personal and intimate way than the United States, by helping "Frank" be a good governor.

By this time Al thought of himself as old, experienced, and wise in politics and administration. He wasn't much older than Roosevelt, but he felt older and more experienced. He had a protective instinct toward Roosevelt, because he was a younger man and because he had been sick and weak and crippled and had been through a terrific experience of isolation. Smith rose to this idea with simplicity and friendliness.

The days immediately after the gubernatorial election were hard for Al Smith. They were interesting for Franklin Roosevelt. Smith could not help but regret his loss of status in the state and was reluctant to take his hand off its work. It was a perfectly natural human feeling. His days were clouded with sadness.

On the other hand, Franklin Roosevelt, the newcomer, had just been elected when it seemed impossible, when his party had gone down in defeat and he was the only one who had pulled through in New York. It was a time of excitement for him. He was in the challenging situation of beginning to plan, while Al Smith was wondering about his own future and that of the beloved state to which he had given such true service.

Out of this situation arose a natural tension between the two—never conscious or expressed by either man. But Smith, as he cleaned up one piece of work after another preparatory to leaving the Executive Chamber, was inevitably making notes to "tell Frank" what to do about this and that.

When Roosevelt came back from Warm Springs, they began to have brief conferences over the telephone. For Roosevelt, like every newly elected officer of government, was besieged by the thousand and one small politicians who wanted to see him about something.

It was clear that Smith had many well-worked-out ideas, and Roosevelt was receptive to them. There was no doubt that he anticipated following Al Smith's advice. Al Smith had demonstrated while he was the standard bearer that social and humanitarian legislation would always bring popular political support. Franklin Roosevelt was to carry on these ideas. He believed in them. He wanted to do what Al had done and perhaps do it better.

Toward the end of this interim period Smith began to recommend appointees and advisers to Roosevelt. Some of the people he recommended Roosevelt didn't like. A case in point was Robert Moses. Smith was devoted to Moses, a man of undoubted talents, and Smith had been helped greatly by his activities and advice. Roosevelt did not like Moses; Moses "bothered" him. Moses bothered many people, but he was an able public-spirited citizen. He had his peculiarities. There were others too for whom Smith had respect and admiration whom Roosevelt did not understand.

Al Smith had, in the later years of his governorship, the advice and help of Belle Moskowitz, an able, high-minded woman of energy and shrewdness. She believed in social reform and labor legislation and had wanted to help the Governor make them realities. The fact that her first association with Smith was based on a violent reaction against Charles Whitman, who was Governor from 1916 to 1918 and who treated her and her ideas rudely and faithlessly, ought not to be minimized. She had been a lifelong Republican, but now she was "sore" at Whitman. She wanted somehow to square off with him and at the same time promote a program of social progress in which she was truly interested.

She went over to Al Smith publicly in the very last days of his first campaign for governor (1918) and arranged for him one meeting with a group of influential people whom he otherwise would not have known. Smith accepted her invitation to speak to the University Women on my recommendation. I introduced them to each other in the automobile on the way to the meeting. She liked him. He was glad to have a new recruit and was cordial. The campaign was over in a few days, but not before Mrs. Moskowitz had established herself at party headquarters with the record of having been one of the campaign workers.

After the campaign she developed a good idea for the Governor's approach to state problems. She brought it to me for political comment, just as she must have consulted many others.

It was a plan for the reconstruction period. World War I was just over, and obviously many things had been done in the state during the war that would have to be modified or adapted to the regular pattern of state government. Her project was a plan for a reconstruction program under a Reconstruction Commission made up of some of the ablest citizens of the state. She had been impressed with the effectiveness of the Factory Investigation Commission. For the Reconstruction Commission, she revived the idea of bringing the people and the experts, along with the legislature, into the planning of changes. The idea was excellent. Eventually she asked me to make it possible for her to present it to Governor-elect Smith, and I did.

He gave us a date on a certain evening, and then she suggested that other people be brought in until we had a company of twenty or so intelligent people to discuss the program. With a naïve, old-fashioned courtesy—women were new in politics—Smith asked his wife and his mother to come, since there would be "ladies present." She made a brilliant presentation. We endorsed it and the Governor-elect took an immediate liking to it.

This reconstruction program was one of the best things Smith ever did. It started his administration with a good program and a good performance.

After the program was launched, Mrs. Moskowitz, of course, became its most effective sparkplug. That began her long and fruitful collaboration with Governor Smith, which was absolutely loyal on both sides. She was of inestimable help to him. He supported her loyally, gave her his friendship, and was able and willing to carry out in the political field many of the ideas she developed.

Governor Smith naturally thought her of prime importance in the scheme of his administration, and though she had held no elective or regularly appointed office, he felt her essential to the progress of his programs. He took it for granted that Roosevelt would want her to carry on. I think he therefore talked very little about it; simply took it for granted.

Mrs. Roosevelt had worked with Mrs. Moskowitz on campaign committees and they had become friends. Governor-elect Roosevelt probably did not know her well—but what he knew about her was to her credit.

During these years, however, Mrs. Moskowitz had become a vigorous and domineering woman. She had become accustomed to power, to having the yes and no, to "fixing things." She knew how to manage men, programs, and politics with extraordinary success. People who wanted to convince Smith of something would see her first, and she sometimes said to a disappointed proponent of some good cause, "Why didn't you ring me up? It's too late now. You should have seen me." The wise ones did.

Whether or not some of that quality of masterfulness conveyed itself to Roosevelt I shall never know. Whether he had any doubts about her personally I do not know. He never said anything to me that would indicate that he had anything but respect for her.

Smith said to him one day, "Now, Frank, you will want Mrs. Moskowitz, of course, and I think the best thing you can do is to appoint her as the Governor's Secretary. Everybody knows then what her duties and responsibilities are, it gives her a good place from which to work, and she will be of invaluable assistance. That's what I think you had better do. I just want to make that suggestion and I am sure she is willing to do it for you."

There was talk about her ability and reliability. Roosevelt gave assent to that, but didn't commit himself. The episode appears to have made a special impression on his mind with respect to his relation to Al Smith and Al Smith's personal and political associates.

Later on when I went, at Smith's request, to raise the question with him once more, Roosevelt said, "You know, I've thought about that a great deal. I admire Mrs. Moskowitz. I think she is very, very able. I think she did a great deal for Al. I am sure she could do a great deal for any man who is Governor, but—" Here he looked off out the window, and for the first time I realized how much he had gained in self-analysis and self-knowledge. "You know, I didn't feel able to make this campaign for governor, but I made it. I didn't feel that I was sufficiently recovered to undertake the duties of Governor of New York, but here I am. After Al said that to me I thought about myself and I realized that I've *got* to be Governor of the State of New York and I have got to be it MYSELF. If I weren't, if I didn't do it myself, something would be wrong in here." He tapped his chest. "I've got to do it myself and I feel sure that if I had Belle Moskowitz there, she is so accustomed to running and planning everything, she would inevitably plan and develop the work of the Governor of New York in such a way that I would not really put *myself* into it. I have to do it this way by myself without Mrs. Moskowitz. I am awfully sorry if it hurts anybody, particularly Al."

I have always thought that if Al had been elected and gone to Washington to be President of the United States, he would have been completely absorbed in planning his national work. But, as it was, he could not take his mind off the comparison between his own experience and wisdom and Roosevelt's new and perhaps amateurish approaches to New York state political and administrative problems. He brooded over the idea that Roosevelt was making a mistake in not taking Mrs. Moskowitz as his secretary. He spoke to me about it many times.

I have also thought, and I know from conversations with Mrs. Moskowitz and Louis Howe, that she and Howe both kept the fire alive. Mrs. Moskowitz naturally resented the situation, and she could hardly help building up resentment within Al Smith. This, I think, had more to do with separating the two men than any other one thing. If Governor Al could only have realized that

Roosevelt, because he had been a sick man, needed more than most men to demonstrate that he could and would do it alone, he would not have attempted to handle him by remote control.

On the eve of Inauguration Day, Roosevelt told Al Smith that he had decided to appoint Guernsey Cross as Secretary to the Governor. He said, "You know I need a great, big, strong man as secretary. I need someone whom I can lean on physically, if necessary, and I think it will be better, Al." A self-conscious tension began between the two men.

With Roosevelt taking over the Governor's office and mansion, appointing his own aides and becoming informed on the problems and the administration, it was soon clear that Al would rarely be consulted on state affairs. Roosevelt was going it alone with his own advisers, friends, and ideas.

5.

NEW BOSS

When Franklin Roosevelt was elected Governor of New York in 1928, I had been a public official in the Department of Labor in that state since 1919. Al Smith had appointed me to the new Industrial Board in 1919, and in 1924 he named me Chairman. I therefore had had some experience in the development and administration of labor laws. Naturally I gave the gubernatorial candidate for use in his campaign such help as I could on details of labor legislation and administration. It should be made clear that the Industrial Commissioner headed the administrative end of the Department of Labor, while the Industrial Board was responsible for the judicial and legislative side. From 1925 to 1928 the Industrial Commissioner was James A. Hamilton, who had been appointed by Governor Smith on strong recommendation but had proved disappointing. Smith knew this and had tried to deal with it in courteous ways. He had asked me to take charge of the preparation of the budget for the Department, although that duty was outside the responsibilities of the Chairman of the Industrial Board. He had asked me to handle the legislative program of the Department, by-passing the Commissioner, and had suggested I carry on conferences with insurance companies, labor unions, and manufacturers preliminary to the preparation of bills. I had become familiar with the administrative problems and knew, to some extent, what the defects in the situation were. Thus, by one device or another, the weakness of the Industrial Commissioner had been covered, and the Department of Labor was well thought of by the people.

Governor Smith told Governor-elect Roosevelt that the Industrial Commissioner would have to be replaced.

Roosevelt said, "I was thinking of appointing Frances to that post. What do you think?"

Smith replied, "Well, she is first class, I know her. I appointed her. I appointed her when women had never been appointed to anything. You know that. I recognized her, first, because women got the vote in 1918, and second, because I knew her and thought she knew about labor matters, and she is fair. She could be trusted to do the right thing and had good common sense, and she talked so you could understand her."

"Well," said Roosevelt, "I know all that, and it appears to me that it might be a good idea to make her Industrial Commissioner. What do you think?"

Al's reply, according to his story and Roosevelt's was, "Well, you should give it a lot of thought. When she is Commissioner she will have charge of administering the whole Department of Labor—all the men who work as factory inspectors and on the compensation boards. I have always thought that, as a rule, men will take advice from a woman, but it is hard for them to take orders from a woman."

A few weeks later when Roosevelt asked me to be Industrial Commissioner he told me this with a chuckle, adding, "You see, Al's a good progressive fellow but I am willing to take more chances. I've got more nerve about women and their status in the world than Al has."

I laughed too, but I could not resist the temptation to say, "But it was more of a victory for Al to bring himself to appoint a woman, never appointed before, when I was unknown, than it is for you when I have a record as a responsible public officer for almost ten years."

It was characteristic of Roosevelt that when he wanted to discuss my being Industrial Commissioner he asked me to Hyde Park. After lunch he took me riding around the place in his hand-operated automobile, which he could drive himself. He pointed out the new trees and the farm improvements and discussed industrial problems. He was just as interested in the trees as in the State of New York.

In talking with him about the Industrial Commissionership, I made it clear that there would have to be some serious reorganization. I was quite sure we would find carelessness and inexcusable delays in the handling of workmen's compensation cases and perhaps some things that were quite wrong in the administration of the Factory Act. We might stumble across corruption.

I told him that I didn't think we would find anything wrong in the factory inspection work because we had two leaders among the factory inspectors who hated each other so intensely that each watched for the mistakes of the other and reported them before there was time for anything serious to happen.

He laughed and said, "Well, that is a principle of government I never heard before. I recommend a thorough investigation."

I felt sure we should find some wrongdoing. Some people involved would turn out to have strong political ties. Although I had no idea who might be involved, I could foresee trouble. That is always the way in an investigation. Sooner or later I knew we should have to begin explaining to some political leader why one of his favorites had to be removed. I wanted to be sure Roosevelt knew before I let him in for that kind of situation. He understood and assented. I also pointed out that in some instances powerful insurance companies would have grave objections to the findings of the investigations and that in groups here and there inside the labor unions we might find people who, I thought, were responsible for "throwing" cases.

He saw that there might be a fight, but he said, "All right."

I remember doing then what I did with him hundreds of times afterward—repeating it all before I left.

"Now do I understand that you want me to go ahead on this program of investigation?" I said. "And after we go through with it, what if we find corruption? You say it is all right to fire people. Is that understood?"

He repeated it after me. He added, "Sure, that's all right. Now we understand each other."

Later we did run into the things I had foreseen. He never forgot.

"Yes," he said, "I told her to go ahead. It has to be done."

As we discussed the possible difficulties of reorganization in the Department of Labor, he gave his approval, and for the first time I registered definitely that this man was becoming my superior officer. I had to learn to know him in a different way from that of a political associate in campaign time, which does not give one the test of the true capacity of individuals to cooperate and carry out joint programs.

I was not too anxious to accept the post of Industrial Commissioner. I had, as Chairman of the Industrial Board, the perfect job. It was fascinating and gave one all the authority one wanted. There was no obligation in that post to untangle administrative problems. The job was to adopt codes that had the effect of law with regard to factory conditions and labor matters, and also provided an opportunity to act as judge in workmen's compensation cases and to set up the final standards which should prevail for the referees. The job required one to be the court of appeals. It was a job that fully occupied all of one's talents—it was creative, and one could make constant progress toward practical achievement of social justice, not only in a large way but in the application of its principles to the problems of individual workers, individual employers, and individual situations in factories.

I was not anxious to be the Industrial Commissioner. That office, I knew, had all the problems and complications of administration. However, it seemed to be the right thing to do. I had been taught long ago by my grandmother that if anybody opens a door, one should always go through. Opportunity comes that way.

It was probably my real preference for my old job, despite the pull of a sense of obligation and adventure to take the new one, that made me say to Roosevelt as I left, "Now, Governor, if between now and Inauguration Day you change your mind about this, or if you find there is objection on the part of the politicians, or if for any reason at all it becomes something that had better not be done, don't give me a moment's thought. Just tell me it is all over and that's fine, because I am quite happy doing what I am doing now."

He laughed and said, "Oh, well, that's all right."

I learned afterward that he mentioned it to a number of people. Apparently it gave him confidence in me that he wouldn't otherwise have had—a confidence that I wasn't self-seeking and that I would not press him beyond endurance for my own support and promotion.

We talked about a good many things that day as we rode around the place. We talked about the legislative program, and he gave me the signal to go ahead on proposed legislation for the reduction of women's working hours, for the correction of defects in the workmen's compensation system, for greater controls over the labor of children, for the abolition of home work or sweated-out work, for the prohibition of night work by women, and for a series of codes under the labor law which were bound to be painful for some people, particularly the codes on mercantile establishments which had been hanging fire for years and on which little, if any, progress had been made. These and other matters he talked about with great simplicity and clarity.

"Go ahead," he said. "I am in favor of the program. I want all these things done. Make all your plans—go as far as you can. When you need help, come to me and I will do everything I can. I am for the program—all of it. Keep me posted so I won't make mistakes when I don't know exactly what is going on."

Our conversation also touched on techniques of administration, and he gave me some good pointers on how to handle politically minded people. "Always ask their advice," he remarked, "whether you take it or not."

This brought us to the discussion of the use we might make of the Advisory Board in the Department of Labor. It had been set up by law during a Republican administration, largely because the Republicans who backed a reorganization of the Department of Labor didn't quite trust the Labor Commissioner to make appointments to Civil Service jobs in the Department, fearing that he would appoint only labor people. They provided a Labor Advisory Board including labor people, employers, and some members of the general public. The Board had been a dead letter. It scarcely ever met, it had no program, and it had been of little use to the commissioners after it was appointed.

I talked to him about the possibility of getting the members to resign and setting up a new group, selected because they could give the work some time. Then they could be true advisers. We could give them an agenda, have them hold regular meetings, and seek their advice on real problems before the Department. I hoped also to utilize them to educate the people concerning problems of the Labor Department's administration and to ask them, as a Board, to make studies of the administrative problems of a number of sections and bureaus in the Department.

Roosevelt was enthusiastic about this idea, and it led him into a discussion of how valuable had been the Factory Commission and Al Smith's Reconstruction Commission. They had brought representatives of the public and the affected parties into advisory participation in the development and administration of laws intended for their benefit. In the past such laws had been administered without consideration for the knowledge and wisdom of the people affected.

He urged me to go ahead with the development of this technique and indicated that he meant to use it more himself, as indeed he did. It was an indication of a new technique in the representative democratic process. The idea that the people should be involved in administrative law from the beginning continued to grow in his mind, and colored many things he did later.

This conviction that he learned early in his gubernatorial administration became a fixed principle: the people must be in the picture in the administrative end of government.

6.

DOMESTIC CIRCLE

The natural hospitality of the Roosevelts was called upon in overabundance during Roosevelt's public life as Governor. They entertained a great deal, inviting people to dinner from all over the state. If a person came from a distance, there was often an invitation to spend the night at the Executive Mansion. Night after night every bed was full, and visiting friends of long acquaintance were asked to double up.

Wherever the Roosevelts lived, whether at Hyde Park, the Executive Mansion in Albany, or the White House, there was always the sense of a big family. Their own children were a considerable company, and there were others who seemed like members of the family. Louis Howe was in and out, as though he belonged, as indeed he did. Marguerite LeHand and Grace Tully, secretaries who came to work for Mr. and Mrs. Roosevelt at Albany, were treated like young sisters. Nancy Cook and Marion Dickerman, living in a cottage at Hyde Park near the big house, were accepted the same way. Visitors seemed to come and go almost at their own invitation and were always apparently expected. There were nieces, nephews, cousins, school friends of the Roosevelt boys, who assumed a right to a parking place.

Roosevelt moved in this family commotion with joyous relish. Having so many people around did not seem to get on his nerves. He was responsive, courteous, very much the paterfamilias, giving advice freely to members of the family with an amiability that was not diminished if the suggestions were ignored or even openly derided.

Visiting at the Executive Mansion, which I often did in Albany, was like staying at an agreeable home furnished in a slightly Victorian manner. The place did not confine the Roosevelts to a formal pattern; they took it in stride. They moved the furniture around, fixed up a cozy little sitting-room upstairs, brought a few things from Hyde Park, and made it look more like home than like the property of the State of New York. Coats, books, and papers were left around all over the Mansion, giving it that pleasantly occupied look.

The servants shared the willingness to take care of visitors at all hours. That is perhaps a part of the atmosphere of an Executive Mansion, but I fancied that it was considerably more spontaneous than in other official residences. Except on evenings of State dinners, there was easy informality. Whoever visited had a good time, and the Roosevelts always seemed to enjoy their guests.

The people of New York have always liked their governors to entertain a good deal, and when invited to a large reception at the Executive Mansion, they came in droves. Roosevelt seemed to enjoy these large evenings. I used to watch him as group after group would sit down beside him for a few minutes. Immediate repartee and laughter would establish an atmosphere of pleasure.

Hyde Park, the family home, was within easy driving distance of Albany; they were there a great deal when Roosevelt was Governor. Here things were a little different, but many people came to visit, stayed for lunch, afternoon tea, or overnight. Many passed by and dropped in. I often stopped at Hyde Park, usually by invitation, for it was convenient to have an informal talk with the Governor and to settle official business quietly and restfully.

He took great pleasure in taking a visitor around in his car to show what the farms of New York looked like and what he was trying to do with this place of his mother's. He loved the road to the river, down over a steep embankment through beautiful woodland. He was interested in the little house Mrs. Roosevelt was building and in the Val Kil industries she was helping to develop on the other side of the property.

In summer and holiday time the children were at home.

There were boys rushing all over the place, riding ponies, practicing hurdle jumps, swinging baseball bats and tennis racquets, filling the air with their shouting.

Large companies would sit down to lunch. The windows would be open, with a pleasant breeze blowing from the Hudson River. Roosevelt would be at the head of the table, talking to everybody, bantering with his children, teasing them and they him. The youngsters would tell preposterous stories to dignified visitors to see if they could get away with them, and would burst into gales of laughter regardless of whether the visitor fell for the story or saw through it. Roosevelt played with his children as though he were one of them; he relished the practical joke of the moment as much as they did.

It couldn't have been easy to bring up children in that atmosphere, with so much publicity playing on them all the time. Moreover, there was Grandmother, a charming woman who doted on her grandchildren and was inclined to help them out of scrapes. On one occasion, as the Governor drove me away from the house, he pointed to two horses grazing in a field.

"I don't know what I am going to do," he exploded. "How can I ever discipline those boys? They did something terrible, absolutely against all the rules. Eleanor and I talked it over and we decided they had to be punished in a way they would remember. So we told them that their pony, which they had always enjoyed very much, was going to be taken away from them and sent to two children on the other side of the town for the summer. They were very depressed about it and we thought we had made some impression. Well, what do you think! Last week my mother buys those two horses for them, two horses, not ponies. Now what am I going to do?"

The boys were strong, healthy, energetic. They played vigorously with all the lads in the neighborhood and even drew into their games the state troopers assigned to guard the house and the Governor.

The house at Hyde Park is a comfortable homelike place. The old-fashioned music room with its dainty Victorian furniture, its hangings, and its crystal lights makes a lovely contrast to the large modern room which was built on and used as a library and living-room. Roosevelt's own study at Hyde Park was always a little room off the back hall. It had been his study as a boy, and it was "plenty good enough for me" when he was Governor. He liked it just that way. The room was small, the desk big. He had a comfortable old chair, a few knickknacks, and the books he wanted near by. "Everything right within reach," he would say cheerfully. He saw all sorts of people there. He did business with state officials, went over budgets, wrote Thanksgiving Day proclamations and messages to the legislature. His mother used to tell me regretfully, "I do wish he'd let me fix him up a nice study, now that he has grown up and is the Governor." But he preferred to keep the old room.

He particularly admired the beautiful view, as did everyone, from the terrace at the southern end of the house. One stepped out long French windows from the living-room-library and onto a green lawn. Many times in summer, when I would be told that "the family was on the lawn," I approached through the library and saw through the open door an unforgettable picture: Mrs. Sara Roosevelt, in a soft, light summery dress with ruffles, her hair charmingly curled, sitting in a wicker chair and reading; Mrs. Roosevelt, in a white dress and white tennis shoes with a velvet band around her head to keep the hair from blowing, sitting with her long-legged, graceful posture in a low chair and knitting, always knitting; Roosevelt looking off down the river at the view he admired, with a book, often unopened, in one hand, and a walking stick in the other; dogs playing near by, and children romping a little farther down the lawn. The scene was like a Currier and Ives print of Life along the Hudson.

Roosevelt's personal habits and way of life were simple to the point of bareness. He had practically no personal luxurious needs or tastes. If he had been a millionaire, I am sure that his hobbies would not have brought him to elegancies of personal equipment. Books, stamps, boats, ship models—these things he spent money on gladly and without thought, but for his personal use he preferred the old to the new—the old sweater, the old coat, the old hat. No fancy desk sets—just a common pen and an ordinary blotter sufficed.

The simplicity of his taste in food is proverbial. Mrs. Roosevelt has often said that if anyone asked him what he wanted to eat, he would think a minute and look up, always with the same innocent look, and say, "Scrambled eggs." It was the only food he could remember. As a matter of fact, he liked all kinds of food, he merely wasn't particular.

Later, in the White House, he continued to live with complete personal simplicity. The building, of course, is a museum piece, open for the world to parade through. The second floor, reserved by tradition for the President's family, is a drafty assemblage of rooms, furnished with no special character. I suppose each presidential family gives them a temporary personal quality, covering the furniture, moving it around, changing the uses of different rooms and making it a home after their fashion. The Roosevelts did the best they could and made themselves comfortable without going to much trouble or expense.

The President chose the Oval Room on the second floor as a study. Here he could have people come in the evening, Sundays, and other unusual times for conferences. Here he could work at a desk near the door to his bedroom, which was the room directly off the study. He often received his secretaries and some close associates in his bedroom in the early morning. Occasionally when he had a cold and I had a matter of important business to transact, I saw him there.

I have a photographic impression of that room. A little too large to be cozy, it was not large enough to be impressive. A heavy dark wardrobe stood against a wall. (There are no closets in the White House and wardrobes are necessary.) A marble mantelpiece of the Victorian type carved with grapes held a collection of miniature pigs—Mexican pigs, Irish pigs, pigs of all kinds, sizes, and colors. Snapshots of children, friends, and expeditions were propped up in back of the pigs. There was an old bureau between the windows, with a plain white towel on top and the things men need for their dressing arrangements. There was an old-fashioned rocking chair, often with a piece of clothing thrown over it. Then there was the bed—not the kind you would expect a President of the United States to have. Roosevelt used a small, narrow white iron bedstead, the kind one sees in the boy's room of many an American house. It had

a thin, hard-looking mattress, a couple of pillows, and an ordinary white seersucker spread. A folded old gray shawl lay
at the foot. "Just the right weight," the President once said.
"Don't like these great heavy things." An old gray sweater,
much the worse for wear, lay close at hand. He wore it over
night clothes to keep his shoulders warm when he had a cold.
A white painted table, the kind one often sees in bathrooms,
stood beside the bed, with a towel over it and with aspirin,
nose drops, a glass of water, stubs of pencils, bits of paper with
telephone numbers, addresses, and memoranda to himself, a
couple of books, a worn old prayer book, a watch, a package
of cigarettes, an ash tray, a couple of telephones, all cluttered
together. Hanging on the walls were a few pictures of the children and favorite familiar scenes. And over the door at the
opposite end of the room hung a horse's tail. When one asked
what that was, he would say, "Why, that's Gloucester's tail."
Gloucester, a horse raised by the President's father, had been
regarded by the family as one of the finest examples of horse-
flesh in the world.

The Oval Study, a beautiful room in its proportions and
design, had for a few weeks after he took over a magnificent
air. He soon began to fill it up with everything that came his
way—a Jefferson chair, another bookcase, another bench, another table, ship models and books and papers piled on the
floor. Any room he used invariably got that lived-in and over-
crowded look which indicated the complexity and variety of
his interests and intentions.

Campaign times were particularly exciting in the Roosevelt
family and household. Vast numbers of people came and went
at Hyde Park or at the East 65th Street house in New York City.
Delegations from various parts of the country, particularly in
1932, came to see what manner of man this was. I remember
particularly a group of miners who, somewhat doubtful of
John Lewis's rock-ribbed Republicanism in support of Hoover,
came to have a chat with this candidate.

During his gubernatorial campaign in 1928, and again in
1930, when he was re-elected, the house and grounds at Hyde
Park looked almost like a public recreation ground. Mrs. Sara

Roosevelt, to whom political campaigns were something new, proved herself up to the demands. Her devotion to her son in his, to her, almost incomprehensible taste for politics was sufficient to take her over the hurdles. She was on friendly terms with people the like of whom she had never met. She asked these political callers about their homes, families, and journeyings with a solicitude which endeared her to them. She remained completely maternal in her attitude and once told me, "I have always believed that a mother should be friends with her children's friends."

A few days after one of these campaigns in which her house had been overrun for weeks, I stopped in, on my way from Albany to New York, to pick up a portfolio of papers I had left the week before. I found her alone and went in to pay a brief call. I thanked her for all she had done to make the campaign successful, expressed my admiration for her ability to entertain so many people, and said I feared she must be tired.

"Oh, no," she said, "it was nice. I enjoyed it. I lived here in the country, you know, in the days before automobiles and telephones. We always had to be prepared for visitors driving quite long distances, who would come to call without notice. So I learned early to have ample supplies of food on hand, because one likes to be able to ask one's friends to stay for lunch or dinner. This was a little more rigorous, but I did enjoy seeing Franklin's friends."

Then she looked around the room, which had a slightly exhausted look, and said, "Of course, I must admit it is hard on the furniture to have a campaign go through one's house. I have just sent for the upholsterer and the repair man and I think everything will have to be done over. The hole in the rug"—she pointed to a cigar burn—"can be darned, they say, and I don't think there is much serious damage done."

Eleanor Roosevelt took a very different interest in politics. She was interested in policies, in the objectives of the government, and in the co-operation of political activity. She worked hard in the political campaigns when Al Smith was running for governor and her husband was ill and out of politics. She came to have a shrewd, independent judgment not only about policies but about politicians. She learned how to spend campaign funds to the best advantage. She could discern who could be relied on to carry through a program and who might go away with the campaign money and forget the program.

She was a great help to her husband in his first gubernatorial campaign. She had already developed the ability to go about among people in a natural, simple, cordial way. When they visited the State Fair, Roosevelt, the nominee, would drive around the grounds and shake hands with many people, while Mrs. Roosevelt would go through the buildings where the livestock, the patchwork quilts, the canned vegetables and preserves, the prize ears of corn were shown. She would ask questions about schools and health and recreation facilities. Her unaffected approach to people won friends at every level.

After Roosevelt became President she did not take part in election campaigns, but there can be no doubt that her wide travels and acquaintanceship contributed not only to Roosevelt's popularity but to the demonstration, by example, of the social objectives which were his basic policy and hers. From the time that he campaigned for governor, he turned instinctively to her to find out what was going on in places where he could not go himself. For the rest of his life he relied on her for this kind of co-operation. It was as though he had another self. Thousands of letters were received every week at the White House from individuals who described their problems and predicaments. The President would read some and be torn by them. Many were addressed to Mrs. Roosevelt. Between them they got the idea that while you might not be able to see every family you could find out about their plight by seeing some.

I remember that when Roosevelt was elected President, Mrs. Roosevelt was sad at leaving New York and told her close friends that she "would have nothing to do." As the wife of the Governor she had had an interesting, active life. She knew people in New York. She had made friends with women's organizations throughout the state. She took part in politics and state conferences. She had continued, as a personal activity, her teaching of history and political science in a girls' school. Reasoning from what had happened to wives of other Presidents, she felt she was going to be a prisoner in the White House, with nothing to do except stand in line and receive visitors and preside over official dinners. She realized that Presidents' wives were expected to show no interest in public affairs. She once told me she had great respect for Mrs. Hoover because she had continued her active work in the Girl Scouts, of which she had long been a director. She sent a couple of horses to Washington, planning to ride every day, partly to keep fit and partly to occupy herself. She thought she might study a language, Spanish perhaps. She was going to catch up on her reading. Life promised to be dull.

They had not been in Washington a month before the President asked her to go down into the southern Appalachian region, from which he had had pathetic letters, to see what the problems were and what could be done. Then he asked her to go to a meeting of an organization interested in social progress, to represent him and say on his behalf, as well as on her own, how much they were interested in the program. He gave her many assignments after that. The hardest perhaps was to go to the Pacific front during the war.

The President was enormously proud of her ability, although he rarely talked about it except to someone in whose sympathy he felt complete confidence. He said more than once, "You know, Eleanor really does put it over. She's got great talent with people." In cabinet meetings he would say, "You know my Missus gets around a lot," or "my Missus says that they have typhoid fever in that district," or "my Missus says the people are leaving the dust bowl in droves because they haven't any chance there," or "my Missus says that people are working for wages way below the minimum set by NRA in the town she visited last week."

He had complete reliance in her observations. He often insisted on action that public officials thought unnecessary because Mrs. Roosevelt had seen with her own eyes and had reported so vividly that he too felt he had seen. They were partners.

7.

HE LIKED PEOPLE

Roosevelt's ways of associating himself with many and different kinds of people, which began to show themselves even before he was Governor, endeared him to the common people as they came to know him, and made the common people entirely comprehensible to him. There was a bond between Roosevelt and the ordinary men and women of this country—and beyond that, between him and the ordinary men and women of the world. He was profoundly loyal to them. Even when good reasons were presented for not carrying out a program that would be beneficial to them, he would examine, appreciate, and even understand the arguments against a project, but persist. Too much of an investment; too much government interference; too much control over people's affairs. He could see the logic but he would say, "Yes, but the people need it. They expect it," and he could not let them down.

His power to associate himself with others came to him rather gradually. One could see it develop from his start as Governor and later as President. His early life did not show much of this ability, but as he grew older, as he went through the horror of his illness and crippling, as he met many persons on many levels, he developed the capacity to associate himself with great numbers of people. He did not and could not know them all individually, but he thought of them individually. He thought of them in family groups. He thought of them sitting around on a suburban porch after supper of a summer evening. He thought of them gathered around a dinner table at a family meal. He never thought of them as "the masses."

When he talked on the radio, he saw them gathered in the

little parlor, listening with their neighbors. He was conscious of their faces and hands, their clothes and homes.

His voice and his facial expression as he spoke were those of an intimate friend. After he became President, I often was at the White House when he broadcast, and I realized how unconscious he was of the twenty or thirty of us in that room and how clearly his mind was focused on the people listening at the other end. As he talked his head would nod and his hands would move in simple, natural, comfortable gestures. His face would smile and light up as though he were actually sitting on the front porch or in the parlor with them. People felt this, and it bound them to him in affection.

I have sat in those little parlors and on those porches myself during some of the speeches, and I have seen men and women gathered around the radio, even those who didn't like him or were opposed to him politically, listening with a pleasant, happy feeling of association and friendship. The exchange between them and him through the medium of the radio was very real. I have seen tears come to their eyes as he told them of some tragic episode, of the sufferings of the persecuted people in Europe, of the poverty during unemployment, of the sufferings of the homeless, of the sufferings of people whose sons had been killed in the war, and they were tears of sincerity and recognition and sympathy.

I have also seen them laugh. When he told how Fala, his little dog, had been kicked around, he spoke with naturalness and simplicity. He was so himself in his relation to the dog, based on the average man's experience of the place of a pet in the home, that the laughter of those gathered around radios of the country was a natural, sincere, and affectionate reaching out to this man.

The quality of his being one with the people, of having no artificial or natural barriers between him and them, made it possible for him to be a leader without ever being or thinking of being a dictator. I don't think he fully appreciated this aspect of his nature as a part of his leadership, but he intuitively used it. It was this quality that made the people trust him and do gladly what he explained was necessary for them to do. While some of his political enemies said that these were merely the signs and marks of a slick politician, the more one associated with him the more one knew that however political he might be, and he certainly did have great political skill, this quality was not a political device at all.

The truth is that he liked to broadcast to "my friends." He would rather talk to people than sit at his desk and be President. He wanted to talk to them about the things he thought they cared about. In particular, he wanted to talk everywhere about what could be done to make this a better, more beautiful, and more sustaining country. Among his deepest satisfactions was the evidence that when he did explain matters to the people, they understood and supported him and took the necessary action to solve a problem.

Details for improvement of the state and later of the country interested him enormously. He never ceased to want to look after the tree belt which had been planted experimentally at his suggestion in an effort to counteract the effect of drought, dust storms, and soil erosion in some parts of the country. He was always deeply interested in the development not only of the Tennessee Valley Authority but of a Missouri Valley Authority, and other river developments, believing that it would make the desert blossom and that more people could find happy, comfortable homes in those areas.

Although he had been around a good deal and seen a lot of life, including its seamy side, he remained essentially a trusting person. This was true when he became Governor, and remained true later. He never believed that anyone would willingly wrong or damage him. His tendency to think that everybody was all right exposed him to a considerable amount of intellectual danger. The only people who repelled him were pompous bores who bragged about themselves.

He would not have liked to be thought of as an unsophisticated person. He often told the story of certain comments of Madame Chiang Kai-shek, when the wife of the Chinese leader was visiting in Washington. He told it with such relish that one realized that it revealed a quality of his own nature he was not aware of. He once asked Madame Chiang about Wendell

Willkie's visit to China. She replied courteously that China had enjoyed having him.

Roosevelt said, "What do you really think of Wendell Willkie?"

"Oh, he is very charming," Madame Chiang answered.

"Ah, yes, but what did you *really* think?"

"Well, Mr. President, he is an adolescent, after all."

Roosevelt pursued the subject and tempted fate by saying, "Well, Madame Chiang, so you think Wendell Willkie is an adolescent—what do you think I am?"

"Ah, Mr. President," said Madame Chiang, a very experienced woman, "you are sophisticated."

As Roosevelt told this story there was a gleam of pleasure and, shall I say, simple human vanity in his eyes. His obvious pleasure belied its point.

Most men who have been long in politics have only political friends with the exception of a handful of relatives and the boys they went to school with. But Roosevelt had a great many friends who had no relation whatever to his political life, and the politicians with whom he had real political friendship did not always join the circle in which he took his ease.

He was attracted to so many different people and varying minds that he could not have built all his friendships exclusively among his political adherents and associates. He had a liking for people who had no political contacts at all. He responded to them and to the ideas of their special fields.

This capacity for friendship with a great variety of people who shared no political responsibility or interest with him was partly the result of his complex nature. He was easy of access to many types of minds. Moreover, these various minds stimulated him, and the refreshment he gained from his nonpolitical friends was a considerable factor in his health and happiness.

A daily diet of politicians and government officers gets quite dreary. Mrs. Roosevelt, well aware of the extent to which he was imprisoned by high office, made a point of bringing in, in an informal way, a great many people from all walks of life. Politicians, scholars, writers, churchmen, as well as personal friends, would drop in.

Mrs. Roosevelt also invited many theater people, musicians, artists, scientists, and explorers. Thus the President's natural, varied interests were satisfied, and he was able to endure the relative confinement of his life with more ease and grace. At the same time he could share in intellectual and artistic developments.

I recall that I met Carl Sandburg in Indianapolis early in 1933 and heard him sing from his collection of American folk songs. When I told him how much I had enjoyed the songs, he said, "I think so much of President Roosevelt I would like to do something for him. I don't know what I can do, but perhaps I can bring my guitar and sing some of these songs for him. Do you think he would like it?"

I told Mrs. Roosevelt and she invited Sandburg. He came with his guitar. After a family dinner he played and sang. The President was delighted with the songs and the singer. It was an evening that left him refreshed.

Roosevelt had a great many friends among artists. There was something natural and simple about most of them which made it easy for him to make quick contact with them. When the Civil Works project for work relief was getting under way, the decision to include artists in it was Roosevelt's own. A number of good, successful artists were greatly disturbed by the poverty and total loss of income which came with the depression to very competent painters. Alfred Barr, Director of the Museum of Modern Art, conceived the idea that artists should have the relief that other people were getting. He promoted it at every hand, mentioning it to a young girl who was a member of the family of a cabinet officer. Having no particular judgment about public affairs but being ardent about painting, she persuaded her reluctant parent to take it up with the President.

The President's immediate reaction was, "Why not? They are human beings. They have to live. I guess the only thing they can do is paint and surely there must be some public place where paintings are wanted."

He said paintings would look better than the old photographs and calendars which hung in public offices. So work was given to a great many artists at the standard of fifteen dollars a week that everyone else got. Post offices, town halls, schools, and other public buildings were covered with murals paid for at that wage and a great number of "easel pictures" were turned out in every section of the country. This, of course, led to other projects in the fine arts—music, theater, and historical research.

Roosevelt responded to the idea, not because he had any particular knowledge of the arts but because the people that practiced them were human beings and, like others, must earn a living.

George Biddle, the painter, once said of him, "You know, it is strange. Roosevelt has almost no taste or judgment about painting, and I don't think he gets much enjoyment out of it; yet he has done more for painters in this country than anybody ever did—not only by feeding them when they were down and out but by establishing the idea that paintings are a good thing to have around and that artists are important."

Roosevelt, in fact, did not appreciate paintings. The only pictures he really cared about were pictures of ships, and he judged those by the correctness with which the rigging was arranged and painted and by the details of construction. The pictures he selected from the art project for his office, while not the worst in the collection, were certainly not good.

He was amiable about letting artists paint his portrait, and someone was always wanting to. Again he had little judgment about what constituted a good portrait. I protested once, when we were talking in the Oval Study, about a half-finished portrait of him and said I wished he would have a serious portrait painted by one of our best painters, to leave as his official portrait. "I am going to have Bay Emmett paint that," he replied gaily. "I like her things. They are always nice."

He looked reflectively at a portrait hanging over the door—a portrait by Lydia Emmett of Mrs. Roosevelt when she was very young. He said, "I always liked that portrait of Eleanor."

"Well, it is very sweet," I replied. So it was. It showed a young woman with light, shining, wavy hair, blue eyes, and a sweet smile; it looked like many other charming portraits by Lydia Emmett, who specialized in painting children.

"Yes," I repeated, "sweet."

The President looked at it again. "I always liked it. That's just the way Eleanor looks, you know—lovely hair, pretty eyes." He nodded with reminiscent pleasure, and I made a mental note, "That's hardly art criticism but it is a record of affection any woman would be glad to receive. A woman whose husband still thinks that a flattering portrait made in the freshness of youth is a perfect likeness of her in middle age has a certain satisfaction."

He paused, I remember, to tell me what beautiful hair Eleanor had, and since this was an enthusiasm I shared with him, we discussed it for a moment. I told him I had always admired the way she dressed her hair for the evening. How magnificent she looked with her light brown hair piled on top of her head! He agreed and added, "And she always looks magnificent in evening clothes, doesn't she?" It was true, she does.

These friendships with people in the arts were not only restful and refreshing to Roosevelt but turned out to have political significance. Though that was not the intention, these men and women added their influential voice to the thousands of Americans who believed in Roosevelt and supported him in his political and economic programs.

Jo Davidson, the sculptor, who did a fine, serious head of him in 1934, became a great friend. Being a man of broad interests, he conceived the idea that artists would like to be politically effective. In 1944 he and others organized a strong and lively campaign group—the Independent Voters' Committee of the Arts and Sciences for Roosevelt, now called the Independent Citizens' Committee of the Arts, Sciences, and Professions.

All kinds of people from all parts of the world came to visit at the White House, and Roosevelt rejoiced to have them staying in the President's house, the property of the people of the United States. Favorite guests were put in the Lincoln bedroom and they usually had great satisfaction out of that experience. Lillian Wald, distinguished founder of the Henry Street Settlement and the District Nursing Association, told me that her visit in the last year in which she was able to carry on any active life at all was perhaps the greatest satisfaction she had ever known.

But whoever came was received comfortably and warmly, was made to feel welcome, and for the time that he was under the roof became a part of this large, inclusive family.

When Their Britannic Majesties were coming for their State visit, someone suggested to the President that it would be nice to assemble for the occasion some of the finest examples of early American furniture, rugs, and hangings from museums and private homes, and to furnish Their Majesties' rooms on the second floor of the White House with them. The person making the suggestion pointed out that when Their Majesties had visited Paris the year before, furniture had been brought in from the Louvre and Versailles, and two beautiful suites had been furnished for them with museum pieces which they had greatly admired. Wouldn't it be nice to give Their Majesties a taste of our life of days gone by?

"No," said the President immediately. "I don't think they would like living in a museum. I think it would bore them. You know, I think they will be tired when they get here. They would rather rest than sleep in a museum."

He preferred comfort rather than show and thought they would. He wanted their entertainment to be not only interesting but pleasurable, and he managed to make it so. Their Majesties stayed two days under his roof as house guests, occupying the best guest rooms on the second floor of the White House just as any other visitors do. There were two State dinners, a garden party, a reception by Congress, a formal visit to Mount Vernon. Here the President had managed to make it agreeable and comfortable by going down on the river and driving back by way of the CCC camp, which the President felt sure the King would be curious to see.

The President had asked the ladies of the Mount Vernon Association to make the occasion especially agreeable, and they had indeed. All the restraining ropes were down, with the guests going into Washington's room and sitting down on the chairs and sofas. I shall never forget the Queen sitting at the little spinet in Martha Washington's morning room and playing a tinkling little tune; nor shall I forget the picture of the King of England opening the bookcases in George Washington's library and

browsing among his books. All these little things to make the
visit human the President himself had suggested.

Although they went through State ceremonial performances,
the guests enjoyed themselves. At a dinner given for them by the
President, I sat beside their personal physician, who said, "I've
been delighted with this visit. Their Majesties have relaxed and
rested and there has been no nervous strain at all. Just wonderful. It's that President of yours, Mr. Roosevelt. He just makes
them feel so at ease."

When Their Majesties went to Hyde Park to visit, even greater
simplicity prevailed, because here they were truly house guests
in a private house and there were no State occasions and formal
dinners. There was only the pleasure of visiting a large, pleasant, informal family in the country and being included within
it. Even the picnic which has been so publicized because of the
"hot dogs" was successful. Hot dogs are a nice food for al fresco
meals, and it was charmingly, becomingly, and comfortably
done, in exactly the way the Roosevelts had been giving picnics
for friends and neighbors for years.

This capacity to entertain the great and the simple, the important and the unimportant, of the earth with the same
comfortable hospitality made a contribution not only to international relations, but to the warm friendliness of American
life. Franklin Roosevelt's way of life seemed so American to
ninety-five per cent of the Americans that they felt they too
could have visited in his home and been as comfortable, and
they were right.

The good will which the visit of Their Majesties created in
this country was due to their own charm, good sense, and intelligence, as well as to the easy, affable way in which Roosevelt
introduced them to American life and American people.

The Queen gave Roosevelt pleasure when she sent for Harry
Hopkins's little daughter, Diana, who was staying in the White
House at the time, as her mother had just died. The child, of
course, wanted to see the Queen, and Her Majesty, learning of
this, arranged to receive Diana in the upper hall when she was
dressed for the State dinner in rose tulle with spangles, wearing
the diamond tiara and jewels of State.

"It will mean more to the little girl," she said, "to see me dressed like this than in my traveling frock." It did, and the President told me the story later, adding, "She's a very nice woman— considerate and human."

Not all important visitors were so agreeable. Some were demanding and placed a burden on the staff of the White House and on their host and hostess. But Roosevelt never lost his poise or affability.

Winston Churchill, of course, became a real friend of Roosevelt's though originally Roosevelt was so uncertain about him that when Churchill was asked to form a government in 1940 the President asked several associates what kind of a man he really was. Their friendship grew out of mutual need and a common ability to appreciate the drama of history, as well as out of the burdens of those who must make the history.

He teased Churchill unmercifully, but that was a sign of his being "in the family." It was Roosevelt's habit to indulge in friendly teasing bouts, and he expected to get back as good as he gave.

It never pained him to stretch his family circle and include visitors, friends, cousins, in family festivals. His Christmas habits were traditional and large. He horrified all the safety-first people by insisting on wax tapers lighted on his Christmas tree even in the sacred White House, and he really liked to read Dickens aloud to a large group of family and friends on Christmas Eve.

His zest for people would have kept him from becoming a "stuffed shirt," if there ever had been any such danger. His naturally democratic good manners grew even better after use at the White House. The Roosevelts did all the formal entertaining that is ever done and a lot besides, just to give pleasure to people ordinarily overlooked. I remember once that after a wartime dinner for the cabinet he went and sat down in the Red Room with the wives, remarking, "I want to see all the girls. I haven't seen you in months and I see your husbands too much." It gave them great pleasure.

His manner of greeting people at formal receptions as they came down the receiving line was remarkably warm and gave each person the feeling that the President had just been waiting for him to come along. Those of us who stood in the next room used to notice that people came through the narrow doorway, after shaking the President's hand, smiling and happy. Roosevelt made them feel that way—from dyspeptic ambassadors and gold-braided admirals to timid old-maid government librarians. The only person I remember coming out of F.D.R.'s warming presence with an austere, indifferent, even sneering look on his face was Mr. Justice McReynolds. With few exceptions, even people who regarded themselves as Roosevelt haters felt agreeable toward him in his presence. They could not resist his contagious fondness for people—all kinds of people.

As he grappled with world affairs in the later years of his administration, Roosevelt's mind became preoccupied with the life and welfare of people everywhere. This was shown strikingly by his curiosity about the way of life of ordinary folk in all the countries he visited after the war began.

When he visited Brazil, although it was a State visit, with public officials as his principal point of contact, he noticed how men unloaded ships. He saw what kind of men the longshoremen were. He saw what the houses of poor people down by the waterfront were like. He had an impression that there was overcrowding in the tenements. The faces of the people in the poorer quarters of the city were fresh in his mind weeks later as he described the trip.

His secret trip to Casablanca to meet Churchill, De Gaulle, Giraud, and others was full of sufficient official and military necessity to occupy him, but he found time to note and tell me later about the poverty of the Arab people. He spoke of the frightful shortage of clothing. A man's half-worn shirt, he noted, cost enough to feed a family for days. Coffee and tea were so badly wanted that one clever piece of Allied propaganda was to drop small bags of coffee or tea from airplanes with U.S.A. or U.K. printed on the cloth. The evidences of untreated disease registered with him. He thought both Casablanca and Marrakech very beautiful and loved the sunshine and the climate. He thought it ought to be possible to make North Africa a great resort after the war; then the "people would have work to do and could earn a decent income."

His journey to Teheran was managed so that he had little

opportunity to see the life of the Persian people, and his whole mind and feeling were concentrated on becoming acquainted with and understanding Marshal Stalin and the Russians. He was extremely curious about the Persians and was sorry that he got no opportunity to observe them.

He told me later that he didn't understand why he was not allowed to see the city. He went directly to the American Embassy upon arrival. He knew that the route from the airport to the Embassy had been over back streets, while crowds waited along the principal streets to see him. But that was merely a Secret Service security procedure which he understood. Almost immediately representations were made that it was unsafe for him to stay in the American Embassy, that some kind of plot was afoot. The Russians insisted that he come to their Embassy, which was inside a compound, where he could be guarded more adequately.

He told me he didn't believe there had been any plot and didn't think so at the time, but it was clear that Stalin wanted him to come to the Russian Embassy. Roosevelt was distressed, because to make it possible for him and his large company to move in, Stalin had to move to a small cottage on the Embassy grounds. Being in the Russian Embassy, he saw a lot of Russians, but he didn't see any Persians.

The Russians interested and intrigued him. He couldn't get the servants around the house to talk to him. They rendered efficient service, smiled broadly and charmingly, but said nothing. And although he was accustomed to a gay exchange of personal greetings and ideas with people in other countries, he liked them.

He had gone prepared to like Stalin and determined to make himself liked. He told me the story of his encounter with Stalin while I was trying to talk with him about a particular piece of legislation then in the Congress. He had the look in his eyes I often recognized as being way off somewhere. As I tried to talk about the legislation, he replied, "Um-um."

Then suddenly he turned, as he often did, breaking in with what was on his mind. "You know, the Russians are interesting people. For the first three days I made absolutely no progress. I couldn't get any personal connection with Stalin, although I had done everything he asked me to do. I had stayed at his Embassy, gone to his dinners, been introduced to his ministers and generals. He was correct, stiff, solemn, not smiling, nothing human to get hold of. I felt pretty discouraged. If it was all going to be official paper work, there was no sense in my having made this long journey which the Russians had wanted. They couldn't come to America or any place in Europe for it. I had come there to accommodate Stalin. I felt pretty discouraged because I thought I was making no personal headway. What we were doing could have been done by the foreign ministers.

"I thought it over all night and made up my mind I had to do something desperate. I couldn't stay in Teheran forever. I had to cut through this icy surface so that later I could talk by telephone or letter in a personal way. I had scarcely seen Churchill alone during the conference. I had a feeling that the Russians did not feel right about seeing us conferring together in a language which we understood and they didn't.

"On my way to the conference room that morning we caught up with Winston and I had just a moment to say to him, 'Winston, I hope you won't be sore at me for what I am going to do.'

"Winston just shifted his cigar and grunted. I must say he behaved very decently afterward.

"I began almost as soon as we got into the conference room. I talked privately with Stalin. I didn't say anything that I hadn't said before, but it appeared quite chummy and confidential, enough so that the other Russians joined us to listen. Still no smile.

"Then I said, lifting my hand up to cover a whisper (which of course had to be interpreted), 'Winston is cranky this morning, he got up on the wrong side of the bed.'

"A vague smile passed over Stalin's eyes, and I decided I was on the right track. As soon as I sat down at the conference table, I began to tease Churchill about his Britishness, about John Bull, about his cigars, about his habits. It began to register with Stalin. Winston got red and scowled, and the more he did so, the more Stalin smiled. Finally Stalin broke out into a deep, hearty guffaw, and for the first time in three days I saw light. I kept it up until Stalin was laughing with me, and it was then that I called him 'Uncle Joe.' He would have thought me fresh the day before, but that day he laughed and came over and shook my hand.

"From that time on our relations were personal, and Stalin himself indulged in an occasional witticism. The ice was broken and we talked like men and brothers.

"You know," continued the President, "he was deeply touched by the presentation of the sword which Churchill brought him from the British people. It was a magnificent ceremonial sword on a crimson velvet cushion, and Churchill made one of his best brief speeches. Churchill himself was pretty well worked up with emotion as he expressed the admiration of the British people for the Russians' gallant battle and for Stalin's magnificent leadership.

"As Stalin rose to accept the sword he flushed with a kind of emotional quality which I knew was very real. He put out his hands and took the sword from the crimson cushion. There were tears in his eyes. I saw them myself. He bowed from the hips swiftly and kissed the sword, a ceremonial gesture of great style which I know was unrehearsed. It was really very magnificent, moving, and sincere.

"He is a very interesting man. They say he is a peasant from one of the least progressive parts of Russia, but let me tell you he had an elegance of manner that none of the rest of us had.

"Churchill brought along his daughter Sarah to act as a secretary and assistant. Naturally, she wasn't at the conferences, but one day we were being photographed for the press and Sarah came out on the porch where we were sitting to bring her father something. Marshal Stalin rose at once on the entrance of a lady and looked slightly embarrassed because he wasn't sure who she was.

"Churchill took her by the arm and said, 'Marshal Stalin, may I have the honor to present to you my daughter, Sarah?'

"Stalin bowed from the hips, took her hand and kissed it in the old-fashioned, elegant European manner. The rest of us said, 'Hello, Sarah,' or 'Howdy.' The contrast was marked, and we all somehow felt that the Marshal had the best of that moment."

The President went on reflectively, "I wish I understood the Russians better. Frances, you know the Russians, don't you?"

I replied, "No, I'm sorry to say I only know the ones who have been here at the Embassy and the Russian refugee taxicab drivers in Paris."

"I thought you knew them. I seem to remember you brought some of them to me."

I reminded him that I had brought Colonel Hugh Cooper to see him in 1933. I had met Cooper and had been fascinated by his experiences in building the Dnieprostroy Dam and by his estimate of the Russians, and had introduced him to the President knowing that he wanted to recommend that the U.S.A. recognize Russia officially.

"Well," said the President, "I wish someone would tell me about the Russians. I don't know a good Russian from a bad Russian. I can tell a good Frenchman from a bad Frenchman. I can tell a good Italian from a bad Italian. I know a good Greek when I see one. But I don't understand the Russians. I just don't know what makes them tick. I wish I could study them. Frances, see if you can find out what makes them tick."

"Do you mean that seriously?" I replied.

"Yes, find out all you can and tell me from time to time. I like them and I want to understand them."

Unfortunately, I had no time to make a profound study of the Russians, but I read a few books. I read B. H. Sumners and William Henry Chamberlin and one or two others. I talked with a few people who had lived in Russia, and from time to time I made a little digest about what they said and what the books said.

I did not know the geography of the land until I read it in Sumners. Nor did I realize the relatively recent expansion of the whole Russian population into the grass steppe of the Ukraine and beyond to the East.

The President became interested in these little digests I made for him and often said, "You know, I want to go to Russia myself."

I think he encouraged people to go to Russia from that time on. He was fascinated with the stories they brought back. He was delighted with the description of going to the opera in

Uzbek related by Donald Nelson, war production chief, who went on a mission overseas for the President. He asked questions based on his recently acquired knowledge of the tribes and races in Russia, about the differences in the people in the different parts of the country, and the way the more primitive groups had responded to the new economic system and the educational program of the revolutionary period.

It was the people and what made them develop that interested him. I think he would have gone on studying the Russians for many years. He had gained some insight into the devotion the men he met had for their economic, social, and political system of Communism.

I told him how one American who had lived in Russia a great deal had responded to my question "What makes the Russians tick?" with these words, "The desire to do the Holy Will."

I had reproached my informant with confusing the prerevolutionary and deeply religious Russian with the modern Russian, but he had insisted that the same quality persisted.

When I told this to the President, he said, "You know, there may be something in that. It would explain their almost mystical devotion to this idea which they have developed of the Communist society. They all seem really to want to do what is good for their society instead of wanting to do for themselves. We take care of ourselves and think about the welfare of society afterward."

Perhaps the most striking illustration of his sense of responsibility, his vocation of service to the people, came out in one of the last conversations I had with him. He had just come back from Yalta. He had been flown rather low, at his request, over Saudi Arabia, a desert country. He could observe from the air the meager vegetation and the limited cultivation of the land. A cheerless, dreary place, it seemed, with little local food supply and no more possible because of the aridity.

He turned to one of the Army engineers traveling with him. "Why don't they raise something here? Is the soil absolutely infertile?"

"No," answered the engineer, "it is good soil and could be used if there were any water at all."

"Can't they irrigate?" asked the President.

"They can't irrigate because there isn't any water here to irrigate with," replied the engineer.

"But," said the President, "there must be some water here. The people must drink and the animals must be watered."

"Yes, there are wells here and there in an oasis, but water, as you know, is sold at a high price."

"How do they get the wells? Dig them?"

"That is the answer."

"How far below the surface is the water table?"

"About fifty feet."

"Is there real water there?"

"Yes, I think so. I think there is a lot of water fifty feet below the surface."

"Well, the solution seems to bring out some good Worthington pumps to pump up the water and irrigate the soil."

"That wouldn't do any good," said the engineer. "It is so hot here that the sun would evaporate the water before it had done the soil any good and would leave it caked and dry."

"But the nights are cool. Why not pump the water up and irrigate at night when it will have time to sink into the soil? They really ought to be able to raise food. There must be a way if there is water underneath the soil."

When he met King Ibn Saud of Arabia aboard ship on the way back, Roosevelt told him he thought American companies could be found who would help water the desert.

The King looked blank and uninterested. "I am an old man, agriculture is not for me," he said. "Perhaps my nephew will be interested when he comes to rule."

"But," said the President when he told me about it, "you know, there is something in that idea. The reason the Near East is so explosive is because the people are so poor. They haven't enough to eat. They haven't enough possible occupations. They need a food supply and they need to raise it themselves. That one thing, I think, would do more than anything else to reduce the explosive qualities of these areas. Look what the Jews have done in Palestine. They are inventing new ways of using the desert all the time."

He paused reflectively, then went on, "When I get through being President of the U.S. and this damn war is over, I think Eleanor and I will go to the Near East and see if we can manage to put over an operation like the Tennessee Valley system that will really make something of that country. I would love to do it."

"There is plenty for you to do here," I replied.

"Well, I can't be President forever, and I don't know any people who need someone to help them more than the people in the Near East."

8.

FIGURES CAN'T LIE

As Governor, Franklin Roosevelt early established the habit of holding conferences or informal hearings on matters not yet embodied in bills. Within the first weeks of his administration he held one of these informal conferences in the Executive Chamber in the Capitol at Albany. This room, upholstered in red velvet plush and hung with magnificent curtains with the arms of the State of New York embroidered upon them, was an ornate audience chamber. It had a large desk at which the Governor sat during public hearings. The door by which he entered was a small one leading from his private office. But the desk was a long way from the door. No one had thought to move it; no one had sensed in advance Roosevelt's problem.

About a hundred of us, including many strangers to the Governor, were in the room as he came in, leaning on the arm of Guernsey Cross. In the other hand he carried a stout stick. In those days he did not walk so well as later. It was but natural common courtesy for those in the room to rise and wait until the Governor reached his desk.

It took him a long, long time to reach the desk. The tenseness in the audience grew as it waited in dread, wondering if he would make it. It seemed like a terribly long distance. Painfully, slowly, and awkwardly he walked along with Guernsey Cross. About halfway to the desk he realized the tension of the audience. He began to smile and nod, tossing his head up gaily. He waved the cane, saying cheerfully, "That's all right. I'll make it."

Roosevelt proved easy and co-operative as a working associate. He was responsive to ideas and suggestions, grasped the significance of reports quickly and was stimulated by them. When he undertook to put over a program he did it well and effectively, even if the time of preparation had been short and he had been inadequately briefed. He has often been criticized for this and called superficial by his enemies. To his associates this way of handling things was a boon. He trusted his appointees. He understood the major policies and programs but did not try to make himself a technical expert. He relied on his commissioner or board for that. He was generous, and in talking to a committee or department heads would say, "Commissioner X has worked this out and recommends . . . " Then he would call in Commissioner X to answer detailed questions.

The first months, in fact the first year, of Governor Roosevelt's term were mostly "carry on" months, continuing with the program started in the Smith and Dix administrations. We made progress in the labor legislation and social justice programs. We improved administrative practices in the Labor, Welfare, and Health Departments. We speeded up the workmen's compensation administration. We pushed forward safety codes for factories and mercantile establishments. We developed the industrial hygiene and preventive activities of the Labor Department, strengthened and trained inspection staffs and increased their appropriations.

The Governor supported all these measures and liked to be kept informed of their progress. He wanted me to tell him the human part of the story: how we discovered that men were getting silicosis while polishing the inside of glass milk tanks; how the girls painting luminous dials on clock faces and pointing the fine hair brushes with their lips had contracted radium poisoning; how the old carpenter who lost his arm and settled his compensation claim by agreement with his employer without a hearing had been cheated out of about $5,000, which we discovered by a spot check investigation. When the carpenter was asked why he had settled for so little, he said, "Well, the men in the office were all educated men, and I supposed they knew the law. I never thought that educated men would cheat me."

In the first months of his governorship, even though the depression was yet to come, it was evident to those of us who watched industry closely that there was great irregularity in employment. It was not yet the fall of 1929. Stock prices were still soaring and wild exaggerated spending was still going on, but many people were out of work for longer periods than was comfortable and the turnover was great. The practical thing was to develop some machinery for dealing with this problem. We had inherited an old Public Employment Service, unprogressive and limited in its usefulness to the employers and workers. In addition, there was a tiny branch of the United States Employment Service operated by the Federal Government, which was manned by an ineffective, incompetent staff but which was in competition with the state employment system.

I described the problem to the Governor in human terms. I told him of the dirt and disorder in some of the Public Employment Service offices. I told him about one I had uncovered where applicants for work waited in a dingy second-floor room, 100 feet by 20, with one window, one exit, no chairs or benches and no electric lights because, as the manager said, the men would steal the bulbs and would go to sleep if you gave them benches. Roosevelt reacted to the need. At once he saw the point of developing a good modern well-supported State Public Employment Service, where people would be decently treated and where the business of getting a job could be carried on in an orderly, businesslike, humane way.

The stock market collapse in 1929 brought a sharp accentuation of declining employment. Misleading information was put out, many holding that it was only a money crisis and that industry would soon restore itself. But in New York more people were out of work each month.

The profound long-term economic remedies for unemployment were not so much discussed in those days as they are now. What was clear to Roosevelt and to all of us who had immediate obligations to the people of the state was that we must find *some* answers and stimulate *some* immediate activities.

The solution of unemployment problems became one of Roosevelt's major activities as Governor. He had not made up his mind as to what should be done, but he proved himself a man who could study and learn. No one had many clear recommendations, but the further development and utilization of the Public Employment Service was certainly a number one idea. Other recommendations were to keep children and young people out of the labor market by strict enforcement of the child labor laws and by refusal to grant working papers; to promote the voluntary adoption of the five-day week throughout the state as a method of sharing the work; to recommend to employers that they keep workers employed at least part time, or a few days a week, for as long as possible; to increase old age assistance in the hope of making it possible for older people to retire and so reduce the labor market; and to inaugurate in every locality "made work" drives so that men and women out of work could get some kind of a living out of odd jobs.

Unemployment insurance was talked about a great deal, but an insurance system cannot pay out benefits before it has collected premiums. I became convinced that we ought to have unemployment insurance even if only on a state basis. It would not solve the problem of the depression of the thirties, but it seemed wise that we should attempt to establish the fund as soon as possible as a protection for the future.

In studying the situation for the Governor, I saw that a great deal could be done by a given plant, industry, or community to bring about relatively steady employment and production and to guarantee to employees annual employment or an annual wage. This we called stabilization of employment, and Governor Roosevelt was tremendously interested in it.

There were a number of practical examples of this. The John A. Manning Paper Company in Troy gave a guarantee of steady work on an annual basis and therefore an annual income to its employees. Since it was close at hand and small enough to be studied quickly, I brought it to Roosevelt's attention. He was also interested in the Welch Grape Juice Company in Westfield, New York, based on a seasonal industry. It amused him that their stabilization method had been to add jelly to their products. They had also moved to a shorter work day and week.

The Governor often talked with Ernest Draper of Hills Brothers Company, importer and packer of dates. The owners had reduced seasonal unemployment by installing a cold storage plant so that the packing could be done over a longer period of time; and by developing filler items which would have a constant sale and would make demands upon their production throughout the year, such as shredded coconut and canned figs.

The Governor used to telephone me frequently for quick, immediate reports on changes in employment and unemployment. He was not sufficiently skilled in statistical procedure to realize that one could not get accurate and significant figures more often than weekly, and that we must rely upon the monthly reports from the industries regarding their payrolls and employment.

All sorts of amateurs were putting out estimates of unemployment on a given day and predictions of what it would be a month later. The United States Employment Service, which had no information-collecting technique, announced figures which reflected only the number of placements or applications they had had in a particular week, comparing these figures with those of the previous week. This was an unreliable and misleading procedure, as a measure of unemployment.

We in New York hardly knew what was going on in Washington. We had confidence in the Bureau of Labor Statistics of the United States Department of Labor. We regularly contributed all we knew about employment, unemployment, and payrolls in our state to the Bureau's pool of information. We were fairly sure that these people were making honest, reliable estimates of employment throughout the country.

It became clear that one could never count the unemployed—one could only count the employed. A count of people not doing something at a particular time has no significance. If one is trying to find out the degree of cigarette smoking in the community one counts the smokers.

We greatly improved our techniques for collecting information about the number employed in New York during this period, and the fact that the statistics each month showed that fewer people were employed was sufficient indication of the size of the unemployment problem.

On January 21, 1930, while riding down to the office in the State Building in New York City, I read a story out of Washington on the front page of the *New York Times* that President Herbert Hoover had told the press that there had been a gain in employment in the past week. He indicated that things were much better.

As I read and realized that this came from the President of the United States, I was horrified, for I knew that he had been grossly misinformed. I surmised that the misleading figures from the United States Employment Service had been given to him and that he, the President, an educated and intelligent man, had not taken the precaution of checking them.

As I read the story over again I became more indignant, because I knew it was going to hurt and grieve the people being laid off in great numbers. They would not understand, they would feel betrayed, they would feel that there was something wrong with them personally if the President said that the employment situation was better the country over. A great despair would enter their hearts and they would say, "Why don't I get a job if things are better?" I knew that wives would read the story and reproach their husbands. I knew that young people would read the story and say, "Why doesn't Papa work?"

I know now that I had no proper perspective on the prestige and position of the President of the United States. He seemed to me just another citizen, and I thought that if he was wrong, it was my duty to make a correction since I had access to true information. I think now that what I did would be called "fresh," but I plunged into the task of correcting him with ardor. I sent for Eugene Patton, chief statistician of the state Department of Labor, a member of the Labor Committee of the American Statistical Association, and thoroughly acquainted with the methods used in building up employment indices. I asked him if what we knew about unemployment in New York could be projected over the whole country to enable us to draw a competent conclusion about unemployment in the United States. His answer was that we could easily find out by asking the Bureau of Labor Statistics in Washington to tell us exactly how the unemployment index was moving in other industrial states, and then we could relate it to the figures in New York. We went to work. We spent the whole day at it.

The next day I sent for the press and issued a statement that the President was wrong. Unemployment was increasing, I said; there had been no increase in employment, and things were worse. We gave out an estimate of the decrease in employment borne out by the figures of the Bureau of Labor Statistics, if properly analyzed.

I felt the satisfaction of one who has told the truth. I was astonished to see that my answer made headline news the next day. At once I began to get telegrams and telephone calls thanking or berating me.

In the middle of the morning Governor Roosevelt called. I had forgotten that this was an official situation; I had not even thought of telling the Governor I was going to make this answer. When I heard he was on the wire, I thought, "I suppose I have done the wrong thing, and this puts him in a dreadful predicament."

I went to the telephone full of apologies, only to be greeted by a cheerful voice saying, "Bully for you! That was a fine statement and I am glad you made it."

When I said I was sorry I hadn't told him about it in advance, he said, "Well, I think it was better you didn't. If you had asked me, I would probably have told you not to do it, and I think it is much more wholesome to have it right out in the open."

A great many unemployed workmen, employers, and citizens who were trying to think of ways to solve unemployment problems soon took our side on every proposal because we had told the truth and they knew it was the truth. I think that it may have had a political effect on Roosevelt's presidential campaign, but at that moment the political implications did not occur to us. It had seemed the right thing to do.

I learned in that period that Roosevelt could "get" a problem infinitely better when he had a vicarious experience through a vivid description of a typical case. Proceeding "from the book," no matter how logical, never seemed solid to him. His vivid imagination and sympathy helped him to "see" from a word picture. Later, when the problems of unemployment became even more pressing, he heard many theoretical economic discussions, but he never felt certain about the theory until he saw

a sweater mill located in a small village outside of Poughkeep-
sie which had employed no more than one hundred and fifty
people. Roosevelt talked with the employer, who was in despair. He talked to the workers, who were frightened and confused. In this way he got the economic and human problem all
at once. He had a basis of judging whether a program would be
practical by thinking of how it would apply to the sweater mill.

The mill had made, before the depression, a good quality ladies' knitted sweater which sold at retail for nine or ten dollars.
The workers got fair wages, or at any rate the wages of others
in that industry. Their earnings were enough to be comfortable
in that community. Work was reasonably steady because the
quality of the product was good and the owner had developed
a steady market with a few excellent wholesale houses as customers.

Then the depression began. The wholesale houses began to
give smaller orders than usual because the retailers ordered
one or two sweaters where they used to order a dozen at a
time. The owner had to close down the mill for longer periods
between orders and lay off about half of the employees. The
wholesalers asked if he could make a cheaper sweater. He tried
to. He got small orders for the cheaper sweater, but that did not
bring him enough work.

The employer was a local man and his employees were his
friends. They begged him to do something, for there was no
other work in the vicinity. Their savings were exhausted and
they had to have work. In desperation he went down to the city.
He canvassed the streets where the wholesalers and jobbers
were located and found them equally frantic. They must sell
something or they too would be crushed and out of business
and their people unemployed.

Finally he found a jobber who said, "We just got an order for
five thousand sweaters to sell at two dollars apiece. Can you
fill it?"

The employer gasped. "How could I? You know that doesn't
touch the cost."

"I know," the jobber said. "I hate to suggest it to you, but if
you reduce wages way down, stretch out the hours, and use a
shoddy yarn, you can do it."

The employer, remembering his people, agreed to try. "There will be nothing in this for me," he said.

"Perhaps not," said the jobber. "There won't be much for me either, but see what you can do."

The owner went home, called the people of the mill together, and put it up to them. He would forego profit, he said, and it would give them a few weeks' work at wages he hated to mention. He asked them to figure out the wages they could be paid on a sweater selling at two dollars. The jobber had told him, he said, there were two other firms ready to take the order. The workers finally said they would do it because they had to have something.

When Roosevelt saw the mill, they were working on that order, at wages that netted them about five dollars a week and gave the employer no return on his capital. He realized vividly then how desperate people can become. This experience helped him to understand the economic phrase "the descending spiral." The insight and sympathy that were such powerful forces in enabling him to support his principles as President throughout a critical period of forced recovery were based to a surprising degree upon his total conception of the experience of this one little mill. To get wages back to a point where people could buy something and prices back to where a little businessman could make something on his investment and effort—this was the problem. He grasped the concrete and could make the application to an industry on a general basis.

9.

JOBS FOR SOME

The situation continued to grow worse. Local communities were meeting the situation as best they could, but it was obvious that they could not stem the tide of distress.

By this time the Governor was seeing people from all over the state. I used to bring labor leaders from every community to tell him about the predicament of the working people in their towns. I brought in employers, who in almost heartbroken tones would tell him how they had been obliged to close down.

Committees from communities interested in relief also came. "Our town can't carry it alone any longer," they said. "We are an industrial town. Everybody is out of work. The people who had money have lost so much in the stock market that we have almost no one to appeal to for contributions. Our tax system won't hold any more taxation."

In 1930 the Governor agreed with me that we ought to make an attempt to educate the people as well as ourselves about the things that could be done, not only to relieve this crisis, but to prevent unemployment in the future, or at least to mitigate its drastic effect upon those who could least bear the burden. The Governor readily agreed to the appointment of a Commission on Stabilization of Employment.

It was called "Stabilization of Employment" and not an "Unemployment Commission" because Roosevelt had already developed what became a consistent attitude, namely, an emphasis on the positive. He did not like to appoint a committee against anything. He did not like to make a recommendation *not* to do something. He liked to recommend things to be done. It was a quality of his leadership which, I think, has been too little appreciated.

The plan of the Commission on the Stabilization of Employment was to inquire into the causes of the crisis, with the idea that out of that inquiry, as well as from a study of earlier crises of unemployment and of the economy of the community, recommendations might come which would tend to develop steady production, steady employment, and income to the working people in steady business and trade.

I made it a point to share with Roosevelt, as much as I could, the detailed information I picked up as Industrial Commissioner.

The Governor was greatly impressed by the success of the Manning Paper Company, to which I have previously referred. Perhaps he did not appreciate how much more difficult such an achievement might be in different industries. The Manning plant, employing three hundred, made industrial abrasive papers. It dealt almost entirely with other manufacturers who could estimate their needs in advance and would do so in return for a favorable price and prompt, regular deliveries.

The Procter & Gamble Company had a guarantee of forty-eight weeks of work per year to each employee. Of course, they put out a small standard object, soap, which could be made in advance and stored in the warehouse, but they had the idea of selling it to their retailers or jobbers on an annual contract, with monthly deliveries, so that the retailer or jobber was not required to provide his own storage space and yet would give an estimate and order for a year in advance. Roosevelt was interested because here was a large plant operating in many states with the same standard of an annual program of guaranteed employment.

Years later, in 1944, Roosevelt as President recommended what he had begun to call "an annual wage." The annual wage is nothing but guaranteed annual employment. In supporting an annual wage, he was once more letting an idea filter in from a concrete experience, giving it a constantly simpler expression and aiming it in the direction of a positive program which could be understood by all. While the phrase "stabilization of employment" is undoubtedly more exact, it would not have won so easily the hearty support of the workingmen of the United States as the idea of an annual wage. The annual wage or stabilized employment is impossible for some industries—building trades, for instance, in which it would be highly desirable if anyone could think of ways of working it out. The President always shot over this idea of impracticability. He believed that people could work out ways of doing desirable things if they but harnessed their wills to the objective they had agreed was sound and moral.

In 1930, at the Governor's suggestion, I asked Henry Bruère to be chairman of the Commission on the Stabilization of Employment. Before World War I, when there had been a serious period of unemployment in New York City, Mr. Bruère had been Chamberlain of the City in the administration of Mayor Mitchel, and had undertaken the handling of the unemployment problem. He had opened and operated the famous "Hotel DeGink" on the Bowery, which provided a temporary, friendly, noninstitutional lodging and eating place for countless unemployed transients who poured into the city. He had operated a reasonably good "make work" program and had tried to start a public works program on a local basis.

"It is just the same old unemployment problem that it was back in 1914," he said in 1930.

I had to admit it was the same old unemployment problem.

"Has anything serious ever been done about it in the meantime?" he asked.

I replied that very little had been done.

He suggested that we get out the 1918 report (in which I had participated in a minor way) and see what we had recommended then.

"Probably," he said, "with some review we can recommend the same things now."

I pointed out that we were now dealing with the state, not the city, an immensely more complicated industrial picture. We were in the midst of a world-wide economic crisis, stemming partly from the economic aftermath of the war and representing partly one of the periodic crises in our economy. There were more data on the causes of unemployment and a greater experience of what could be done to mitigate its hardships.

The Governor was aware of these changes and wanted fresh consideration of the problem. He also wanted to conduct the studies so that the people as well as the Commission would be educated. He followed the work of the Commission closely. He asked me to spend a great deal of my time on it and to be sure that we came to practical conclusions. We held hearings in every part of the state. We met regularly and debated the many suggestions for relieving the immediate crisis and for preventing unemployment in the future.

Roosevelt absorbed the ideas that were passing through our minds as I retailed them to him. He became familiar with many of the tentative recommendations and used to suggest them himself for discussion and stimulus to employers and labor people who came to see him.

After a period of hearings and studies the Commission, or a good many of its members, began to be impressed with the fact that in an industrial system as complicated as ours, unemployment is just as much of an industrial hazard as accidents, and should therefore be insured in advance. That individuals should not suffer the total, crushing cost of unemployment.

The State of New York was accustomed to taking advanced steps in legislation, but unemployment compensation or insurance was something quite new. It was bound to be expensive, and it was questionable whether one state could carry the burden alone when competing, neighboring states did not carry unemployment insurance by law as part of the cost of doing business. We discussed within the Commission the possibility of joining with neighboring states where great interest had been shown in our work and inquiry.

In 1946 it seems odd that none of us at that time thought in terms of a federal law. But in 1931 there was no federal labor legislation, and attempts at labor and social legislation on a federal basis had been declared unconstitutional by the Supreme Court. It seemed wise to explore the unemployment problem with other eastern industrial states which had similar problems and which were aroused over the conditions of people in their own states.

We took up with Governor Roosevelt the question of calling an interstate conference on unemployment. He was immediately responsive, although he realized that it would mean a heavy burden of work and leadership for him. He was cautious about the possibility of giving offense to the other governors. "Heads of sovereign states, you know," he said. He told me first to ask the labor commissioners of each state whether the governors would be willing to come. After that he telephoned each governor informally before a public invitation was issued.

It was typical of Roosevelt that he should foresee the possibility of appearing to diminish the status of the other governors. He thought of them as people, not as wooden images symbolizing the state, and he was careful of their feelings, not entirely out of political astuteness but out of a sensitivity for human feelings and good fellowship.

We were fortunate that there were at that time modern, alert governors in near-by states anxious to make headway against the terrific problems of unemployment. Among them were Joseph B. Ely of Massachusetts; Norman S. Case of Rhode Island; Wilbur L. Cross of Connecticut; Morgan F. Larson of New Jersey; Gifford Pinchot of Pennsylvania; George White of Ohio; William Tudor Gardiner of Maine, and John G. Winant of New Hampshire.

The idea that there were common industrial and economic problems appealed to these men. Knowing there would be a ready response, Governor Roosevelt formally invited them to Albany for a three-day conference on unemployment problems.

The Governor emphasized that it must be done well or not at all. I telegraphed Paul H. Douglas of the University of Chicago, a young, intelligent, forceful economist, asking if he would come to help cast the economic material into practical, digestible form and to assist in presenting the problem to the assembled governors. He came. I presented him to Governor Roosevelt. The Governor liked him at once and trusted him. He liked his clear, concise approach to problems. Douglas was a prodigious worker. In a few days he had prepared a conference program that I could conscientiously recommend to Governor Roosevelt and that the members of the Stabilization Commission thought well of.

The governors assembled. Here was one of the tests of Franklin Roosevelt's powers of leadership. For the most part he did not know them. They were willing to come at his invitation because they were in the same predicament. However, no man in politics likes to acknowledge the leadership or superiority of any other person of equal rank. Roosevelt was another politician and might be a political rival.

Roosevelt understood that his first problem was to disarm these governors, to present himself to them as truly disinterested, a public official charged with a grave duty, honestly trying to find an answer and asking their help and co-operation. The brilliance and sincerity of Roosevelt became clear at that time. I remember with what satisfaction men like Henry Bruère, then president of the Bowery Savings Bank, and Maxwell Wheeler, president of the Larkin Company in Buffalo and of Associated Industries, who had not seen him in action before, realized that he was rising to the situation. He was master of the material which we had piled up in such quantities that it was almost too much to expect him to know what was in the report. He mastered it by simplifying it. That was his technique, and he was always good at it. He simplified every question that I raised and every point that I made in the outline I had prepared for him. He raised questions himself in a modest and inquiring way. He illustrated and illuminated some of the problems for the governors by referring to concrete cases, always in a graceful, consultative manner which indicated to the governors that he wanted to hear from them, not just to tell them.

This conference proved to be one of the highlights of his prepresidential career. He disarmed his critics. He made his position clear and didn't do all the talking or all the work himself. Politically speaking, it turned out to be a practical move for him, although I am sure no such thought entered his mind when he agreed to call the conference. It was one of the things that had to be done to help the people in our part of the country out of the predicament of mass unemployment.

He made the acquaintance of John Gilbert Winant and other governors and they became his friends and supporters, ready to help him do in the future everything that could be done to improve the lot of the working people of the United States. They later became his supporters in the annual Conference of Governors. They became supporters of the idea that unemployment insurance might be a good thing and that it was possible to make some headway in establishing it in this country. They became interested in the idea that a great deal could be done in establishing a common area of labor and social legislation through interstate compacts.

If in later years, when Roosevelt was President, there had not been discovered a method by which federal labor legislation could be written so as to be constitutional, I feel sure we should have fallen back upon these ideas of interstate compacts. It was one of the ideas in his mind when, as President, he began exploring what could be done to put a floor under wages and a ceiling over hours, what could be done to make a sound program of accident prevention that would be applicable in all parts of the country, what could be done to build a program of unemployment and old-age insurance which would protect the people against the worst economic hazards.

The conference was also one of Roosevelt's important educative experiences. He was growing rapidly. More and more he found in himself the capacity to lead people and guide their thinking. It interested me to see him come by degrees to the realization that he had a responsibility for what happened to people beyond state limits. He began to grow on the idea of one nation. We had not begun then to talk about "one world."

By the time he had digested the report of the conference on unemployment and the report of his Commission on the Stabilization of Industry, he had become convinced that unemployment insurance was necessary for the country and that we would come to it sooner or later. Whether it should be state by state, by interstate compact, or by the Federal Government, he had not made up his mind. When he went to Salt Lake City to make a speech before the Conference of Governors, he had become convinced that he must take a stand. It seemed a big stand at the time.

I wrote three or four pages about unemployment insurance to be included in the speech. He cut it. I listened to him over the radio and was slightly disappointed. He had not stated it emphatically enough, it seemed to me.

But his judgment proved to be right. He had toned it exactly right for absorption and approval by the governors. The fact that every newspaper played it as "Governor Roosevelt Comes Out for Unemployment Insurance" showed his power to gauge the public reaction. If he had been more emphatic, there would have been an immediate shying away by all except the already convinced.

Roosevelt had also become clear in his mind that unemployment insurance was not enough, that it alone would not keep our economy on an even keel. He felt that people in every walk of life—government, labor unions, businessmen, and political leaders, as well as economic thinkers—would have to think, plan, and experiment to overcome this hazard to our industrial society. He was fully appreciative of the enormous advances in the standard of living which had come about through the utilization of machinery, efficiency, and system under private ownership and management. But he could not accept the cruel philosophy then being peddled in some quarters that, since the system was so good on the whole, the only thing to do when it struck one of its periodic crises was to let it plunge to the bottom where it would right itself and gradually begin to move up again.

I once saw Roosevelt listening to this argument from a man he had known for years and who called himself an economist. I shall never forget the gray look of horror on his face as he turned on this man and said, "People aren't cattle, you know!"

The conceptions he was building up in 1930, 1931, and 1932, learning by experience and by facing problems as they came, led him to the actions he took as President, not only in promoting social security legislation but in planning in 1944 and 1945, when the end of the war was in sight, for cancellation of contracts, tax adjustments, and prompt settlement of government bills, all in such a way as to prevent the unemployment he foresaw as one of the hazards of the postwar period.

It is interesting to note that his insistence with labor leaders, employers, government colleagues, and congressmen that some way be found to prevent unemployment resulted in the Full Employment Bill, which he lived to see introduced but which he did not live to see become a law.

PART THREE

THE NATION

POLITICS

As the 1932 national conventions approached, it was clear that there was a movement under way to nominate Roosevelt for President on the Democratic ticket. Jim Farley had undoubtedly been at work for months. Louis Howe had been thinking and planning along these lines for years. But among many of us working with Roosevelt in Albany, these things were not much discussed. My knowledge of what was happening was implicit rather than explicit.

Roosevelt had tremendously vigorous and earnest supporters, in addition to the organization politicians, whom Farley dealt with. Many who backed Roosevelt before the convention were touched by the ideas that had moved both Roosevelt and Al Smith. They believed affirmatively in the possibilities of life in this century on this continent.

With the nomination secured, Roosevelt launched into his campaign. He had thought that Herbert Hoover would be easy to beat, but as the campaign developed he found that he would have to work hard at it. A newcomer in the national field, Roosevelt had to get out and become known. He saw thousands of Americans. The freshness of his approach made friends among them. He found he liked national campaigning, and that liking for the big political arena stayed with him.

He said little about Hoover personally, either in campaign time or later. Like other kindhearted, liberal people, Roosevelt had been shocked by President Hoover's orders to drive veterans of World War I out of Anacostia Flats in Washington and to burn their encampment when they had marched there in protest in 1931. He had been shocked that the President should fear his fellow citizens. His instinct had cried out that veterans in an illegal encampment in Washington, even if difficult and undesirable, must all be faced in a humane and decent way. He had said little, had just shaken his head and shuddered, when the incident took place.

When the veterans came to Washington in March 1933, in a similar, if smaller, march on the capital followed by an encampment, Roosevelt drove out and showed himself, waving his hat at them. He asked Mrs. Roosevelt and Louis Howe to go. "Above all," he said to them, "be sure there is plenty of good coffee. No questions asked. Just let free coffee flow all the time. There is nothing like it to make people feel better and feel welcome."

After the veterans in 1933 had the free coffee and a visit from Mrs. Roosevelt, they were willing to send a committee to talk with Howe. Gradually they began to go home, and relief funds were found to help them start back.

Campaigns always stimulated Roosevelt enormously. He liked going around the country. He enjoyed the freedom and getting out among the people. He used to come back and describe individuals in the crowd—a woman with a baby, an old fellow, small boys scampering in the throng. He associated them sometimes with the town, county, and state in which he had seen them. His personal relationship with crowds was on a warm, simple level of a friendly, neighborly exchange of affection.

Having watched him a long time, I know that that feeling was sincere. It became natural to him, but it was a lesson he learned. He learned to love people by trying to understand them and to find the common denominator between him and everyone with whom he had contact. His affection for people bore no resemblance to the social worker's professional approach or the parson's pious respect. He just liked them for themselves, the way they were, and, of course, he liked and was sustained by the affection they returned.

Roosevelt's campaign speeches were of major importance to his advisers. As I see it now, we all had pride in him. Each of us wanted Roosevelt to do superlatively well, particularly with the matters that were our special concern. Each of us, having his own audience and following, was conscious of what our particular group would want to hear from Roosevelt. I think it was affection and jealousy for him and his reputation that caused so much sparring among his associates over what should be in a speech.

He was courtesy itself in receiving suggestions from his advisers. Some suggestions, I am sure, he had not the slightest intention of using, but he would receive the pages of proposed oratory with great good will. He did rely completely, however, upon factual information supplied him by his associates. Every figure, date, and statement had to be correct, for he was likely to use them without further rechecking. He had a right to expect this service, and he got it. The men in his immediate group who whacked the speeches into shape used the material we submitted. Then Roosevelt mulled over the product and rewrote it with his personal ideas and conclusions.

In one campaign he asked me to write a speech in which he wanted to stress what had been done in social security and why, and to sketch the future of this program. I summed up one section by saying, "We are trying to construct a more inclusive society." I heard that speech over the radio some weeks later, and this is how he, with his instinct for simplicity, wound up that section: "We are going to make a country in which no one is left out."

In the 1944 campaign, which we dreaded because the President's strength was not what it had been and because we feared the effects of the strain upon him, he let Governor Dewey, the Republican candidate, get two or three speeches up on him. He just didn't seem to care, he'd get around to it in time. Long before, he had made a date to speak at a dinner of the Teamsters' Union in Washington. He had made this date with Dan Tobin, president of the Teamsters, because he liked Dan and wanted to oblige Dan by making his "labor speech" at his meeting.

Aware that the President would probably do this, Dewey made his labor speech a few nights earlier. It was a good speech and put the Republican party on record in favor of everything the New Deal had done in the way of labor and social legislation and recognition of labor, and he promised to do more. He delivered it effectively, as though he meant it.

The President had asked me to contribute some material for his labor speech. He had also asked Isador Lubin, then working in the White House, whom he trusted greatly. I expect he also asked a good many others to contribute something. He turned all the material over to Sam Rosenman, who dug away and made further attempts to write a good labor speech.

After Dewey's speech we consulted and wondered what in the world the President could say to point out sufficiently that his opponent's promises merely repeated Roosevelt's actions. How could the President make a new and affirmative stand of his own?

Two days before the dinner I sent over some additional material and then telephoned to say I didn't think he ought to use it, since it would be difficult to make a labor speech without appearing merely to answer Dewey. The President was easy and relaxed. "You don't need to worry," he said. "I'm not going to use any of the stuff you sent me. Put it away, maybe we'll use it some other time, but not now. I have got my mind on something else, and I'm going to have a good time at Tobin's dinner."

One listened with some trepidation that night. It was the now famous speech in which Roosevelt told of the persecution of his little dog, Fala; they were calling Fala names and Fala didn't like it. While I was not among those who thought it a great speech, I recognized, as I heard everybody on the streets saying it was the greatest speech he had ever made, that he had done the effective thing. In a witty and undisturbed way he had put his finger on all the dirty, mean attacks on individuals being circulated underground. He had treated the problem perfectly. It was no longer a danger to his candidacy.

I have often been asked what Roosevelt thought of his presidential rivals. It is impossible to say with finality, but he did think Hoover a solemn defeatist, with little hope and with no consciousness of people as human beings or of their needs. Alfred Landon he considered a nice fellow who didn't know much—just a figurehead in what Roosevelt thought the Republicans knew was a hopeless campaign.

When he asked Landon to come in to see him after the 1936

campaign, to give the picture of a united country and to bury the hatchet, Roosevelt was entirely sincere and mentioned Landon's good will, although he spoke rather slightingly of his intellectual and political attainments. There had been much bitterness in a small element of the Republican party, but Roosevelt was not disturbed by the Liberty League crowd's extreme charges. The Republican campaign with its talk of "grass roots," its sunflower symbol, its use of "Oh, Susanna" as a battle song, amused him by its futility. He regarded Landon as a nicer fellow and a more patriotic American than some of his supporters. However, he was surprised that Landon accepted his invitation to come to the White House.

Roosevelt's general policy was never to mention the name of the opposing candidate, a theory with which Jim Farley agreed. "Call him the gentleman from Indiana," Roosevelt would say with a smile. "Call him the candidate of the Republican party. Call him our opponent. Call him anything, but never call him bad names. That creates an unfavorable impression among Americans. And never mention his name. Many people, hundreds of people, just cannot remember names. If they don't hear the opponent's name, that is clear gain for us. They have heard my name so often and so long that it in itself is a political asset, and you can trust them, particularly the Roosevelt haters, to say my name plenty of times. In the end, lots of people go to the polls and look the list of candidates over and make up their minds after they get into the ballot booth. I know that sounds feeble-minded, but I know it's true. When they look over the list they vote for people whose names they know. We don't want to do anything to advertise the name of the opposing candidate."

Wendell Willkie, I think, was more disturbing to Roosevelt as a rival than anyone who ran against him. He recognized that the elements which forced Willkie's nomination were not oldline Republicans but people with some progressive ideas, who, under other circumstances, might have been converted to the Roosevelt cause. As the campaign wore on and Willkie proved to be a vigorous, but not good, campaigner, the President grew a little supercilious. The ostentatious effort to make Willkie appear a simple small-town boy with the rigged-up visits to Elwood, Indiana, where he hadn't been for years and had no real attachment, rather annoyed the President. As Willkie's campaign went more badly, Roosevelt took mischievous glee in the discomfiture of the Republicans, who would grit their teeth because of some trifling defect in campaign technique.

Roosevelt regarded himself as an experienced campaigner and polished politician, and it rather offended him to see mistakes made in the art of political campaigning. I think he tended to overlook the drawing power of Willkie's sincerity, and he underrated the strength of the appeal against the third term, which was a great talking point in the 1940 campaign.

Willkie made his labor speech in Pittsburgh before an audience largely of labor men. I thought it was pretty good. He put himself on record in favor of the things that labor traditionally wanted, but we would have expected any politician to do that in 1940. Then he worked up to what he would do as President in improving the labor laws and their administration. He was not specific, except on one point. He said, "I will appoint a Secretary of Labor directly from the ranks of organized labor." This was sure of a big hand, as the labor leaders tended to believe that the post belonged to them. Although they had, with few exceptions, co-operated with me in my period of office, it was natural for them to believe, as I did, that the post should go to labor. So far so good. But when the cheers had died down in the audience, largely of men, Willkie continued, hoping to get another hand—and he did—"And it will not be a woman either."

The President, listening to the speech on the radio, was quick to catch the blunder. Although the audience of men applauded loudly and Willkie undoubtedly left the hall thinking he had made a hit, women in the United States, including Republican women, were pained and insulted.

The President said to me, "That was a boner Willkie pulled. He was all right. He was going good when he said his appointment of a Secretary of Labor would come from labor's ranks. That was legitimate political talk, but why didn't he have sense enough to leave well enough alone? Why did he have to insult every woman in the United States? It will make them mad, it will lose him votes."

"You'll be surprised to know, Mr. President," I said, "that I already have about five hundred telegrams and letters from women, expressing irritation, and more than half of them tell me they are Republican women."

"He's sure to make other boners as time goes on," Roosevelt said. "If we don't do anything to break the spell, I'm pretty sure he will talk himself out of enough votes to carry me without much effort."

However, when the campaign was over, Roosevelt recognized Willkie as the leader of an important section of the population. He had rolled up a large vote. The President, feeling as he always did the necessity for unity in the United States, particularly with the war becoming daily closer and more dangerous to us, asked Willkie to come and see him.

The interesting thing is that he took an immediate liking to Willkie and he hadn't expected to. Whether it was Willkie's charm, sincerity, or vigor, I cannot say, but Roosevelt liked him. The next day he talked to me about it.

"You know, he is a very good fellow. He has lots of talent. I want to use him somehow. I want to offer him an important post in the government. Can you think of one? I want it to be an independent job. I don't want him to be a member of the cabinet or anything like that. I don't want him right around with us. I want him to do something where the effort is nonpolitical but important. But I'd like to use him, and I think it would be a good thing for the country, it would help us to a feeling of unity."

We were about to form the Defense Labor Board, which preceded the War Labor Board. The Board was to have labor and employer representatives. For the chairmanship we wanted a man not connected either with labor or industry. I suggested Willkie, and the President agreed.

I telephoned Willkie at once and offered him the job in the President's name. He declined. He told me that, although he wasn't against doing something in the service of his country, he didn't propose to take on anything so controversial as that.

But the President had him in mind, and when he asked Willkie to go to England as his personal representative, it was, I think, one of his intuitive judgments. It was an instinctive feeling that a hearty, likable fellow who could say "We feel sorry for you" without being offensive, and who would be understood by the common people, would give courage and hope to our British friends. Roosevelt also felt that the leader of the opposition party would carry more reassurance than a political friend of the President's. Nor was it lost on Roosevelt that Willkie would be affected by the sight of war. For a long time it had been clear in Roosevelt's mind that our foreign policy, with the possibility that we might have to enter the war, must be not the province of one party or of a President, but the conviction of both parties and their leaders. Roosevelt knew that Willkie's trip would help toward unity.

Many people thought Roosevelt would be jealous of the attention Willkie got. I watched him closely, and I am sure he wasn't. He was pleased with the effect Willkie had in England, and it was a considerable effect. He was also deeply interested in the convictions Willkie arrived at through personal contact with the war.

Willkie's quick trip around the world added to his convictions. Some people tended to conclude that he had accepted what he was told without reflection. But Roosevelt did not underestimate Willkie. His was a mind Roosevelt understood. He had some of the same characteristics himself, and he recognized the validity of opinions based upon a combination of feeling, personal observation, and descriptive analysis made by others. He was always interested in how the Republicans would treat Willkie later, and he felt sympathy for him when they shouldered him out of the way so quickly at the next convention.

Roosevelt once said to me, "You know, Willkie would have made a good Democrat. Too bad we lost him."

For Dewey, Republican candidate in 1944, Roosevelt had little respect. He expected him to make a bad campaign and was surprised when it turned out to be excellent, revealing preparation, thought, and good advice. Dewey made a minimum of mistakes and some good plays.

The 1944 Republican platform, of course, was of great interest to us, and I remember the discussion at cabinet meeting.

One member said, "Disgusting, disgusting, so insincere and pretentious."

I replied, "Well, I think we should be grateful for that platform. It means that the New Deal has won forever. The country has adopted as a permanent program those items which, when we introduced them, were supposed to be radical, revolutionary, and temporary. Now the Republican party has adopted as its formal platform most of these items which we have called New Deal items, and have merely promised to make them better, extend them, and, of course, administer them better."

"I think you're right," Roosevelt said, "but it isn't going to be any easier to make a campaign against a man who says he is for the same things that we boast about as being our contribution."

Roosevelt in 1944 did not intend to make a real campaign. The official national decisions he had to make were all-absorbing. He was older and not so strong physically as in years past. He had no intention of taking his eyes or his mind off the war. I heard him say this over and over again.

Under normal circumstances Roosevelt would not have run in 1944. But his experience and his knowledge of our resources and plans and of those of our allies made it imperative. I think there was no question in his mind, after we entered the war, that it would be necessary unless the war had finished. His hope had been that the war would be over before the next presidential election and that his contribution in ensuing years would be in representing his government in some way in the international organization for peace. As the months wore on, it was obvious that the war would not be over in 1944, and he reconciled himself, as all of us did, to the idea that he must continue.

When he began to get reports from the field that Dewey was gaining, he changed his mind about the necessity for campaigning and announced one day at cabinet meeting that he was going to make an old-fashioned rough-and-tumble campaign. He had to go everywhere, he had to show himself, he said. "There has been this constant rumor that I'll not live if I am re-elected, and people have been asked to believe that I am all worn out and sick. You all know that is not so, but apparently I have to face them to prove it. Apparently 'Papa has to tell them.' That is the way politics go in this country, and I am going right after Dewey and make a real campaign."

He began what was one of the most vigorous campaigns of his life, even if it was short. He loved campaigning, and always had. He had such a good time that he gained twelve pounds in weight, generally brightened his naturally hopeful outlook on the war and postwar life, and came back stimulated and invigorated from the contact with people. Riding around New York City in the pouring rain didn't hurt him. His contact with the crowd, his sense of belonging, gave him happiness. "It kept me warm, you know," he told me, "and I didn't know I was wet through."

Roosevelt's campaigns were stimulating and illuminating to him. From each he learned. In 1932 he discovered anew the power and influence of the women's vote. He was much impressed by the political activities of the Women's Division of the Democratic National Committee under Mary Dewson. She proved to be a remarkable organizer and campaign director. She knew the woman voter as distinguished from the woman member of the local political party group. She knew that the average woman voter had intellectual curiosity and made up her mind about candidates on the basis of principles.

Roosevelt, like Farley, was pleased with what she did in making the women of America politically conscious. By 1936 he was insistent that the Democratic National Committee should give a generous appropriation to the Women's Division, and he backed the Division in everything it did. It pleased him that the "Rainbow Dodgers," campaign literature put out by the women, had a wider and more effective circulation than anything else issued.

"Make it simple enough for the women to understand," he would say after that, "and then the men will understand it."

The 1936 campaign was a political education for the Democratic party. The convention was like a love feast, with no doubt that Roosevelt and Garner would be renominated, but there had been some sparring over the platform. The collapse of the Agricultural Adjustment program and the National Recovery Administration under adverse Supreme Court decisions had created a difficult political situation, for both programs had been popular with the electorate. The platform included promises to find a way to restore the essentials of these programs.

When the Democratic politicians started on their speeches, they discovered that all they had to talk about of their first four years in office since Wilson were the social and labor advances under the "New Deal." Headquarters ground out speeches, memoranda, outlines, dodgers, and campaign literature on this theme. One of the most circulated speeches, published in the Democratic campaign book as a model for others, was by Representative William Bankhead of Alabama, in which he lauded the New Deal to the skies. It was a good speech. Roosevelt always believed that the liberal forces in the southern states were strong and would eventually come to have an influence. He was grateful for Bankhead's political endorsement, but he went out of his way to find southern leaders who practiced these campaign pronouncements. There are many—O. Max Gardner, former Governor of North Carolina; Clark Foreman of Georgia; Frank P. Graham, president of the University of North Carolina; Josephus Daniels and his son Jonathan of North Carolina; Alexander Guerry, president of the University of Tennessee, and many others.

Before 1936 few practical politicians had been particularly concerned about "doing good" to labor except the President and Senator Wagner. It was, of course, my special field, and the conservative press had denounced me along with the President. After every state except Maine and Vermont went Democratic, more politicians strove to take part in the social and labor program. This, I suppose, was the discovery of the labor vote, although, as a matter of fact, ordinary people everywhere, whether members of organized labor or not, voted overwhelmingly for this program in 1936. There could be no doubt that Roosevelt's attitude had been endorsed by this election, in which there was really just one question—"Do you want the Roosevelt policies continued?"

Roosevelt in 1936 was on the top of the wave. The country

had revived under his leadership. The Democratic convention in Philadelphia had been a great success. Nothing had marred the spirit of unity save the new phrase "economic royalist," which Roosevelt had used in his speech of acceptance.

As I read the speech now, I find myself bewildered that it should have caused such resentment. I heard the speech and understood the argument perfectly. He pointed out that we in America had shaken off the power of royalists in the political field. He was thinking of sovereignty as deriving from the people through the democratic processes we had developed in a free, representative republic. Then he went on to point out that there still existed controls: the power to give or not to give jobs, the power to charge high or low prices, the power to permit or not to permit new, competing firms. These controls, he tried to indicate, were economic, not political. In a burst of literary creativeness he said "that this control was the control of economic royalists."

I was sitting on the platform very close to him. I heard the words, I saw the expression of his face, I knew what he meant. He was talking about the unwarranted power exercised by those who had control, not by virtue of wealth but by virtue of aggressive exercise of power stemming from ownership of factories, electric power production, or distributive enterprises. Even though I understood that point, I remember saying to Mary Dewson, who sat next to me, "I think this is going to be used against him."

She shook her head. "Oh, no, oh, no."

But it was used against him, and almost immediately. Many rich persons, even widows who derived their income from trust funds over which they had no control and from investments in enterprises in whose conservative management they could take no part, began to whimper, "Roosevelt calls me bad names. He calls me an economic royalist."

People who ought to have known better jumped to the conclusion that he was declaring himself an enemy of every rich person, whether one's riches accrued from old land holdings in whose development and management one took no part or from portfolios of investments which had come to one under Grandfather's will.

Even people who earned large incomes by intellectual or artistic activities, who actually contributed to the economic life and progress of the country, were inclined to believe that he meant them in his condemnation of "economic royalists." This reaction, of course, was typically American; it was not literate or urbane, but in some subtle way, I suppose, it expressed a more widely distributed guilty conscience than anyone realized. I remember explaining to two rich women, personal friends of mine, that they were not economic royalists; that they had no control over anything; that they merely lived off the profits which farsighted fathers and husbands had secured for them.

Roosevelt was both the gainer and the loser from his use of this challenging phrase—the gainer because people who were not rich reacted like those who were rich but not powerful. I told him that these two women, also friends of his, were deeply disturbed. He laughed. "Of course, they did not know what I had in mind, but perhaps it was a lucky choice of words. Anyhow, I don't think people ought to be *too* rich."

He said "too rich" in an emphatic tone of voice. I never knew what he meant by "too rich" and I doubt that he did. It was probably a hark-back to the older and simpler American scene before the appearance of the multimillionaire, who was a puzzle and embarrassment to the old-fashioned "well-to-do" and often seemed like an aggressor to the poor.

Roosevelt did not fear experiment. I remember coming back from a trip to California when Upton Sinclair was running for Governor in a hot campaign, and his program, known as EPIC (End Poverty In California), was gaining adherence. Sober liberals in California were horrified. They begged me to tell the President that help would be needed from him to stem the tide of votes for Sinclair.

I went to see him and told him the program was fanatic. I said there was danger that Sinclair might be elected and EPIC imposed, and that it would ruin the California banking system, according to the judgment of our friends in California.

He thought a minute. "Well, they might be elected in California. Perhaps they'll get EPIC in California. What difference, I ask you, would that make in Dutchess County, New York, or Lincoln County, Maine? The beauty of our state-federal system is that the people can experiment. If it has fatal consequences in one place, it has little effect upon the rest of the country. If a new, apparently fanatical, program works well, it will be copied. If it doesn't, you won't hear of it again."

Nor was Roosevelt afraid to try bold political ventures. When he undertook the "purge" in 1938, he thought he might use presidential prestige to eliminate a number of Democratic congressmen who had consistently voted against his policies and "must bills." He underestimated the strength and sincerity of the Democratic party organizations in the local communities, and was a little on the reckless side; but by taking that intransigent attitude he undoubtedly evoked in the electorate itself the beginnings of a new standard for candidates for office.

The boldest of precedent-breaking ventures was the third term, but it was made with profound reluctance and heart-searching.

Roosevelt has often been blamed for not coming out earlier and more frankly for or against the third term. Those of us who were associated with him in this period have differing views as to when he made up his mind. Certainly he discussed the problem with many people. With me he was always negative.

If I said to him, "I recommend that next year you do this and that," he would laugh and say, "Don't you know I'm through in January 1941?" Or, "You will have to speak to the next President about that."

I never urged him because I had real doubts about the wisdom of third terms as a matter of principle. However, the European war had already begun, and Roosevelt was deeply aware of the problems that seemed sure to engulf us, in the Pacific as well as in Europe. I felt that this was an emergency situation in which the wisdom of continuing him in office had to be considered. Here was a man who had, I knew for certain, no intention of building up permanent personal power; a man who wouldn't make the great sacrifice of personal freedom necessary even for a benevolent dictatorship. He was too flexible, voluble, curious, and exploratory; he had too much sense of proportion and humor. He had long ago discovered, along with Mr. Justice Holmes, "that he was not God."

A strange light on this third term came one evening when I went with Daniel Tobin of the Teamsters' Union to see the President. I cannot recall now why we went. We finished our business shortly. The President, seated in his second-floor study, was in a relaxed mood.

As we prolonged our visit in pleasant conversation, Dan said, "Mr. President, you just have to run for the third term, you know you do. Don't talk to me about your fishing trips next winter—you are going to be right here in the White House."

"No," said the President, "no, Dan. I just can't do it. I tell you, I have been here a long time. I am tired. I really am. You don't know what it's like. And besides, I have to take care of myself. This sinus trouble I've got, the Washington climate makes it dreadful. It's the Washington disease. I never had it until I came here. How can I get over it? The doctors say I have to go into the hospital for a month of steady treatment. But I can't do that, you know. When a President does that, the bottom drops out of the stock market, the Japs take advantage of what they think is a serious illness, the Germans start propaganda that I am dying and that the United States is in a panic. No, I can't be President again. I have to get over this sinus. I have to have a rest. I want to go home to Hyde Park. I want to take care of my trees. I have a big planting there, Dan. I want to make the farm pay. I want to finish my little house on the hill. I want to write history. No, I just can't do it, Dan."

Tobin expostulated, giving his emotional arguments. The President laughed. "You know, the people don't like the third term either."

"That's all right," said Tobin. "Labor will stand by you."

The President laughed again at some private joke.

"I want to tell you two a very interesting thing," he said. "About two months ago John Lewis came to see me one evening. He was in a most amiable mood, and he talked about the third term too, Dan, just the way you have, only much smoother." Roosevelt could not resist teasing a friend. "When I told him what I told you, that the people wouldn't like a third term and that it would be very hard going politically, what do you think he said, Dan? He said, 'Mr. President, I have thought

of all of that and I have a suggestion to make for you to consider. If the vice-presidential candidate on your ticket should
happen to be John L. Lewis, those objections would disappear.
A strong labor man would insure full support, not only of all
the labor people but of all the liberals who worry about such
things as third terms.'"

The President paused. He could see Dan was astonished. "Can
you beat it?" he said. "What do you think of it?"

Tobin exploded. "Why, Mr. President, he isn't even a Democrat. How does he think he'll get the nomination?"

We were both curious. Tobin asked the question. "How did
you answer him, Mr. President?"

"Why, he didn't press me," said the President, "he didn't press
me. He just asked me to think it over and give it consideration."

As I drove home that night I recalled that only a few days
earlier I had conferred with Lewis about some labor legislation
and had suggested that the support of the labor organizations
ought to be forthcoming. He had said that he did not wish to
commit himself on this legislation *yet*. Then he observed, in a
very ceremonious way, "I have made some suggestions to the
President and I think that I shouldn't commit myself until he
has time to think about them and come to some conclusions."

Whether Lewis had any expectation of being nominated
for Vice-President at the Chicago convention in 1940 I do not
know. I doubt it. He was there but left early, after making an
appearance before the Platform Committee. I met him in one
of the hotels just before he left. He was friendly and said he was
well satisfied with his treatment.

Tobin and I, perhaps the only people to whom Roosevelt told
the story, commented that Lewis apparently had given up the
struggle gracefully. We thought he would continue to support
Roosevelt. I feel sure now that this explains why he came out
against Roosevelt when the campaign was at its height.

Lewis tried to turn the miners' votes against Roosevelt in
1940 and 1944. He failed. We showed Roosevelt an analysis of
mining district votes—they had gone overwhelmingly for him.
Roosevelt's comment was, "Well, Lewis learned."

I have never been sure when Roosevelt made up his mind to
a third term. Frank Walker and others responsible for the cam-

paign certainly knew, perhaps in March or April, that he would be willing to have a third term if it could be handled properly. They were pledged to keep it secret, and the result was that a great many moves were started for different individuals as candidates for President, perfectly legitimate in a period when a President has served two terms and the convention against the third term is being observed.

This caused a great deal of heartburning later, because men who would not have attempted to win the nomination against Roosevelt felt they had been left out on a limb. The indignation began to be clear when we got to the convention. By this time Walker was telling those who had a right to know that the candidate was Roosevelt, and the lines were being laid for the nomination, which would have to be made to appear a universal demand. Indeed, as far as the people were concerned, it was a universal demand. But it is in the nature of political parties and delegates to like change. With change there is a chance for new people. The sparring for posts and nominations is one of the major activities at a convention.

Before those of the cabinet who were going to the convention left Washington, we had a talk with Roosevelt about the desirability of his appearance at Chicago. He said he had definitely made up his mind that he would not go. The situation, domestic and foreign, required his complete attention in Washington. He thought it wouldn't look well and would appear that he was putting on pressure. He was even opposed to flying out at the last minute as he had to the 1932 convention. Yet those who were promoting his candidacy, men like Senator Guffey and Walker, felt his appearance would please the delegates and focus the enthusiasm which must go into a campaign.

Harry Hopkins, certainly not an old-line Democratic politician, but a shrewd man who had become acquainted with a lot of Democratic politicians while administering relief and the WPA, was to be in charge of Roosevelt headquarters at the Blackstone Hotel. He was to make decisions and keep in touch with the delegates during the convention. This irked many of the old-line politicians. They hate to see an "amateur" coming into the technical or professional side of politics.

But Hopkins was there with a private wire to Washington,

and with plenty of people to help him. There was a continuous procession of delegates to his office from the day he arrived. The bitterness around the corridors was keen as prospective candidates and the delegates pledged to them realized that Roosevelt was going to run. They had to devise an appropriate strategic retreat or make a fight on the floor of the convention, which was universally dreaded.

This was the year Mayor Kelly of Chicago planted men in the basement of the auditorium, in front of microphones connected with loud-speakers concealed throughout the convention hall. Whenever Roosevelt's name was mentioned, the boys in the basement would let loose a bedlam of cheers. The delegates did not know what was going on. Those on the platform had no idea that the enthusiasm did not come from the delegates. On the second day the delegates realized there was something remarkable about it, and by the third day the secret was out. People were angry.

They were angry for other reasons too. They were angry because of the patronage that had been denied them for eight years. They were angry that so many strangers and amateurs had come into political life. They were angry about the purge, which had hurt some of them and some of their friends. Some were deeply disturbed over the Supreme Court fight, in which honorable men had differed with the President. Some thought that we had had enough of the New Deal, and that it was time to call a halt.

Another cause of distress was the many candidates for Vice-President. Garner had announced that he was not running for a third term, although there were some who thought he could be persuaded. Roosevelt clearly did not want him. Everybody wanted to know whom he did want. Harry Hopkins didn't know, nor did Roosevelt's closest advisers in the cabinet. I had talked about it with him and had asked whether he wanted Henry Wallace. Did he think Wallace would make a good running mate? Wallace was very able, clear-thinking, high-minded, a man of patriotism and nobility of character. He had a following among farmers. He was one of the few people with an agricultural background who had begun to make himself comprehensible to the industrial working people of the country, and he had a real following among the liberal thinkers in every section and walk of life. He might strengthen the ticket.

"Yes," the President had replied, "he might strengthen it politically, and one has to think of it, he would be a good man if something happened to the President. He is no isolationist. He knows what we are up against in this war that is so rapidly engulfing the world." He was indefinite, however, and did not commit himself.

In Chicago I was disturbed by the bad feeling. It seemed to me unfortunate for Roosevelt to enter a campaign for a third term with a burden of ill will. Not that one doubted he would be nominated. But one had doubt as to the good will with which it would be done.

The deals were being made for candidates to withdraw, and some of them were holding out bitterly. Senator John Bankhead withdrew in a beautiful speech of renunciation, which must have cost him a good deal. So it went down the line. One after the other withdrew, but not without shouts from the floor indicating that people didn't like this kind of thing. Those of us who were friendly were doing our best to be diplomatic, to see everybody, and to ease the tension. But feeling was sour.

A number of reporters spoke to me about it, as did personal friends of Roosevelt.

Early one morning I had a telephone call from a young man who was so excited he neglected to tell me his name until I pulled it out of him. It was Bob Allen, of the Pearson and Allen "Washington Merry-Go-Round" team. I did not know whether Allen was looking for news or was playing a part. But he had a good deal to say to me.

The gist of it was: The situation was terrible. It might end in a riot. It would certainly end in a terrific increase of Roosevelt haters in the Democratic party. Something must be done. The people who were representing Roosevelt were not making friends for him. I have called you, Miss Perkins, because I think you will do something. I think Roosevelt will listen to you, if you tell him he must come out here. He knows you are a friend of his, and I think you have the nerve to tell him that he ought to come out.

I admitted that I was disturbed too. I agreed that the situation was unfortunate and that if the President came, his courageous, simple, and openhearted way would capture the delegates and help them to re-establish their own feeling of good will which was so important for everyone.

I had not known Allen was a Roosevelt adherent, but I was willing to believe any of the newspapermen might be, because there was a good deal of warmth and affection in their dealings with him. I learned later that Allen had predicted in his column that Roosevelt would come to Chicago. I suppose he liked to have his "inside dope" proved right. It is not unlikely that he was pressuring other people to help his prediction come true. However, I do not question that he was honestly concerned and was trying to give good advice.

I thought about it for half an hour. I decided to call Roosevelt. It was a good time of day. The President wouldn't yet be deeply occupied. He was always easy to get on the phone and willing to interrupt whatever he was doing to talk to one of his associates. I put in a call and soon got the President. He wanted to know how things were going. I said he would be renominated and then told him about the bitterness and crossness of the delegates, about the difficulties, confusion, and near fights. I told him that if he could come out to Chicago it would be a wonderful help. I told him of Allen's call. I urged him as strongly as I could.

"No, no, I have given it full consideration," he said. "I thought it all through both ways. I know I am right, Frances. It will be worse if I go. People will get promises out of me that I ought not to make. If I don't make promises, I will make new enemies. If I do make promises, they'll be mistakes. I'll be pinned down on things I just don't want to be pinned down on *now*. I am sure that it is better not to go. I am sure it will come out better the other way."

"Can't you suggest something?" I said. "What can we do?"

"How would it be if Eleanor came?" he asked.

"I think it would make an excellent impression."

"You know Eleanor always makes people feel right," he said. "She has a fine way with her. Would you like her to come?"

"Yes."

"Telephone her. I'll speak to her too, but you tell her so that she will know I am not sending her on my own hunch, but that some of the rest of you want her. Talk to one or two others before you speak to her." He paused. "How is the vice-presidential fracas coming on?"

I mentioned the great number of candidates and said the lines were getting tense.

"Haven't you made up your mind yet?" I asked. "If you can possibly say today whom you would like, I believe it would ease the tension. If you have made up your mind, I think you ought to let us know."

"I really haven't made up my mind," he said. "What do you think about Henry Wallace?"

I said that I hoped he remembered I had always thought extremely well of Wallace.

"How do you think he will go at the convention?"

"Well," I said, "nothing has been tried. One can't tell. I don't think he would lift a finger if he thought it would embarrass you or if he thought you didn't want him. So there is no sign of a Wallace campaign, and one cannot gauge the effect. He has a following and he is making friends all the time."

"I think Wallace is good," said Roosevelt. "I like him. He is the kind of a man I like to have around. He is good to work with and he knows a lot, you can trust his information. He digs to the bottom of things and gets the facts. He is honest as the day is long. He thinks right. He has the general ideas we have. He is the kind of man who can do something in politics. He can help the people with their political thinking. Yes, I think it had better be Wallace."

I said, "Are you making up your mind?"

"Yes," he said, "it's Wallace, I guess. Yes, it will be Wallace. I think I'll stick to that."

"That's fine," I said. "What shall I do?"

"Would you mind going over to tell Harry? What hotel are you in?"

I told him the Stevens.

"You'd better not telephone. Probably someone is listening in on Harry's wires. You'd better go over yourself and tell him. Will you? That I have decided on Wallace."

"All right, Mr. President."

Harry Hopkins was somewhat surprised, though by no means in disagreement. He had had no indication; in fact, the previous night he had called the President and could get no answer out of him.

Hopkins called the President for verification. Then he told the newspapermen that the vice-presidential candidate was likely to be Wallace. I don't remember whether anybody thought to tell Wallace but I think I finally called him. I then proceeded to make the preliminary arrangements for Mrs. Roosevelt to come out. She did sweeten the convention. She made friends, shook hands with thousands of people, and made a pleasant, spirited, and high-minded speech which put the political tone where it ought to be—on patriotism and leadership rather than on patronage.

Roosevelt felt badly when Jim Farley parted company with him on the grounds of the third term. There isn't any question but that Jim's conviction was sincere. He thought that for political and constitutional reasons the third term was bad. He once told me that a party is built up and kept in line by expectations. Everybody thinks that some time or other he is going to have a place in government; that is an incentive for the people who do the work and hold the party together between campaigns. If you have three terms, people get discouraged. They will feel out of it. It is true that so long as one man remains in the presidency the people underneath are not likely to be changed in great numbers. Another President in the same party would bring in a new crowd, and more Democrats would take part in government. Perhaps Farley had more serious reasons. Having expounded them to the President and been disagreed with, he decided to part company. Farley's decision was deeply painful to Roosevelt. He was fond of Farley and expected political friendship to endure through anything.

When Farley later retired as chairman of the New York State

Democratic Committee, some of his friends decided to give a
dinner in his honor. I was invited to attend, and my immediate
instinct was to say yes. I had great affection for Farley and respected his work as a politician and as Postmaster General. I
accepted the invitation, and then it occurred to me that perhaps
I ought to speak to the President.

"I have been invited to this dinner," I told Roosevelt, "and I
am planning to go. Any objections? Will it embarrass you in
any way?"

"No," he replied, "not at all. It is a good idea. Say something
nice about Jim. He is a good scout, you know."

Early in his presidency, Roosevelt had John Garner sit in on
cabinet meetings. We all learned a lot from Garner—about politics, about the functioning of the government and the mind of
Congress. His talk was racy and amusing. But after a bit the
President became convinced that Garner "leaked." First he told
a few cronies, then others, what had been said in cabinet meetings, and indeed a change came over the cabinet, a drawing in
of horns, a limitation on the free and vigorous expression of
opinion.

Garner had a colorful phrase for many things. Since cabinet
members didn't want uncompleted programs and half developed ideas spread around before they were ready, they got into
the habit of staying behind to talk privately to the President.
Garner called the practice "staying for prayer meeting."

I never knew whether or not the President regretted the
innovation of inviting the Vice-President to sit in on cabinet
meetings. When Wallace was Vice-President he felt supported
by his point of view. At the same time he realized that Wallace
was able to do comparatively little toward promoting legislation in the Senate. Garner, with his long experience and know-
how of politics and congressional techniques, undoubtedly did
a great deal to put the original "New Deal" legislation on the
statute books just as he probably hampered it later on. After
the first batch of New Deal laws had passed, his principal advice was, "Mr. President, you know you've got to let the cattle
graze."

Roosevelt's interest in politics never flagged. The way the game was being played, the state of the Democratic party's thinking in various parts of the country, the attitude, purposes, and plans of the Republican party, always interested him. When a cabinet member took even a brief trip, Roosevelt always wanted information when he came back. He used us all as eyes and ears. He wanted to see the country through our eyes. He liked to get vivid descriptions of places, people, events—not long-drawn-out encyclopedic reports, but the high spots that one would tell one's family after an interesting trip.

He was deeply touched by reports that railroad workers, hotel clerks, and other people whom any traveler would be bound to meet sent messages of affection to him. I am sure that he had a sense of support, moral and personal rather than political, from these evidences of good will.

Because I was Secretary of Labor I met, in my travels around the country, more working people than other cabinet officers. I made it a point, no matter what the purpose of my visit to a community, to arrange in advance to see the working people, preferably in their own union halls. On their own ground they would express themselves and ask questions. Roosevelt took great interest in my reports of these meetings. For the participants were not big professional labor leaders. They were the men who worked at the benches and in the mills. He felt that from them he had a real picture of American life.

He also liked to have my reports of what the women said. I went to a good many women's meetings and club meetings, and I met a cross section of the women of America. He was quick to appreciate that in all the women's organizations I found women of well-to-do Republican families who confessed to an admiration for him and a liking for what he had done.

When he prepared his political speeches during campaigns, he thought about the women's and labor's vote. Instead of going after it on the ward politician's theory that handing out one job makes ten votes, he appealed more subtly to their moral sense and their social feelings. He was convinced that women as well as working people have an emotional slant that fixes itself upon faith in community life and in social good will among the various elements.

Once when I was trying to resign, he wrinkled up his nose in the way he sometimes did when he was trying to be funny and said, "Well, I don't think it would be so good politically. I notice that we haven't lost the labor vote or the women's vote on your account."

As a matter of fact, the votes in these two fields had greatly increased in the years of the New Deal. It was characteristic of him that he had noticed those things and had realized that, however much of a pain I might be to some people, the majority of the voters had not reacted unfavorably to my programs.

There was rarely a cabinet meeting devoted to political talk exclusively, but there was often a great deal of political talk. There was bound to be more of it just before or just after a campaign. On one occasion members of the cabinet who were going on political missions during a campaign raised some questions.

"May we say, Mr. President, that there will be an hours and wages act to take the place of the NRA?"

"May we say, Mr. President, that some method of developing a better judicial interpretation of our laws will be found?"

"May we say, Mr. President, that you will, if elected, maintain economic stability?"

"May we say that work relief will be continued?"

"May we say that there will be an extension of public works?"

He said "Yes" to most questions, then dismissed the problem with, "Say what you please. Use your own judgment. But if it turns out wrong, the blood be on your own head."

If you wanted to go out on a limb for some hobby or theory, he would never say no. He kept an open mind as to whether it was wise or unwise, but he reserved the right not to go out and rescue you if you got into trouble. He wanted you to understand that. Many, too timid to defend their own position, resented this.

A sober consideration of politics indicates that this was good judgment. Otherwise, how could a man keep himself open to new ideas? How could he judge political timeliness and

wisdom unless he permitted those who were ardent in support
of new ideas to express themselves so that he might see the reaction? Roosevelt was sympathetic to a lot of new ideas that failed
to get popular approval, but he knew it was important to wait
for the moment when the people were ready for a program.

He was a great believer in alternatives. He rarely got himself
sewed tight to a program from which there was no turning
back. Supreme Court reform, of course, was one program to
which he did get himself sewed tight. I have reason to think he
later regretted it, although he made the best of his defeat and
consoled himself with the belief that some good came out of
the disturbance. Whatever happened, he loved the great game
of politics, and he played it like a master.

The flight to the Chicago convention in 1932, for example,
was a sign of the mastery that grew with the years. It gave the
1932 campaign a brilliant launching. It led to victory, and victory meant facing the gravest problems ever to confront a President of the United States.

II.

FAITH OF HIS FATHERS

On Saturday, March 4, 1933, Franklin Roosevelt was sworn in as President of the United States. On the morning of the Inaugural there had been a service at St. John's Church. Not in the plans for the Inauguration, it had been arranged at Roosevelt's sudden decision, I think, as an afterthought. Late on the eve of the Inauguration, we had had a telephone message from one of his secretaries that Roosevelt would like the members of the cabinet and their families to meet him for worship and intercession at St. John's at ten o'clock on the morning of Inauguration Day. We went, only the members of the new cabinet, their wives, and their grown sons and daughters who happened to be with them. The President was accompanied by his mother, his uncle, his wife, and such children as were in town. It was a simple but memorable service, following the outline of the Book of Common Prayer, with the hymns and Psalms chosen by Roosevelt after conference with Dr. Endicott Peabody, the head of Groton, his boyhood school, who had come down for the occasion.

We were in a terrible situation. Banks were closing. The economic life of the country was almost at a standstill. Roosevelt had to take control of the government of the United States that day. If ever a man wanted to pray, that was the day. He did want to pray, and he wanted everyone to pray for him. It was a closely kept secret, and it was days before the world knew that the President had gone to church before his Inauguration.

It was impressive. Everybody prayed, it seemed, as Dr. Peabody read out the prayer for grace and help for "Thy servant, Franklin, about to become President of these United States." We

were Catholics, Protestants, Jews, but I doubt that anyone remembered the difference. On succeeding Inauguration Day an-
niversaries each year he went to St. John's to repeat the prayers
and service of his first Inaugural. The President grew to have
great faith in this particular service and to feel rewarded and
strengthened by it. The number of persons invited became
larger, but always there was a sense of intimacy. No pictures
were taken, and little mention was made of it in the press.

On the last Inauguration Day in 1945, the service was held at
the White House, not at St. John's, for the Secret Service had
prohibited the President from going to any public building during the war. It was all right, but not so intimate and not so holy
in atmosphere as the service in the church. He said good-by to
almost all who were at the service that day, instead of leaving
first as by protocol he should have done. He said to Mrs. Roosevelt and to the Secret Service men who were standing by to
escort him out, "No, I'll stay here and speak to the people."

And so, as they went, they stopped to speak to him as he sat
in his chair near the door. In one way it was exhausting, I suppose, and in another way it was refreshing to him, for he was
so cut off in the years of the war from ordinary social contacts.
He was grateful for the opportunity to shake a hand and exchange a smile and a word of cheer with the people in the East
Room that day. Mostly they were people who cared about him.

Most of them, of course, did not know that he was going
away the next day. The cabinet members knew or inferred that
he was departing on a high mission of State, although we
did not know where. I went to say good-by, thinking that it
would be difficult to see him after Inauguration. He shook my
hand warmly. "I am sorry you are going," I said. "I hope everything will be all right."

He said, under his breath, "You'd better pray for me, Frances."

This was the only time I knew him to speak of the need of the
petitions of others, but he was always grateful for them. Lots of
people used to send him word they were praying for him. They
sent him telegrams and letters, and he saved and showed me a
good many. He was touched by them, and he liked to tell me
about it because he knew I shared his religious faith.

In Franklin Roosevelt's religious life his essential humanity was clear. I remember noticing him one evening, when he was Governor of New York, at a dinner party at the Executive Mansion to which a lot of people he didn't know had been invited. He had had an exhausting day, but these people had come a long way and he knew that they wanted to see and talk with their Governor. He asked Mrs. Roosevelt to bring one or another to sit down beside him and talk intimately for a few moments. I knew he was tired. I knew these people were not very interesting. I sat on the other side of the room and observed him making a real effort to be not only charming, but concerned about each one's problems. He was doing this not because it gave him pleasure or because it was a political technique, but because they needed his support and friendship and understanding.

I remember saying to Mrs. Roosevelt, "You know, Franklin is really a very simple Christian."

She thought a moment and, with a quizzical lift of her eyebrows, said, "Yes, a *very simple* Christian."

I never developed the point further with her, but as I watched him and thought about him from time to time, I realized that his Christian faith was absolutely simple. As far as I can make out, he had no doubts. He just believed with a certainty and simplicity that gave him no pangs or struggles.

The problems of the higher criticism, of the application of scientific discoveries to the traditional teachings of the Christian faith and the Biblical record, bothered him not in the least. He knew what religion was and he followed it.

It was more than a code of ethics to him. It was a real relationship of man to God, and he felt as certain of it as of the reality of his life.

His sense of religion was so complete that he was able to associate himself without any conflict with all expressions of religious worship. Catholic, Protestant, and Jew alike were comprehensible to him, and their religious aspirations seemed natural and much the same as his own. He had little, if any, intellectual or theological understanding of the doctrinal basis of the major religions. But he had a deep conception of the effect of religious experience upon a man's life, attitudes, moral sense, and aspirations.

In the journey back from Yalta, when General Watson, his secretary and aide, was stricken, it was Roosevelt who arranged with the Roman Catholic chaplain aboard the ship to receive Watson into the Roman Catholic faith. The President knew that the matter of going into the Roman Church had been on Watson's mind for a long time and that he had made up his mind to do it. Watson's wife was a Roman Catholic, and it was natural for him to expect to do this. Roosevelt didn't have a profound theological argument with himself about it, but as he told me afterward, "I just thought 'Pa' would like it, and so I spoke to the Chaplain and asked if it could be arranged."

Roosevelt was intrigued by the story that Stalin, in his youth, has been destined for the priesthood and had gone to a theological seminary for a number of years before he joined the revolutionary forces. Roosevelt always wondered about that. Two or three times he asked me, "Don't you suppose that made some kind of a difference in Stalin? Doesn't that explain part of the sympathetic quality in his nature which we all feel?"

This idea that religion was important to a man stuck with him always. The conception of Freedom of Religion in the Four Freedoms of the Atlantic Charter was Roosevelt's own. He thought of Freedom of Religion in its real sense—freedom of each man or group to worship God in his or its own way. It never crossed his mind, I think, that there would be people who, in the name of his Freedoms, would make a deliberate practice of not worshiping or of propagandizing people not to worship God.

To him, man's relation to God seemed based upon nature. In this, of course, he reflected the teaching of the natural law, although he was probably almost unaware of that teaching. But it was strongly embedded in his mind. It was not political or Roman Catholic pressures that caused him, when he was negotiating with Maxim Litvinoff for the recognition of the Russian government by the United States in 1933, to insist that freedom of worship was a condition of recognition. It seemed to him a natural moral guarantee.

His own story of how he talked with Litvinoff about this matter illustrates the simplicity of his mind on the subject. According to Roosevelt, Litvinoff said that they had all the freedom of religion they needed in Russia; nobody was punished any more for going to church; they just discouraged it.

And according to Roosevelt's own story, he said to Litvinoff, "Well now, Max, you know what I mean by religion. You know what religion gives a man. You know the difference between the religious and the irreligious person. Why, you must know, Max. You were brought up by pious parents. Look here, some time you are going to die, and when you come to die, Max, you are going to remember your old father and mother—good, pious Jewish people who believed in God and taught you to pray to God. You had a religious bringing up, and when you come to die, Max, that's what is going to come before you, that is what you are going to think about, that's what you are going to grasp for. You know it's important."

Roosevelt always thought he had made an impression upon Litvinoff. He said, "You know, Max got red and fumbled and seemed embarrassed and just didn't know quite what to say."

A more cynical person might feel that Litvinoff was embarrassed because he didn't agree with Roosevelt at all and was trying to find some way out of the rather intimate personal pressure which Roosevelt had put on him.

This naturalness of the appeal to religion, I believe, explains many of the attitudes Roosevelt took and much of his faith in the possibilities of man, whom he never thought of as divorced from God in his struggle to improve his life upon this planet. He saw the betterment of life and people as part of God's work, and he felt that man's devotion to God expressed itself by serving his fellow men.

Roosevelt had not only a well-developed sense of religion in its true and important sense, but also real love for the Church in which he was brought up. He read the Bible a good deal. He knew a good many phrases and passages by heart. He loved the Book of Common Prayer, read it frequently, and often quoted from it. His Thanksgiving Day proclamations on at least two occasions when he was Governor of New York were drawn

largely from prayer book sources, one of them being a para-
phrase of the General Thanksgiving. The hymns, Psalms, and
canticles of common use in the Church were all a satisfaction
and comfort to him.

He loved the system of the Church and its order. When he
was at Hyde Park he always went to church. He took great interest in the progress of the parish, the maintenance of the
building, the investment of its endowments, and the selection
of the objects of charitable activity.

He was always trying to buy good safe United States government bonds that would pay about four and one-half per cent
for a $10,000 legacy which had come to St. James's in Hyde
Park. It was one of his perpetual jokes with Henry Morgenthau
to "complain" that the New Deal had ruined the interest rate
for worthy investors. Whenever Morgenthau would report a
new issue of government bonds, Roosevelt would say, "Got
anything that carries four and a half per cent for my parish?"

It was a source of some criticism in Washington that he was
rarely seen in the local churches. During World War I he had
been a junior vestryman at St. Thomas's Church, and it was
anticipated, indeed he anticipated, that he would go there regularly. He did go on a few occasions in his early days as President.

He said to me once, "I can do almost everything in the
'Goldfish Bowl' of the President's life, but I'll be hanged if I can
say my prayers in it. It bothers me to feel like something in the
zoo being looked at by all the tourists in Washington when I go
to church.

"Do you know," he went on, "what they rigged up in that
church? I know it was meant in good part, but they put red
plush cushions in a couple of pews way down front in the middle aisle. They also put a red silk cord and tassels around those
pews to reserve them for the President of the United States. Can
you beat that?

"No privacy in that kind of going to church, and by the time
I have gotten into that pew and settled down with everybody
looking at me, I don't feel like saying my prayers at all."

His affliction made him doubly conspicuous and doubly a
point of curiosity. But he tried to do his duty, and when the

Bishop of Washington in the first year of the Roosevelt administration asked the President and his cabinet to come to the National Cathedral on a Sunday morning for a special service of intercession, the President agreed and sent word to us to attend.

There we were, and so was the rest of Washington, and so were the tourists. It was indeed difficult to concentrate upon the mighty act of worship when people who didn't come to worship God but to see the sights were hopping up and down, pointing out distinguished people. We managed, however, and the President joined heartily in singing the hymns and making the responses. I am sure the Bishop was pleased.

At the end of the service the Bishop, as is customary in cathedral churches, came to the portal to greet the President and wish him well in his work. Roosevelt stopped to have a brief chat with him, and the Bishop walked out to his car beside him. But the Bishop took advantage of that little interlude to press a point dear to his heart, for he loved his cathedral and was anxious that it should be increasingly a center of interest in the capital.

He reminded Roosevelt that President Wilson and Ambassador Kellogg were buried in the crypt and suggested that Roosevelt at once make out a memorandum that he too wished to be buried there. This apparently horrified Roosevelt. On the way home he muttered to his secretary, "The old body snatcher, the old body snatcher."

That evening he dictated a memorandum to his heirs and assigns, directing them that under no circumstances should his body be buried in the National Cathedral or any other cathedral but should lie peacefully in the ground at Hyde Park. Years later when he was driving me around Hyde Park one day he said, "That's where I'm going to be buried, Frances. Right there— when I am dead. Don't you ever let anybody try to bury me in any cathedral."

Somebody once reproached him because on Christmas Days, when he was in Washington, instead of going to his own church he was in the habit of going to one of the big Methodist or Baptist churches. "What's the matter?" he replied. "I like to sing hymns with the Methodys."

The year he took Winston Churchill with him, he said, "It is good for Winston to sing hymns with the Methodys."

He had relatively little interest, as I have said, in the philosophical concepts which absorb those who approach religion from the intellectual point of view, but in the last year of his life he ran into one theological concept that was important to him because it explained what made the Nazis the way they were. He spoke of it a number of times, so that one may assume it was an important intellectual experience for him.

The Reverend Howard Johnson, a young curate at St. John's Church, whom Mrs. Roosevelt had met at a Young People's Club in February 1944, was invited by her to come to dinner some evening. He was surprised and delighted. When a few weeks passed and no invitation was forthcoming, he decided to be bold and presume upon his cloth. He called the White House and told Mrs. Helm, the social secretary, that Mrs. Roosevelt had invited him to dinner. I am sure he did it very courteously. He confessed to me, by implication, that he was stirred by a kind of evangelical fervor.

He received a note the next day inviting him to dinner that evening at seven-fifteen. He arrived on the dot, assuming he had been asked to a large party where he would be an extra man. He found the driveway and entrance hall empty. The usher took him to the upstairs sitting-room, where he found the President alone. Johnson said he was at a loss as to what to say or do.

The President knew the circumstances of the invitation and with charming grace put him at ease at once, talking to him about St. John's Church, its history and architecture. Mrs. Roosevelt came in twenty minutes later full of apologies for being late. She was accompanied by a young woman, who, he gathered from the conversation, was a relative, and by a young soldier, the son of an old friend.

Dinner was served at the end of the hall *en famille*. The conversation was intimate and gay and drifted to the detective stories of Dorothy Sayers. The President spoke of them enthusiastically.

Johnson, still in an evangelistic mood, said to the President, "You know, of course, that Dorothy Sayers is even more important for her theological writings."

The President had never heard of her theological writings. He questioned Johnson about them, and this led to a discussion of her theological point of view.

Johnson said, "You know, of course, that many moderns like Dorothy Sayers derive from Kierkegaard."

"Who is Kierkegaard?" the President asked.

Johnson sketched the little that is known about this Danish theologian, now dead a hundred years. He described his philosophy and its influence on modern thinking—man's natural sinfulness and his helplessness to reform himself except by the grace and help of God. This was the inner core of Kierkegaardian teaching. In short, it was a fresh emphasis on the doctrine of original sin and its implications for man. Johnson pointed out that the recent interest in Kierkegaard was chargeable to the current break-up of the humanistic illusion under which men had been laboring for a hundred years or so.

The President asked many questions, jotted down names of books by Kierkegaard, kept Johnson, who is by way of being a Kierkegaard expert, late, and listened more than he talked.

Some weeks later I happened to be reporting to Roosevelt on problems concerning the War Labor Board. He was looking at me, nodding his head, and, I thought, following my report, but suddenly he interrupted me. "Frances, have you ever read Kierkegaard?"

"Very little—mostly reviews of his writings."

"Well, you ought to read him," he said with enthusiasm. "It will teach you something."

I thought perhaps he meant it would teach me something about the War Labor Board.

"It will teach you about the Nazis," he said. "Kierkegaard explains the Nazis to me as nothing else ever has. I have never been able to make out why people who are obviously human beings could behave like that. They are human, yet they behave like demons. Kierkegaard gives you an understanding of what it is in man that makes it possible for these Germans to be so evil. This fellow, Johnson, over at St. John's, knows a lot about Kierkegaard and his theories. You'd better read him."

Johnson had another experience which illustrated the President's varied religious attitudes. It fell to young Mr. Johnson's lot to arrange the services at St. John's Church on March 4, 1944, the anniversary of the President's Inauguration. He felt the heavy responsibility of having to arrange this service in the absence of the pastor and took pains with it. He was guided by the 1933 service, but he selected other Lessons, Psalms, and hymns and chose prayers appropriate for the period. To the usual intercessions and blessings he added the *"Prayer for Our Enemies"* written by the Most Reverend William Temple, Archbishop of Canterbury, at the beginning of the war.

Older clergymen told him that would never do. The White House would never authorize it in wartime; it would be misunderstood throughout the country; the publicity would be terrible, since the Christian injunction to pray for our enemies was scarcely understood, even by Christians in this country. With stubborn determination Johnson submitted the service to the White House for approval. The service came back approved, and for this particular prayer the President had written in the margin in his own hand, "Very good—I like it."

12.

A MIND IN THE MAKING

One morning late in February 1933 Roosevelt's secretary telephoned and asked me to call at the East 65th Street house that evening. My appointment was for eight, but I arrived early.

The place was a shambles. Ever since the nomination six months before, a great many visitors, from cranks to persons destined to play important roles in the Roosevelt administration, had converged on the house for conferences or to seek favors from the President-elect. The press had established a base of operations on the first floor.

The constant flow of visitors left the small staff of servants powerless to retain any semblance of order. Furniture was broken. Rugs were rolled up and piled in a corner. Overshoes and muddy rubbers were in a heap near the door. The floor was littered with newspapers. Trunks were jammed into one corner, and in another stood boxes containing Roosevelt's papers which had just been sent down from Albany and had to be sorted and filed for reshipment to Washington.

I made my way to the comfortable second floor where Roosevelt had his study. I was greeted by a secretary, who asked me to have a seat. A stocky blond man whom I did not know was sitting on a sofa. Shortly he was invited into Mr. Roosevelt's study. Finally my turn came.

Roosevelt gave me a friendly greeting and, extending his hand toward the stocky blond man, said, "Frances, don't you know Harold?"

"Shall I just call him Harold or do you want to tell me his last name?"

"It's Ickes," he laughed. "Harold L. Ickes."

That was my introduction to the only person other than my-self who was to serve in the Roosevelt cabinet from its first to its last day. Ickes had been practicing law in the Middle West. A former leader of the Progressive party, he had done yeoman work for Roosevelt in the campaign. Now he had agreed to serve as Secretary of the Interior.

After Ickes left, Roosevelt came right to the point. "I've been thinking things over and I've decided I want you to be Secre-tary of Labor."

His words came as no great surprise to me. The newspapers had been speculating on this for days. Moreover, I knew that he wanted to establish the precedent of appointing a woman to his cabinet. Since the call from his secretary, I had been going over arguments to convince him that he should not appoint me.

I led off with my chief argument, that I was not a bona fide labor person. I pointed out that labor had always had, and would expect to have, one of its own people as Secretary. Roose-velt's answer was that it was time to consider all working peo-ple, organized and unorganized.

I told him that it might be a good thing to have a woman in the cabinet if she were best for the job, but I thought a woman Secretary of Labor ought to be a labor woman. He replied he had considered that and was going on my record as Industrial Commissioner of New York. He said he thought we could ac-complish for the nation the things we had done for the state.

Since I seemed to be making little headway, I tried a new ap-proach. I said that if I accepted the position of Secretary of Labor I should want to do a great deal. I outlined a program of labor legislation and economic improvement. None of it was radical. It had all been tried in certain states and foreign countries. But I thought that Roosevelt might consider it too ambitious to be undertaken when the United States was deep in depression and unemployment.

In broad terms, I proposed immediate federal aid to the states for direct unemployment relief, an extensive program of public works, a study and an approach to the establishment by federal law of minimum wages, maximum hours, true unemployment and old-age insurance, abolition of child labor, and the creation of a federal employment service.

The program received Roosevelt's hearty endorsement, and he told me he wanted me to carry it out.

"But," I said, "have you considered that to launch such a program we must think out, frame, and develop labor and social legislation, which then might be considered unconstitutional?"

"Well, that's a problem," Mr. Roosevelt admitted, "but we can work out something when the time comes."

And so I agreed to become Secretary of Labor after a conversation that lasted but an hour.

On Sunday, March 5, Mr. Justice Cardozo of the Supreme Court administered the oath of office to the new cabinet, and we solemnly swore "to support and defend the Constitution of the United States."

I was apprehensive and on guard at the first official cabinet meeting. As the only woman member, I did not want my colleagues to get the impression that I was too talkative. I resolved not to speak unless asked to do so. We sat stiffly and solemnly; we were not yet entirely acquainted with one another and we had not acquired official poise.

The President asked questions around the table and commented on the replies. Finally, he turned to me. "Frances, don't you want to say something?"

I didn't want to, but I knew I had to. There was silence. My colleagues looked at me with tense curiosity. I think some weren't sure I could speak.

I said what I had to say, quickly and briefly. I announced that I had called a conference of labor leaders and experts to draft recommendations for relief of unemployment. I said a program of public works should be one of the first steps.

The details do not matter here. As far as Roosevelt was concerned, I was one of the team. The men in the cabinet, from the beginning, treated me as a colleague and an equal. There was no special deference, beyond the ordinary daily amenities, because I was a woman. Nor was there any suggestion of a patronizing note. I recall that once Claude Swanson, the Secretary of the Navy, wondered whether he should tell a certain story since there was "a lady present."

"Go on, Claude," said the President, "she's dying to hear it."

Those early meetings were full of excitement, and always there was an easy give and take. Roosevelt wanted to have his advisers' reactions. He did not expect yes-men around him. He wanted a free expression of opinion, and it took place, under his leadership, in a stimulating atmosphere.

I saw his mind continuing its growth in this period, as I had seen it develop in previous years and as I was to see it take on further depth and stature in the years ahead.

Roosevelt's mentality was not intellectual in the sense in which that word is ordinarily used. He was a man of high intelligence, but he used *all* his faculties when he was thinking about a subject. He did not enjoy the intellectual process for its own sake as many educated, perhaps overeducated, men do. He did not enjoy debate and argument based on principles of logic so as to achieve superior position by marshaling facts and overcoming an opponent.

This was not the way his mind operated. He had to have feeling as well as thought. His emotions, his intuitive understanding, his imagination, his moral and traditional bias, his sense of right and wrong—all entered into his thinking, and unless these flowed freely through his mind as he considered a subject, he was unlikely to come to any clear conclusion or even to a clear understanding.

The popular literary picture of a statesman is a man who reads, far into the night, volumes of information, studies profound reports, compares the views of experts, analyzes the details of their agreement and disagreement, and then by a process of pure logic arrives at a conclusion. I have never seen a man of action proceed in this way, which is the technique of the legal analyst who prepares a case for the senior member of the law firm who must argue it in court.

Certainly Roosevelt never proceeded like that. His imagination and his sympathy entered into every subject he had to think about.

Of course, he followed a pattern of logic in his thinking, arraying the facts, comparing them, and drawing conclusions, but he did not rely solely upon logic as a guide to action. On one occasion when I was describing a French political situation after a visit to France, he said, "How ridiculous for them to do a thing like that. It is bound to hurt everybody concerned."

"Yes, Mr. President," I replied, "but it is logical, and that, as you know, has a great appeal to the French mind."

I remarked that logic is an instrument which assists man in his thinking but is not a reliable guide to action, and that man acting on pure logic is often untrue to his nature.

The President said, "That is exactly right, that is the way I feel."

In the light of all that modern psychologists have said about the frustrations, confusions, and defeats that come to modern man when he relies exclusively upon his intellectual processes, one cannot but wonder if Roosevelt's utilization of all of his faculties did not result in a healthier mind.

His way was that of the common man as opposed to the intellectual and uncommon man. The common people understood Franklin Roosevelt and he understood them, largely, I think, because their processes of looking at things and coming to conclusions were almost the same. This probably was why they trusted him even in situations where he took an action they didn't like.

In 1943 when there seemed to be a threat of a railroad strike, Roosevelt stepped in, on the advice of James Byrnes, then Director of War Mobilization, and attempted an arbitrary settlement of the dispute between the brotherhoods and operators.

The railroad workers were angry: first, because he attempted a settlement by direction; second, because he seemed not to understand that although they had gone through the motions of taking a strike vote, they did not intend to strike; third, because he didn't refer the problem back to the machinery of the Railway Labor Act, asking for another report, by one of the committees.

Roosevelt had just returned from Teheran. Because time was short, he acted as recommended. He did not fully comprehend the situation.

The railroad men came to my office in protest the next day. Despite their resentment, they said, "You know the President never would have done this if he had understood the case. He didn't have the thing straight. That's why he did it."

One man put in, "You know, he was using his arithmetic mind and not what his heart told him was the right thing to do."

His way of thinking, of course, had some blind spots. Roosevelt never understood the point of view of the business community, nor could he make out why it didn't like him. He did not hold that everything should be judged by whether or not it makes money, and this made the business people incomprehensible to him, except for the few who were philosophical in their approach or who shared, as many of them do, the prejudices, moral qualities, and ethical slants of the common man.

Many of his detractors have said that this was the aristocratic attitude of one who did not have to earn his living and therefore did not sufficiently understand the importance of making everything pay a profit. There may be something in this theory, but at least it gave him a freedom to think in fields in which the common people needed to have their leaders think. It spared him a great deal of cynicism as he rejected the "practical" or money-making line of judgment on issues he had to decide. His question always was, "Will it work, will it do some good?" He sometimes asked, "Will it ruin us financially?" If it clearly would not ruin us financially, it did not seem to him important that it did not promote the immediate financial situation of particular groups.

Again, he never could understand or comprehend the dictators. He used to laugh, as I did too, at the dire predictions that he would make himself a dictator. He was totally incapable of comprehending what a dictator is, how he operates, how he thinks, how he gets anything done. A man like Mussolini was a puzzle to him, Hitler worse than a puzzle. He didn't like concentrated responsibility. Agreement with other people who he thought were good, right-minded, and trying to do the right thing by the world was almost as necessary to him as air to breathe. I never knew him to take an action or inaugurate a program in which he did not have agreement with some people he respected. If a substantial number of persons were in agreement, his sense of the fitness of things was even better satisfied.

This leads to a question—if a great many people are for a certain project, is it necessarily right? If the vast majority is for it, is it even more certainly right? This, to be sure, is one of the tricky points of democracy. The minority often turns out to be right, and though one believes in the efficacy of the democratic process, one has also to recognize that the demand of the many for a particular project at a particular time may mean only disaster. Roosevelt knew and felt these things, but he was always tempted to go along with the great majority.

Inevitably he could not understand the Soviet purge of generals and politicians. It was difficult to tell from the newspapers just what had happened, but the persons liquidated had been members of the Communist party.

He shook his head, puzzled. "I just can't make it out. Why would they want to get rid of people in their own party?"

Some sophisticated cynic answered, "Why, Mr. President, it is as though the New Deal Democrats should decide that the other Democrats were too much and order them all put in jail or shot at dawn."

He smiled at the jest, but he rubbed his head in that bewildered way he sometimes had. "It just doesn't make sense."

Another blind spot was his inability to comprehend disloyalty. He counted on his opponents to fight him at every turn with every weapon and misrepresentation, but he was never prepared for the disloyalty and defection of people who called themselves his friends.

He had the naïve idea that those who had joined up with him politically, or personally, were really on his side, belonged to his club, so to speak, and were with him through thick and thin. We would take the sweet with the bitter. We would take strength and weakness. We would agree to disagree and still work for the same general program without loss of affection or loyalty.

Al Smith's decision to "take a walk" in 1936 hurt Roosevelt keenly. He was sore about that, I think, and never quite understood it. It pained Roosevelt to see Smith going with the Liberty

League and standing against what Roosevelt believed was a program Al Smith should have favored.

"I just can't understand it," Roosevelt would say. "Practically all the things we've done in the Federal Government are like things Al Smith did as Governor of New York. They're things he would have done if he had been President of the United States. What in the world is the matter? Why can't Al see this is the program he ought to be for?"

I saw Smith from time to time when I was in New York. Roosevelt knew that I saw him and would ask, "How is the old boy?" Once he said, "I'd like to see him sometime." He all but sent messages of affection.

Smith, for his part, inquired about "Frank" and his family and said, "Well, I wish you'd give Frank my love. I don't agree with him and we have had political differences, but I think a lot of him."

Al Smith stopped in Washington, once if not twice, to call on the President in the White House and to have a little visit with Mrs. Roosevelt, with whom he never broke his personal friendship. I don't know what the two men talked about. I am told that they both laughed over some things. But there was no real reconciliation or understanding, which was one of the political tragedies of the times.

Roosevelt felt loyal about his friends and expected them to feel the same way about him. He did not analyze political or personal friendship too closely. He could, of course, read the "Beware of the Dog" sign and appreciate the fact that an individual had become disloyal or was disaffected. When a person once turned against him, Roosevelt rarely mentioned his name again. It was one of those things he wanted to keep away from.

The disaffection of John L. Lewis, when it occurred so suddenly in January 1937, was a great surprise to him. He had not thought much about why John L. Lewis had come out for him in the 1936 campaign. He took it for granted that Lewis and all labor people were on our side. He was so sure that the New Deal was right, it seemed obvious to him that the good people, certainly working people, would be for it.

In January 1937 Lewis was in my office one day by my invitation. I planned to discuss with him some of the legislation we had pending. He was moody, uncommunicative, formal, quite unlike himself, for he had always been helpful as a consultant on legislation and administrative enterprises. Something was out of joint, but I did not think it wise to ask what it might be.

Finally, without any warning, he turned on me. "Why do you take the trouble to ask the opinion of John L. Lewis on these matters? Surely my advice is not wanted by anyone. Surely what I have to say is of no consequence whatever to you or anyone else in the administration."

I protested, "Of course I want your advice."

"But the President has not sent for me," he said somberly. "Doesn't he want my advice?"

"What do you mean, Mr. Lewis? Why should he send for you?"

"It is now two months since the election and he has not sent for John L. Lewis," he replied. He proceeded to berate the President soundly, calling him all sorts of names, saying he had eaten labor's bread and now failed to stand by labor. It was a long, melodramatic tirade. He walked up and down the floor of my office making a public address to me.

I interrupted to ask why he was suddenly so angry. He told me that Jim Farley had called him up during the last weeks of the 1936 campaign, knowing that the United Mine Workers had large cash accounts in various banks. Farley had told him, he said, that the campaign committee was short of funds and requested Lewis to make a hundred thousand dollars available immediately. As Lewis told it, he gave me the impression that he had contributed the money to the campaign fund. I called Farley later for verification, and he told me that it was a loan, not a gift, and that it would be repaid promptly.[*]

I tried to explain to Lewis that there was no particular reason why Roosevelt should have sent for him, since the program for the immediate future had been announced in the party platform and campaign pledges. "Ah," he retorted, "but when J.P. Morgan was the principal contributor to the Republican party

* This $100,000 was returned. Earlier in the campaign, Lewis had been responsible for contributions from a variety of sources amounting to $156,000.

he certainly had constant access to the President and told him exactly what he wanted done. The tables are reversed now, and I expected to be consulted in the same way."

I tried in vain to point out that it was ridiculous to believe that J.P. Morgan or any other large contributor had ever dictated to a President. It might be true that Morgan's political thinking and that of a President ran parallel, but, I said, I should assume the same would be the case with labor and Roosevelt.

I pointed out how destructive to our form of government it would be to have persons who were not the elected representatives of the people attempting to settle legislation and administrative policies. He was scornful of the idea that labor and labor leaders should not attempt to do this but should help to preserve the representative responsibility of our government. Clearly it was his view that money talks in politics, and he was going to insist upon it, if possible. His language was picturesque and was almost identical with the statement he made to the press a week later and in a prepared address on Labor Day, 1937, which created such a sensation. It was as though he had given me a dress rehearsal.

I was quite sure that the President did not know that Lewis had made a loan to the Democratic campaign fund out of the funds of the United Mine Workers. I later verified this and found that Roosevelt had never heard of it. But it would have made no difference if he had. He wanted to see labor leaders from time to time; he wanted to see business and farm leaders. He liked to hear their ideas about legislation and test his own convictions about proposed bills by talking with them. But of this I am certain: the fact that a man or a group had made a campaign contribution gave his opinion no more weight or importance than anyone else's view in Roosevelt's mind.

No other labor leaders were disturbed because Roosevelt had not seen them in six weeks. They knew it had been the practice since the beginning of the Roosevelt administration for the Secretary of Labor to talk over proposed legislation with them well in advance of its introduction and to convey their opinions to the President. They knew, too, that from time to time the Secretary arranged for them to see the President briefly.

I have never thought it wise or helpful to carry reports of ill-natured comments. In this case, however, I made up my mind that it would be best to tell the President at least part of the story, lest he inadvertently say or do something which would precipitate a crisis. I told the President before Lewis made his public statement. The President was astonished, but he said calmly, "It is something to remember and we had better not talk about it."

Whether Lewis expected to alarm me by his outburst, or wanted me to tell the President, I do not know; but when he erupted in the press it was not news to us, although the country, and even Roosevelt's opponents, were shocked. Until that time Lewis, who is a man of ability, had been increasingly well spoken of by the press, by government officials, even by employers. But this intemperate attack made many people turn against Lewis, not Roosevelt.

An extremely important factor in Roosevelt's mental equipment was the faculty known as memory. His memory embraced a vast store of things, not assorted in a systematic, logical way, but extraordinarily responsive to the stimulus of the subject and the key word. Yet there were whole areas in which his memory was defective. One of the things about which one speculates, in looking back at him now that he is gone, is the pattern of his memory. The psychologists might say Roosevelt remembered the things he wanted to remember and forgot the others.

To one who observed him over a long period this seemed not to be so. It is true that he conveniently forgot a lot of unpleasant things. He forgot attacks growing out of ill will; he forgot defection; he forgot a good many quarrels—not all of them however. I suppose that he himself could hardly have analyzed how he exercised his memory, but it was an element in his make-up on which he relied over and over again.

I came to regard it as of vital importance in my dealings with him. I learned to prepare material so that it would photograph itself upon his memory. I habitually prepared a complete memorandum which any subordinate might read; but I also prepared not over two pages, preferably one page, of strictly

structural outline material. It was the kind of academic outline that is so tiresome to the average reader but so helpful to
one who must recall the principal steps in an argument. Under
headings I, II, and III, with subordinate a, b, and c, one could,
if one tried, boil things down. With that in his hand and under
his eye, I discussed the matter with him. I answered all his
questions. I undertook to tell him the opposition to the argument. I persuaded him to read some of the larger memoranda,
but to hold the outline in his hand as he read or discussed them
with me.

When he had been over the outline, asked his questions, heard
explanations, jotted a pencil note on the margin of the outline,
I would put the question to him: "Do you authorize me to go
ahead with this? Are you sure?" Then we might have a brief
discussion of the propriety or timing of the program or the political technique to be used.

I always told him frankly who was opposed and why, as well
as who was in favor and why. After that kind of discussion he
might say, "Yes, this is all right. I am in favor of that program.
Go ahead with it."

After a few more moments of conversation I would always
make the occasion to go over the outline with him a second
time. "Are you sure you want item number one? Do you want
items number two and three? You understand that this is what
we do and this is who is opposed?"

With that clearly photographed on his mind, he would say,
"Yes, go ahead."

Then I knew I could safely proceed. I never sewed him up
formally to a program, however, without asking him once
more, just before it was actually launched, "Do you remember
you agreed you thought well of the plan to do one, two, and
three? Is that all right? Is it still okay?"

When he said "Yes" again I never had the slightest doubt of
his support.

It is my final testimony that he *never let me down.*

There are others who say that Roosevelt sometimes let them
down after he had told them he was in favor of a particular
project. My own belief is that they did not sufficiently prepare
it for him. They did not tell him what the opposition was.

He remembered when you told him. I have had the strange experience, two or three years after an interview, of hearing him, without preparation, make a complete statement, with dates and statistics, based upon the information given him when the program was inaugurated.

Too many people acted as though the President were all-wise. Some of the best of them did this. I was startled that people who ought to have known better should say, "The President must know what the situation is better than I do." How could he know the situation? He had no informant except the public official in question.

Some public officials, it seemed to me, were quite willing to get him sold and tied up to their ideas. They would get gleeful satisfaction because they had put something over and hadn't been called to terms for an explanation of the opposing point of view. Some felt that if they could get the President to endorse something, it was launched. They would take their chances on being stopped elsewhere, and they were perfectly willing to embarrass him for the sake of getting their own view over. He often came to distrust these people, and coolness and separation followed.

In the use of his faculties Roosevelt had almost the quality of a creative artist. One would say that it is the quality of the modern artist as distinct from the classical artist. The name for it in the graphic arts is automatism. It describes an artist who begins his picture without a clear idea of what he intends to paint or how it shall be laid out upon the canvas, but begins anyhow, and then, as he paints, his plan evolves out of the material he is painting. So Roosevelt worked with the materials and problems at hand. As he worked one phase, the next evolved.

Roosevelt's plans were never thoroughly thought out. They were burgeoning plans; they were next steps; they were something to do next week or next year. One plan grew out of another. Gradually they fitted together and supplemented one another.

As he worked on the problems of statecraft and developed the plan of action which was necessary in the days and years of his leadership, he worked within human and moral values.

He worked with his instincts. He relied upon his intuitive judgment. He drew upon his memory. He exercised his imagination.
He followed a logical and analytical method when helpful, and
he came to his decision and judgment by a combination of all
these qualities.

Overshadowing them all was his feeling that nothing in human
judgment is final. One may courageously take the step that seems
right today because it can be modified tomorrow if it does not
work well. It was this faculty which released him from the driven,
frightened psychosis of the period. Since it is a normal human
reaction, most people felt as he did and gladly followed when he
said, "We can do it. At least let's try."

Roosevelt could always force himself to face the most dreary
and discouraging facts and situations. Often he ended such a
contemplation by saying, "This is very bad, but one thing is
sure. We have to do something. We have to do the best we know
how to do at the moment." Then he would add, "If it doesn't
turn out right, we can modify it as we go along."

This kind of mentality develops a man who is more an instrument than an engineer. The prophets of Israel would have
called him an instrument of the Lord. The prophets of today
could only explain his type of mind in terms of psychology,
about which they know so pitiably little. He was able to use the
feeling and aspiration of all people as a general guide. He could
and did express these hopes in concrete projects. To know that
he was the instrument of the hopes of men, as well as of the will
of God, would, I think, have given him contentment with his
life and achievement.

Illustrative of these qualities is the way in which, after one or
two interviews, he accepted the abstruse and almost incomprehensible report of Dr. Albert Einstein on the possibility of developing an atomic bomb from the theories and slender accumulation
of knowledge of nuclear physics and fission. Roosevelt had a
meager scientific education and could not possibly have understood and followed Einstein's scientific arguments. But Einstein
is also a warm, human, imaginative personality, and the sympathy that sprang up between them made it possible, in part, for
Roosevelt to accept his theoretical explanation.

He gave the signal to go ahead on the exploration and development of the atomic bomb because of his hunch that Einstein, like his fellow scientists, was truthful and wise. He had seen him on Henry Wallace's recommendation, and he knew Wallace, a man of scientific understanding, was also truthful and wise.

But that audacious decision lay far ahead. The crisis that faced him in the first weeks of his administration gave tremendous scope for the play and expansion of his remarkable mind and personality.

13.

NEW DEAL

When Franklin Roosevelt and his administration began their work in Washington in March 1933, the New Deal was not a plan with form and content. It was a happy phrase he had coined during the campaign, and its value was psychological. It made people feel better, and in that terrible period of depression they needed to feel better.

As Roosevelt described it, the "new deal" meant that the forgotten man, the little man, the man nobody knew much about, was going to be dealt better cards to play with.

The idea was not specific; it was general, but it was potent. On Roosevelt's part it was truly and profoundly felt. He understood that the suffering of the depression had fallen with terrific impact upon the people least able to bear it. He knew that the rich had been hit hard too, but at least they had something left. But the little merchant, the small householder and home owner, the farmer who worked the soil by himself, the man who worked for wages—these people were desperate. And Roosevelt saw them as principal citizens of the United States, numerically and in their importance to the maintenance of the ideals of American democracy.

That phrase, "new deal," which gave courage to all sorts of people, was merely a statement of policy and emphasis. It expressed a new attitude, not a fixed program. When he got to Washington he had no fixed program.

The notion that the New Deal had a preconceived theoretical position is ridiculous. The pattern it was to assume was not clear or specific in Roosevelt's mind, in the mind of the Democratic party, or in the mind of anyone else taking part in the 1932 campaign. There were no preliminary conferences of party leaders to work out details and arrive at agreements.

The general situation, however, was clear in Roosevelt's mind and in the minds of his supporters and party. He represented the humanitarian trend. The idea was that all the political and practical forces of the community should and could be directed to making life better for ordinary people. This was accepted by most of the dominant elements in the Democratic party in 1933.

Though no one can tell how much the Smith campaign in 1928 had affected the thinking of the Democratic party, it was understood in 1933 that the Democratic party had a mission to the disadvantaged people of America. Even the old-fashioned Southern Democrats had accepted this—as an idea.

I remember clearly something that happened in the first months of the Roosevelt administration. Some question was before the cabinet, and the President was inquiring about the attitude of those present. John Garner, the Vice-President, sitting at the end of the table next to me, spoke up.

"Mr. President," he said, "I think that when we were campaigning we sort of made promises that we would do something for the poorer kind of people, and I think we have to do something for them. We have to remember them. We have to take account of that."

This led Garner to approve in cabinet meeting the idea that we should recommend at once federal aid for relief. Postmaster General Jim Farley, a practical politician, constantly upheld the necessity of a public works program as well as other approaches to doing something for "the poorer kind of people." George Dern, the Secretary of War, who had been Governor of Utah and who represented, in a way, the thinking of Democrats in the western part of the country, urged the same things.

The advice of fundamentally conservative men like Garner, Farley, and Dern meant a great deal to Roosevelt. He recognized that he himself was perhaps to the left of center and that he belonged to the younger branch of the party, the branch devoted to the promotion of social justice. He was still feeling his way, still making up his mind, but a number of fundamental ideas were clear. That I know, because he talked about them to me during the campaign and afterward.

He was going to work with the states. He was going to break down the conflict which so often existed between state and federal government. He was going to take the governors into his confidence and invoke their co-operation. He had thought a great deal about state-federal relationships because as Governor of New York he had been obliged to.

As Governor of a rich, self-sustaining state, he had operated in a community where the phrase "sovereign state" meant something. The state could take care of itself and tended to assert its sovereignty at every point. New York usually thought that such federal programs as were carried on in that state were more rigid, less useful, and less effective than the state programs.

That was about the correct view in 1930. The New York State Health Department was strong and did much more than the Federal Public Health Service for the people. The federally-operated United States Employment Service was a feeble nonentity in New York, where we had a good Public Employment Office.

New York also had a fine Department of Education. The emphasis was upon local educational enterprises, but they were bound together by the standards of the Department's Board of Regents. This guaranteed a strong and uniform public-school system.

The state, having valuable timber and mineral deposits, had a large Conservation Department. It had no need of federal help in that field. The state's Department of Public Welfare was one of the best in the country. Until the depression began, no one thought about getting aid from Washington in the field of charitable assistance.

As one of the thirteen colonies, New York had an historical background. Many of its people were descendants of early settlers, and they had that sense of pride and continuity which accumulates around people whose great-grandparents are buried in the town in which they live.

It was, to be sure, also a state which had perhaps a larger element of foreign-born, and first generation descendants of foreign-born, than any in the country. The cities of New York and Buffalo held millions of such persons. But these people, perhaps more even than old settlers, tended to think of the locality in which they lived as the whole of America. They were bound to be provincial in their feelings. All that an immigrant child learned about American life he learned from the single community where he lived and went to school.

Washington, until the Roosevelt administration, was not interesting or important to the people of New York. They looked to Albany rather than Washington as the place of power. If there were grievances to be redressed, it was to Albany that their thinking and planning turned.

The local newspapers, and they were very good, printed a great deal of illuminating information about the political situation in the state and about the proceedings in the Assembly and Senate. The decisions of New York's courts were studied and quoted all over the country. The Supreme Court of the U.S.A. was something far off.

Roosevelt shared this attitude, but his experience in the Wilson administration had given him a broader outlook. His tour of the country as vice-presidential candidate in 1920 had shown him that in the West there is a much greater concentration upon Washington as the place of power and government.

I made this discovery for myself during the 1928 Smith campaign, when local leaders would indicate that they had no confidence whatever in their own state capital or governor or health department. They looked to Washington for help.

In some western states there was resentment that they were a "long way off" and that nobody in Washington paid any attention to them. And they wanted attention. Before 1932 no one in New York or New England, as far as I could discover, and I had lived there all my life, expected someone to come from Washington to solve a problem.

As we discussed this question once, Roosevelt found a private, personal explanation. We recalled that a number of western states had been settled not by people who went adventuring, but by people who were asked by the government and the railroad companies to go out and settle. Some midwestern states were settled when the issues of slavery and antislavery were so acute that there was a constant effort to people new areas quickly, make them states, and give them a vote. All sorts of promises had been made to these early settlers, and there had been help from Washington for one problem or another. That soon passed, but the attitude that Washington ought to "do something about us" was carried on.

Even while he was Governor of New York, Roosevelt began to believe that Washington ought to assume more responsibility for the leadership and development of the country. He once pointed out to me that a state like Georgia had meager tax resources. There was no possibility in such states of building up the financial resources which enabled New York to do so much for its people.

People in the northern industrial states, where tax values were high and budgets could be reasonably good, opposed further extensions of the grant-in-aid principle whereby the Federal Government, for instance, had financed road building throughout the United States. There was a constant outcry in states like New York and Massachusetts that grants-in-aid to states of limited means for road building merely meant that the citizens of New York and Massachusetts paid taxes to the Federal Government for other states' roads.

Roosevelt never held that view. I heard him explain frequently, not only to the members of the state legislature but to protesting private acquaintances, how essential and desirable it was that taxes should be collected where the money was and that part of it should be spent where it could do the most good in the United States. He had great pride in New York and liked to see New York take the lead. However, his Georgia experience had taught him the desirability of spending federal money there for economic and social improvements. This, he thought, would enable a state like Georgia to become richer and have greater tax values of its own in time.

He came right up against the problem of state-federal relationship in the St. Lawrence waterway development. New York could not go ahead with its plans to use the power of the St. Lawrence River, a pet project of Smith's and Roosevelt's, unless the Federal Government made a treaty with Canada.

He became deeply interested in the idea of a greater co-operation between the states and the Federal Government. He wanted the states to advise the Federal Government of their experience and problems in a systematic way long before a crisis was reached. Having been a governor rather than a senator of the United States, he considered governors a natural line of communication with the Federal Government.

When we tried to operate this idea of state-federal co-operation after he became President, I realized that the Senator is the ambassador from his state to the United States Government and is very jealous of this prerogative. He expects to be the medium of communication and co-operation with his state.

One of the first jobs Roosevelt asked me to undertake was to arrange the preliminaries of a governors' conference and to make out part of the agenda. There was no opposition yet from the senators to the idea of the President's dealing directly with the governors on matters of state co-operation with the Federal Government. Perhaps because the country was in such distress, most officials were glad to have responsibility upon other shoulders. The senators' objections became evident a little later when we began to operate programs where the Federal Government was spending money in co-operation with a state government with the governor's advice. Then, indeed, we discovered that the senators have, or believe they should have, the full and final say on all problems, not only of policy but of specific projects to be adopted and personnel to be selected for a job in their states.

I remember describing such a situation to Roosevelt and saying how unprepared I had been for it. "Of course," he said, "of course. I understand, now that I think of it. Every governor, particularly in states where the governor's salary is about $3,000, looks forward to being United States Senator. No United States Senator, even if he belongs to the same party, likes to be ousted by the superior prestige and patronage which the expenditure of federal money may get for the governor. Well, *that* is something to remember."

Another procedure Roosevelt had in mind before he went to Washington was regular co-operation with Congress. I suppose every President-elect has gone to Washington with the best of resolutions to co-operate with Congress. Roosevelt had observed the failure in a number of cases, and he had a plan of his own. He told me he would call in the leaders regularly and would invite committees of Congress to the White House. He meant to keep the Congress informed of what was going on in the President's mind before legislation was formulated.

He was clear that the duty of Congress was to legislate and the duty of the President to execute. He expected to make it clear that he relied on Congress. But he also had solid ideas about the place of the President's office in our American scheme of things, and he felt that the failure of some Presidents to assert the leadership which came to them by right of their election by the entire nation had been a mistake.

He recognized that to assert leadership and to develop a plan for legislation required tact, and that it had to be done slowly. The President, he thought, should be responsible for developing and recommending a program for the good of the whole country. Members of Congress had a narrower responsibility. But the combination of the President, elected as the direct representative of all the people, and the Congress, representing different states and localities but charged with duties of national legislation, should prove fruitful.

He had ideas about party responsibility. Keenly aware of the two-party system under which American democracy thrives, he felt that there should be more internal party unity. He pointed out the weakness with which the Democrats went into campaigns because there was not an agreed-upon program. The platform, yes, but the platform was not taken too seriously either by the people or the candidates after they had been elected to office. He believed that through conferences among the congressional and state political leaders and the President the needs of the country could be gradually canvassed. He believed a party program must be worked out to get the adherence of the rank and file. He often said that we must work out a method whereby the enthusiasm and political intelligence evoked among the voters during campaigns would be kept alive, harnessed, and put to work between campaigns. Then we would have, he said, a democratic representative way of expressing the will of the people to the Congress.

But these were ideas for procedure, not a total pattern for the New Deal. It is important to repeat, the New Deal was not a plan, not even an agreement, and it was certainly not a plot, as was later charged. Most of the programs later called the New Deal arose out of the emergency which Roosevelt faced when he took office at the low point of the depression.

Undoubtedly he agreed with those chosen for the cabinet upon general policy and immediate steps. I had such an understanding with him, but it began with emergency rescue measures. Clearly he had a pattern of fiscal control in mind. I am pretty sure that there was some understanding with Henry Wallace about the Agricultural Adjustment program, which also was a form of rescue work. But there was no central unified plan. There wasn't time or organization for that. The New Deal grew out of these emerging and necessary rescue actions. The intellectual and spiritual climate was Roosevelt's general attitude that *the people mattered.* Government programs designed to give reality to that attitude developed and fitted into one another out of the necessities of the times. The pattern emerged from the necessary action. The action was not projected from a central pattern, but the people mattered.

By midsummer of 1933, however, the New Deal had developed from a general idea into several courses of action. In these first few months Roosevelt gave his quick attention, his imaginative understanding, and his intuitive and positive response to a considerable program.

First, there was a general relief program.

The Civilian Conservation Corps was put on the statute books.

The Reconstruction Finance Corporation was directed by Roosevelt to loosen up its policy to include loans to small enterprises and to enterprises that would put people to work.

The Home Owners' Loan Corporation was formed to save small property-owners.

The battle to have a real public works program was won.

The United States Employment Service was renovated.

A program of farm relief was inaugurated.

The Agricultural Adjustment program was launched to save farmers from extinction.

The NRA was a new, vigorous, and imaginative approach to the problem of reviving industry and overcoming unemployment.

There was also an energetic fiscal policy. The banks were closed, reorganized, and reopened. A law for the insurance of bank deposits was set up to protect the people's funds.

Numerous activities of whose genesis I know little were also emerging in those early months of the Roosevelt administration. The Securities and Exchange Bill was set up to protect investors. The Tennessee Valley Authority plan was developed, and a vast, integrated power, soil, conservation, and settlement program grew out of it. Then came rural electrification and the farm resettlement programs.

A vital aspect of these first few months was the revival of our international intercourse with the rest of the world. Ramsay MacDonald of Britain, Edouard Herriot of France, and many others were invited to visit the White House to confer on world economic affairs. This eventuated in a World Economic Congress held in London later in the year. The Congress was a failure for a variety of reasons which others will write about with more authority.

But approaches to it restored our interest in international affairs and awoke our consciousness of responsibility. Our people began to look out and see that the depression was world-wide and that mutual aid among the nations might be a good idea.

In this first year too, Roosevelt established formal international relations with Soviet Russia. Cordell Hull and Sumner Welles of the State Department were beginning to work out a Good Neighbor policy with Latin America. Hull was opening discussions on reciprocal trade agreements. We applied for membership in the International Labor Organization.

Those who look back upon the period and say that not enough consideration was given to these measures can hardly remember how gray and bleak and desperate were the people

of this country in the period between election day and Inauguration Day, 1933. They longed for a cure. It was a period of
social danger. Fortunately it was Roosevelt, rather than a Huey
Long, who appeared as the "deliverer." Bankers and businessmen, mine operators and laborers, truck drivers and lawyers,
said to one another, "We must pull our belts in and hold out
until March 4."

Roosevelt moved fast to demonstrate that something could
be done. He took action that was needed, but, more than that,
he explained over the radio what the action was, how it was
going to be taken, what he hoped it would do, and what the
people's role would be.

He did not think we had discovered any panaceas. He knew
these were temporary emergency measures. He once said at a
cabinet meeting, about a proposal for further expenditure for
public works or WPA, "We have to do it. It is like putting all
you've got into stopping up the hole in the dike. You have to
keep that hole from getting any larger. We must do what we
can at this time. We haven't any more time."

Even with the benefit of hindsight and with an awareness
of the problems that arose and still haunt us from NRA, I say
that Roosevelt's hunch was right. The speedy enactment of the
program that came to be known as the New Deal revived the
faith of the people. It put us back on the upgrade. It gave us
knowledge of industrial processes and complications which
had never been in the possession of the government before. It
constituted an education for the American people and for their
government.

Those aspects of the New Deal and its aftermath which I shall
tell about are only the ones I knew at firsthand, either from
sharing in the cabinet discussion or from the work of the Department of Labor. I shall not attempt a full chronological
record. The immediate relief measures, such as CCC and WPA,
come first as examples of the emergency steps which had to
be taken in the crisis. The NRA, in turn, was part of a larger
recovery program and leads on naturally to the story of the
new status for labor in America, culminating in the National

Labor Relations Board and the Wages and Hours Act. I shall tell what I can of this story before returning to the other recovery measures, represented by public works, and to the long-range program of social security, though all of these programs went forward together in those years.

14.

CIVILIAN
CONSERVATION CORPS

In one of my conversations with the President in March 1933, he brought up the idea that became the Civilian Conservation Corps. Roosevelt loved trees and hated to see them cut and not replaced. It was natural for him to wish to put large numbers of the unemployed to repairing such devastation. His enthusiasm for this project, which was really all his own, led him to some exaggeration of what could be accomplished. He saw it big. He thought any man or boy would rejoice to leave the city and work in the woods.

It was characteristic of him that he conceived the project, boldly rushed it through, and happily left it to others to worry about the details. And there were some difficult details.

First, there was the question of who should go into the CCC. The President agreed, after some argument, that care must be exercised in the selection of the men. Some unemployed men would not be physically fit for the rigors of outdoor life; others who had family responsibilities ought not to be encouraged to go away; still others might prove to be unsuitable, perhaps dangerous, in co-operative camp living.

The attitude of the trade unions had to be considered. They were disturbed about this program, which they feared would put all workers under a "dollar a day" regimentation merely because they were unemployed. They feared it would take men from their trades and skills.

Then there were the problems of controlling and protecting large numbers of men in the woods and remote places. City men unaccustomed to the woods would get into trouble. You couldn't just open the forest and say to the unemployed, "Go on in and we will pay you a dollar a day."

The rate of a dollar a day was proposed as wages plus board and keep. It was low as wages but high as relief. It was bound to be attractive to some of the more undesirable characters in the big cities who were also unemployed.

I suggested that the Army be assigned to take care of the men going into the woods. The Department of Agriculture Forestry Service could plan and supervise the work, but it had no facilities for housing, feeding, clothing, transporting, doctoring, and keeping order among such a large group. The President thought that was all right.

The labor people were upset that the Army was in the picture. Yet no other agency in the government could take care of so many men. The Army had tents, trucks, cots, blankets, shoes, underwear, sweaters, wash basins, soap, kitchen equipment, and officers trained in the organization of sanitary, orderly camps and in the business of being responsible for large groups of men.

When the President heard of labor's opposition to the Army's role, he said, "Oh, well, that can't be. I'll tell you what, the Department of Labor will recruit these men."

"Mr. President," I said, "you know as well as I do that the Department of Labor has no facilities for recruiting, selecting, and transporting these men. There are three thousand employees in the Department, and not one is trained for this. What's more, we have no tents, no cots, no kitchens."

"Do it through the United States Employment Service," he said.

I had just told him that the Employment Service was practically nonexistent although its name was still on a letterhead. I had asked his permission to seek funds to resurrect and reorganize it. We were trying to assist in the passage of the Wagner-Peyser bill in Congress, which would in time make an effective agency out of the service.

Because the opposition seemed to him to have some validity, Roosevelt insisted that the Department of Labor take charge of

CCC. He said, "Resurrect the Employment Service right away. Use the Labor Department to recruit and select these men."

I was to learn that he often did that kind of thing. It was in line with his 1942 request for sixty thousand airplanes. It had to be done, so he put the dynamite under the people who had to do the job and let them fumble for their own methods.

At any rate, we thought and worked quickly. I wired for Frank Persons, whom I had known as an able organizer in the Red Cross during World War I. He came, and in three days we had set up an agency known as the National Re-employment Service, received a special appropriation attached to the CCC bill to finance it on a temporary basis, and proceeded to make the rules for selecting 250,000 unemployed men for forestry work.

The Forestry Service entered into the work eagerly, happy that it had a President who appreciated forestry. They laid out work programs and selected the sites. They called back former foresters and recruited and trained junior foresters to supervise the work in the field.

We had to call upon the Army to supply and manage the camps and commissaries, to provide equipment and transportation. George Dern, Secretary of War, reconciled the Army to this limited but important function. The Army called back reserve officers in great numbers to take charge. The first canvass showed that many reserve officers, themselves out of work and with meager resources, were growing desperate. They were glad to come back and entered sympathetically into the rush program. It was a new problem for conventionally trained officers, for Secretary Dern announced that there was to be no military discipline, since the men were not enlisted soldiers but civilians.

A year later Secretary Dern reported at a cabinet meeting that he thought the experience of handling the CCC had been the most valuable the Army had ever had.

"They have had to learn," he said, "to govern men by leadership, explanation, and diplomacy rather than discipline. That knowledge is priceless to the American Army."

The Army became enthusiastic about the training in the

camps, saying it was an admirable substitute for citizen military training. The things learned were the basic essentials of Army knowledge; namely, how to live in companies of men; how to live under rules and time schedules; how to take care of yourself and your equipment; how to keep clean; how to obey orders and work with precision. The work, exercise, good plain Army food, and regular sleep built up the health and strength of the men until they were, in physical toughness and mental alertness, the equal of men with a year of military training.

As one enthusiastic colonel said, "Learning how to shoot and take care of a gun is not the basic training. It could be taught quickly to men in top physical and mental condition, as these men are."

The Labor Department, Army, and Forestry Service each had a representative on the committee in charge of CCC, and they drew up the rules. At the President's request I kept close to the whole program and reported to him from time to time. He thought a lot of this project and wanted to be sure that nothing happened to give it a bad name or diminish the public's enthusiasm for it.

Characteristically, he had decided to appoint a labor leader as director on the theory that that would make organized labor well disposed to the project. Robert Fechner, vice-president of the Machinists' Union, had had some experience serving on government advisory committees in his home state. He had also lectured on labor questions at Harvard and Dartmouth. The President had known him in the Wilson administration. He was appointed, and the Roosevelt theory proved correct. Labor was satisfied that there was no disguised regimentation, and it was uncritically in favor of CCC from that time on.

The fact that this set-up might not make for efficient administration did not trouble Roosevelt. When it was pointed out to him, he said, "Oh, that doesn't matter. The Army and the Forestry Service will really run the show. The Secretary of Labor will select the men and make the rules and Fechner will 'go along' and give everybody satisfaction and confidence."

It is a technique of administration which drives professors of political science almost mad—but government in a representative democracy has to be adapted to human feelings. Roosevelt could accommodate the objections of labor, liberals, and those suspicious of the military without any conflict within himself on grounds of efficiency or logic. His idea to establish a Civilian Conservation Corps proved to be felicitous, and it operated with great success.

15.

RELIEF

It is hard today to reconstruct the atmosphere of 1933 and to evoke the terror caused by unrelieved poverty and prolonged unemployment. The funds of many states and localities were exhausted. The legal debt limit of many states had been reached, and they could borrow no more, even for so urgent a matter as relief. The situation was grim in city, county, and state. Public welfare officers had reached the end of their rope, and special committees, appointed by governors, mayors, and county officials, had exhausted their imagination as well as their funds. The Federal Government and its taxing power were all one could think of.

Whatever plans the Roosevelt government might make to revive the normal economic life of the country, the urgent need was for direct relief to the unemployed. During the Democratic campaign Roosevelt had placed considerable emphasis upon this need. It had been basic in the appeal for votes that suffering would be relieved immediately.

Unemployment had been increasing steadily since the autumn of 1929. When Roosevelt took office in March 1933, it had reached its peak. No one has ever known the exact number out of work and in need. The kind of statistical information now capable of giving us a fairly good answer to that question was not available, but the estimates of persons out of work ranged from 13,300,000 to 17,900,000. The true figure is probably somewhere between, and the number in actual distress approached seventy-five per cent of the unemployed.

In Pennsylvania a fairly full report was available, thanks to Governor Gifford Pinchot. He estimated that Pennsylvania's

unemployed totaled more than 1,500,000 and said that the figure represented an increase of twenty-eight per cent between
July 1932 and March 1933. He pointed out that more than
thirty per cent of the workers of Pennsylvania still employed
were on half time or less and that only two out of five employable persons were on full-time jobs with full pay.

Governor Pinchot appealed to the Federal Government for
assistance. He asked for $45,000,000, saying that it would do
no more than keep Pennsylvania's destitute on an irreducible
minimum of food for six months.

The situation was worse perhaps in Illinois. It was equally
desperate in other states, in direct proportion to the community's dependence on industrial production for the bread and
butter of the wage earners and their families.

As the Roosevelt administration took up its task, the unemployed had just struggled through the third severe winter since
President Hoover had proclaimed, in the summer of 1930, that
"the depression is over." National income had declined from
$81,000,000,000 a year to $39,000,000,000. Banks were
collapsing throughout the nation. Relief stations were closing
down for lack of funds. Hunger marchers were on parade.
Food riots were becoming more common. Crime, born of the
need for food, clothing, and other necessities of life, was on
the upsurge.

There were insecurity and terror in the agricultural regions,
where sober farm people forcibly prevented sheriffs' sales on
foreclosed mortgages. The increase in petty larceny was alarming. An honorable man like Dan Willard, president of the
Baltimore & Ohio Railroad, when asked at a public meeting
what he thought about the situation, said, "If a man whose
family is hungry steals, I cannot blame him. I think I would do
the same."

Shortly after Inauguration Day, Harry Hopkins and William
Hodson came down from New York to see me. Hopkins was
chairman of the New York State Temporary Emergency Relief
Administration, which had been established by Roosevelt when
he had been Governor. Hodson was director of the Welfare
Council of New York City. Hopkins was not then a close friend

of the President's. He had been appointed to his New York job because he had been recommended by people Roosevelt trusted. In the 1932 campaign Hopkins's support of Roosevelt was confined to activities in behalf of a group of social workers who had endorsed the New York Governor. His later appointment was in no way a reward for political activities.

Washington was so hectic that it was difficult to concentrate on concrete programs. There were on my desk over two thousand plans for federal action to cover unemployment and as many more on the President's.

Hopkins, Hodson, and I met at the Women's University Club, which was jammed. We found a hole under the stairs, and there, in cramped, unlovely quarters, they laid out their plan. It was a plan for the immediate appropriation by the Federal Government of grants-in-aid to the states for unemployment relief. I was impressed by the exactness of their knowledge and the practicability of their plan.

They told me they had not been able to get to the President to present their program. I knew that Secretary Marvin McIntyre was almost frantic trying to arrange appointments for people with political influence, for old friends, job seekers, congressmen, as well as a few people with ideas. Feeling certain of my ground, I cut across the usual formalities and made an appointment for Hopkins and Hodson to see the President immediately, telling McIntyre that these people knew how to operate and had a concrete proposal.

Roosevelt heard their views with interest. He knew about Hopkins's work as relief administrator in New York. In his conversations that day and in later conferences Roosevelt showed that he intended to incorporate some of New York's experience in handling relief into the federal program. After a series of preliminary talks Roosevelt called in Senators Wagner, La Follette, and Costigan, and asked them to draw a bill to establish the Federal Emergency Relief Administration. The three senators were good enough to consult me, chiefly on the New York experience, and the measure was drawn up and approved by the President. Congressional committees conducted hearings on the bill in April, and the Congress passed it early in May. The

President signed the measure on May 12, 1933, and appointed Harry Hopkins as Federal Emergency Relief administrator. FERA opened for business on May 22 with a working capital of $500,000,000.

Half of this appropriation was earmarked to be spent in the states on the basis of one federal dollar for every three dollars from all other public sources. This feature of FERA had been borrowed from the experience in New York, where counties, cities, and towns matched state contributions for relief. The other half allotted to FERA was placed in a discretionary fund which was to be distributed in states where the relief burden was so heavy and funds so depleted that they could not meet the requirement of three dollars for one.

The fortunes of the unemployed took a turn for the better the day FERA began to operate. The original appropriation and an additional $850,000,000 were expended by March 1934, including the Civil Works program. Congress, surveying the results at that time, was generous with FERA.

In its brief span of life FERA received and spent $4,000,000,000 on all projects. It was the first step in the economic pump priming that was to break the back of the depression. FERA spent money for many things, all necessities of life—food, clothing, fuel, shelter, medicine. In an analysis of how the money was spent, Harry Hopkins said, "We can only say that out of every dollar entrusted to us for lessening of distress, the maximum amount humanly possible was put into the people's hands. The money, spent honestly and with constant remembrance of its purpose, bought more of courage than it ever bought of goods."

Thus the relief program was launched. While even its most enthusiastic sponsors never thought it was the complete answer, it kept people alive and instilled courage. In looking back, moreover, one sees that it provided a substantial stimulus to the revival of industry by creating purchasing power in a class previously destitute, and that it had a tremendous effect on raising the standards of living of the poorest and lowest paid people.

Very early in the program Hopkins and his assistants,

Aubrey Williams and David K. Niles, began to explain to those of us who would listen how degrading and humiliating was a program of handouts when Americans wanted, above everything, to work and contribute. There was the story, not lost on Roosevelt, of the elderly man who had been the support of a large family and who was getting fifteen dollars a week on relief. He went out regularly, without being asked, to sweep the streets of his village. "I want to do something in return for what I get," he said.

When Hopkins proposed in the autumn of 1933 that we launch a program which gave work rather than cash relief to the unemployed, he met with a sympathetic response from the President. Roosevelt asked him to come to a cabinet meeting and describe what he had in mind. He had in mind a program, which we called "made work" in New York, of finding useful things for people to do.

The Civil Works Program was intended originally to give employment to about four million unemployed, anticipating that others in distress would have help through direct relief. It was never intended that Civil Works would offer permanent employment. For many families, however, it was the sole source of occupation and income for a considerable period of time. Brief experience with it convinced most observers that it should be continued with careful attention and planning. The effect upon people of having their own money to spend rather than having it doled out to them was good, and their ingenuity in making ends meet was better than that of any social work adviser in a vast majority of cases.

Hopkins handled this program with extraordinary skill in selecting projects, securing the co-operation of local agencies, and managing so that real work was accomplished and people were truly rehabilitated. He was also skillful in his management of the political phases, which were numerous and difficult. When money is to be spent, politicians come into the picture and tensions develop between the adherents of the governor and the senators. Hopkins was wise enough to make allowances for the facts of life, to do the job with honesty and to make friends with politicians at the same time. He did not alienate them from the project and the President. Moreover, he gave the President not only bulk statistics but examples of how a family had been rehabilitated, how a project had resulted in a playground or a swimming pool for a poor community that had never thought of having such a thing; how it brought the cataloguing of a gift of books to a library in a small town so that they became available to readers.

Projects to give work to unemployed teachers, artists, and theatrical people needed enlightened understanding and courage to be endorsed and developed. The President hadn't realized, as perhaps none of us had, the degree to which professional people and artists failed to sustain themselves when the national income had shrunk to the lowest level. People out of work do not give music or dancing lessons to their children nor buy tickets to the theater. The President had a keen feeling for the sensibilities of recipients of this relief.

Thousands of the most respectable groups had to accept it and were deeply grateful for the opportunity to maintain their self-respect. An almost deaf, elderly lawyer, a Harvard graduate, unable to find clients, got a WPA job as assistant caretaker at a small seaside park. He did double the work anyone could have expected of him. He made little extra plantings, arranged charming paths and walks, acted as guide to visitors, supervised children's play, and made himself useful and agreeable to the whole community. I had occasion to see him from time to time, and he would always ask me to take a message to the President—a message of gratitude for a job which paid him fifteen dollars a week and kept him from starving to death. It was an honorable occupation that made him feel useful and not like a bum and derelict, he would say with tears in his eyes.

It was this kind of feeling that Roosevelt cared about. Roosevelt's imagination used to work on these projects, and he was always thinking of things that could be done by the WPA. Wherever he went, he saw the evidences of the improvements wrought by work relief.

Roosevelt supported the Civil Works Administration and later became a great advocate of the Works Progress Administration which grew out of it. The Works Progress Administration, at its peak in the fiscal year July 1938/July 1939, took care of 3,325,000 people, and in the fiscal year 1939, its largest year of expenditure, spent $2,067,972,000 in both federal and sponsors' funds.

The President was always annoyed that so much complaint was made about the WPA. It is granted that there were ridiculous aspects to some of the enterprises and that some parts of the program got out of control. The freedom encouraged in this country led to the selection of some strange plays by local groups, and some congressmen and other citizens protested that the public money was being used to circulate subversive propaganda or to challenge the moral code. Roosevelt bore these accusations without being too disturbed. It amused him that there should be so much protest over play acting, even if supported by public funds. He liked people to have a good time in their own ways. Using unemployed musicians to play at community celebrations and in railroad stations at the rush hours, the existence of little WPA orchestras in almost every community, struck him as modern versions of the town band which bred so many American music lovers.

As the experience under work relief progressed, there was a moment when I feared Roosevelt was going to agree with an idea of Harry Hopkins's that work relief would be better than unemployment insurance and that we might perhaps switch from consideration of unemployment insurance, next on our program, to a permanent work relief, under some other name of course. The President, Hopkins, and I had a long discussion on this point. My argument was that if there were mass unemployment again, political confusion might cause other administrations to prevent unemployment insurance from going into operation soon enough to do any good. Hopkins argued that any unemployment insurance we could devise would not be enough to take care of families in a long depression.

"Well, I don't see why you can't combine both," the President said. "Let's go ahead with the plan for unemployment insurance. I think that's right. Let a man have something definite by law for some weeks and then arrange it so he can have work relief afterward if unemployment continues and he is in need."

Before we left that evening we had doped out a plan. Unemployment insurance benefits should be paid to anyone out of work through no fault of his own after an appropriate legal waiting period. The employers' contributions to the fund should be sufficient so that one could anticipate the possibility of twelve to sixteen weeks of unemployment benefits of one-half to two-thirds of the weekly wages, with a minimum, representing a bare subsistence level, below which no one was to be paid. After the cash benefit was paid and the worker was dismissed from the unemployment insurance rolls, the worker was to keep on looking for a job. If he found no work and exhausted his savings, he could apply for work relief.

"That's right," Roosevelt said. "When he leaves the unemployment insurance rolls, he gets a green ticket and is told he can make another application at another office on this green ticket for work benefits. The job will come to him. First a cash benefit, then use up his savings, then a work benefit. The projects to be used as work benefits ought to be thought out in advance, so our enemies can't yell boondoggling to make fun of a useful job."

The President, I suspect, felt that because we arrived intellectually at this solution, all of it was done. Of course, it has not been done as a matter of law. Unemployment insurance stands alone as the only protection for people out of work.

As times grew better the relief projects were gradually slowed down and closed off. WPA became unpopular in Congress and there was constant protest against further relief appropriations. There remained in this country, however, a core of people, not too many in number, who did better on WPA than ever before in their lives and perhaps better than they are ever likely to. Among these were the handicapped, and it was not until the war years that they were again used to advantage. Many handicapped people got good jobs during the war and did them well. Businessmen learned to use the blind, the deaf, and the lame. Many perhaps have made a place for themselves in industry. One hopes so. One of the items which most interested Roosevelt in reports on labor supply for the war industries was that blind, deaf, and semi-crippled people were being given opportunity to work and were doing well. He was particularly pleased that people in their seventies and eighties were holding jobs, and that no longer did one hear the cry that a man of fifty is too old for industry.

But the people difficult to place remain. They were the last to be hired in the war industries and the least adjustable. They were the people who did better under the kindly prodding, the special case work, and the social supervision of the WPA projects. The WPA had to teach some people the simplest forms of personal reliability, integrity, and cleanliness so that they would be fit to go into a workroom. It started classes, extraordinary as it may seem in a country like this, to teach unemployed women how to wash their hair and their clothes, clean house, tell time, mend, keep themselves neat and tidy. I heard a teacher of such a group say, "If they were cleaning women before, I pity those who were subject to their ministrations."

The unemployables are rarely to be found in the occupations covered by unemployment insurance. They will remain the first load on relief. In 1946 they are undistinguishable because we are on a high level of income and savings, but they are likely to reappear. When they do, the experience with WPA will be of great help to communities everywhere in dealing with them in a constructive way.

The President, I repeat, never regretted the relief program. He never apologized for it. He was proud of what it had done.

And his attitude toward Hopkins changed after the first months. He did not look on Hopkins as a relief administrator exclusively. He regarded him as a man who knew a lot about human nature, who was an exceptionally good executive, and whose judgment was good on almost any question. He proved to be an ideal debating companion for the President. He liked to listen while the President was talking for the purpose of working his own ideas through his own mind until he came out with a practical program. This was exactly the kind of help the President needed. He wanted to use his imagination and yet he wanted to be sure that he checked himself or that somebody else checked him against undue enthusiasm.

Hopkins became not only his relief administrator but his

general assistant as no one had been able to be. In many ways he filled the gap left by Louis Howe's death, but he had a much larger grasp of national and international affairs than did Howe. There was a temperamental sympathy between the men which made their relationship extremely easy as well as faithful and productive. Roosevelt was greatly enriched by Hopkins's knowledge, ability, and humane attitude toward all facets of life.

16.

THIRTY-HOUR WEEK

When we first came to Washington in 1933 the Black bill was already before the Congress. Introduced by Senator Hugo L. Black, it had received support from many parts of the country and from many representatives and senators.

In 1933, and in the two years preceding it, many theoretical analyses of the economic problem had been placed before the country in bills, reports, books, and magazine articles. The Technocrats, a big, vigorous organization, held that the peak of the American capitalist system had been reached and passed. There was a belief that the situation of human beings out of work because of new labor-saving inventions and because of the decline and collapse of business under the periodic fluctuation of production, consumption, and employment, had become firmly established, perhaps permanently. It was said we could not recover without some miracle of control of jobs and production.

How this idea came to Senator Black, a lawyer from Birmingham, Alabama, I do not know. But he had been convinced, as is evidenced by the bill which was his own material and idea. He had worked out a theoretical relationship for the amount of production, the size of the market, the number of jobs, and the total payroll in American life. He conceived of the relationship as static.

This was his major mistake. The relationship is not static. In 1932, when he introduced this bill, it seemed static. The approach of this school of thought to the problem was something like this: We have reached the peak of productivity, and technological advance henceforth would mean a constant decline in the number employed. The Senator therefore reached the conclusion that if everybody who worked for wages in the United States worked thirty hours a week, the number who needed to work for a livelihood would tally with the jobs available at the prevailing level of production. The idea of a dynamic situation where production and jobs might increase did not enter into the conception of the Black thirty-hour bill.

The Black bill then, as it rested before the Congress when Roosevelt became President, provided that there should be a limitation of thirty hours for all persons working in interstate commerce. There were no provisions for emergency variation or for appropriate modifications in different industries dependent upon different natural resources and conditions. There was, moreover, no realization that, if hours were reduced to thirty a week, weekly income from wages would be severely cut. The principle of a minimum wage had not been considered at all.

I told Roosevelt, "This is an important bill and is now before the Congress. It was developed by Democrats before you came into the presidency. It has a great following."

He was startled by its implications. It showed, he thought, ignorance of the industrial process in the United States. It was cold and inhuman. It had no realistic approach to the problem as he saw it. It was a mass approach.

We talked about the possibility of adding a requirement that, when hours were reduced below a certain amount in any industry, a minimum wage board should be set up to pass upon minimum wages in that industry and to base them on the idea of a living standard. There were minimum wages acts in various states, including New York, providing, at the least, for a minimum wage for women and for all low paid workers by implication. This minimum wage was based not only on the hours worked but also on the prevailing minimum standards of living in the community.

Reasoning from the experience of these laws, the President and I agreed that if he were to support the Black bill, provisions for minimum wage regulation must be embodied in it. We agreed that there must also be some understanding of the dif-

ferences in industries. Some industries require continuous operation; others do not; and some must work long hours at peak
seasons. We felt that a government agency must be set up, empowered to grant variations under responsible controls.

The President, with his gift for the concrete, put his finger on
a major difficulty. "What will they do in the dairy industry, the
milk evaporating and canning industry? How can they put that
on a thirty-hour week and still come out square?"

He drew upon his experience as a farmer. "There is not a
great shortage of jobs in my part of the country. There is bad
unemployment in the great cities, but you can't take city men
and put them into dairying. There have to be hours adapted to
the rhythm of the cow."

The "rhythm of the cow" became one of his favorite expressions when he talked about the Black bill at cabinet meetings
and other conferences.

Although sympathetic with the objective, he was doubtful
that this bill would solve the unemployment problem. In fact,
he was quite certain that it wouldn't. He was committed to the
idea of a dynamic economy, an economy of greater expansion
of production and distribution than we had known, rather
than an economy of curtailment of production. He could not
feel that a reduction to thirty hours a week was essential even
for the health and welfare of the people. "Is there any harm,"
he would say, "in people working an eight-hour day and forty-
eight hours a week?"

The President also believed the Black bill unconstitutional.
That had been the view of every attorney we had consulted in
New York and of every lawyer on the federal level, including
the Attorney General.

Roosevelt had a problem. He was in favor of limiting the
hours of labor for humanitarian and possibly for economic reasons and therefore did not want to oppose the bill. At the same
time, he did not feel that it was sound to support it vigorously.
But the agitation for the bill was strong. Its proponent insisted
that it was a vital step toward licking the depression. I said,
"Mr. President, we have to take a position. I'll take the position,
but I want to be sure that it is in harmony with your principles
and policy."

Finally we agreed that I should go before the congressional committee holding hearings on the bill. I would propose amendments to guarantee a floor under wages, that is, some kind of minimum wage machinery. I would point out the necessity for possibilities of variation from the strict application of the thirty-hour week.

Roosevelt was a firm, supporting friend and colleague in these matters. He knew that I had to be the spearhead. He knew that I had to make the appearance, but he was concerned. He took the trouble to talk to me on the telephone in the days preceding my appearance before the committee. Just before the hearing, he telephoned to say that Mrs. Roosevelt and Miss Ishbel MacDonald, daughter of British Prime Minister Ramsay MacDonald, then visiting at the White House, wanted to come to the hearing.

It was characteristic of him to say, "Do you mind? Is it comfortable for you if they come?" Of course it was comfortable, but even in a situation where the publicity would be a reflection of his position, he was considerate of me.

So I went, with his encouragement, to testify. It was a trying experience. Except for my appearance for the bill providing for the Civilian Conservation Corps, it was my first appearance as a cabinet member before a committee of Congress, and this was a full dress affair. Senator Black apparently wanted it that way. Furthermore, the attendance of Miss MacDonald and Mrs. Roosevelt made it a matter of considerable publicity. One could not avoid the ballyhoo of the photographers, the press, the radio, the klieg lights.

I tried to keep within the limits of my agreement with the President. It was extremely important that I do so. The bill in its general outline, I said, was impossible to administer and its results would be doubtful, if not disastrous. But if it were suitably amended, if minimum wage machinery were set up for modifying the hours of labor in different industries after hearing advice from committees made up of employers and workers in those industries, then it might be made into a workable law.

But congressmen and the general public would have preferred to find in some one act a panacea that would solve the whole problem of unemployment. That unemployment could not be solved that way, that it was a complicated phenomenon, that more factors had to be brought into action to overcome it—these were not convincing arguments in those tense days.

At any rate, Roosevelt was fully committed. From that time on, Congress, the newspapers, the people, knew he was in favor of doing something by law to mitigate the hardships of unemployment by techniques of control of hours, wages, and working conditions. He was committed to the principle but not to this particular program.

The Black bill did not go through. Instead, the National Industrial Recovery Act was evolved and adapted. Some biographers of Roosevelt have gone so far as to say that Roosevelt betrayed the Black bill in favor of the National Industrial Recovery Act. They regard this as disloyalty to principle. They say that the Senate committee was about to add a paragraph to the bill which would have set up a minimum wage principle. But those of us who were close to the situation could not detect, at any time, that the adoption of a minimum wage clause was in the making. And, as events showed, the Supreme Court in those days would surely have found the Black bill unconstitutional.

17.

THE BLUE EAGLE

When I talked with the President in April 1933 about the Black bill, his mind was as innocent as a child's of any such program as NRA.[*]

Those of us who favored the enactment of a public works program continually pressed the President on the issue. I would bring the matter up at one session, Jim Farley at the next, Harold Ickes after that—in line with our desire to keep the subject in the President's mind.

The chief opponent of the public works program was Lewis Douglas, Director of the Budget, who had been invited to sit with the cabinet. His arguments were so plausible that those of us who favored public works as a measure for unemployment relief were not able to convince the President to act at once. Douglas always raised doubts in his mind.

One day in April when the matter was brought up in cabinet, Douglas announced, "Mr. President, I have heard in the last few days of a plan being worked out here in Washington. It is so far-reaching, so compelling, so thoughtful, that it takes in every economic factor. I am positive, if it can be developed, that it will do for our economic system in a very short time what could never be done by the public works scheme. It will make all this unnecessary, and the doubt prevailing in the country will be assuaged. It is a wonderful plan."

---

[*] A distinction should be made between the National Recovery Administration (NRA) and the National Industrial Recovery Act (NIRA) which established it. Following common usage, the initials NRA are used in this book for both the Act and the Administration.

I asked for details, but Douglas passed off my inquiry by saying that the authors of the plan were not ready to disclose the details. He said he would give them to the cabinet when the time came.

Meantime, I learned from Isador Lubin, Commissioner of Labor Statistics, that another plan was being worked out by Meyer Jacobstein and Senator Wagner. Jacobstein, a Brookings Institution economist and former congressman from New York, had "sold" his idea to the Senator through Simon Rifkind, Wagner's secretary.

At a cabinet meeting two or three days later, Henry Wallace said, "Mr. President, this morning I ran into this thing that Douglas was talking about the other day. Before you come out in wholehearted endorsement of the Black bill, I wish you would look into this."

The President replied with a laugh, "The Secretary of Labor is going to testify on the Black bill, but not wholeheartedly."

We didn't get any more information at that meeting except that Rex Tugwell had a hand in the plan. After we adjourned, I went to the President and said, "Tugwell and someone else are doing this, and I would like to know why no cabinet member is in on it."

The President assured me that he knew no more about it than I did, but while I was there he called Tugwell and said that if any group was at work on an overall plan or bill, he would like to have me sit in on the next meeting.

I went to an office on an upper floor of the Treasury Department building where Tugwell and Hugh Johnson had been working for weeks under a mutual pledge of secrecy. It was my first meeting with General Johnson. He had been working for Bernard Baruch and, among other things, had prepared Baruch's Railroad Report. In the 1932 campaign Baruch had lent Johnson to the Democratic National Committee. He was an excellent writer and he had worked well with Louis Howe and others in preparing campaign material.

Tugwell and Johnson were anything but pleased to see me. I was the only cabinet officer who had been there. Since the President knew nothing about their program, I insisted upon getting some information. They tried to throw me off with large talk and I got only the barest outline. The scheme seemed to have a good many sound elements, and I felt that it might merit consideration if the Black bill could not be amended.

Later, when Tugwell came to my office, I asked him, "Have you ever talked with anybody at the Brookings Institution?"

"Certainly not," he replied. "The President asked me to explore the whole subject." Tugwell took that as authorization to go ahead. The President thought he was merely investigating some ideas.

At the earliest opportunity I reported to the President that two fairly complete plans were being mapped out—one by Wagner and Jacobstein, the other by Tugwell and Johnson. They both rested on the idea of suspending the effect of the anti-trust laws in return for voluntary agreement by industries for fair competition, minimum wage levels, and maximum hours. I told him that the plans were not very different and both apparently had gotten around constitutional difficulties. The President asked Henry Wallace and me to get the two groups together. That was arranged, and the conferees met daily. When they had completed their draft bill, the President showed it to me. It was novel. It seemed generally satisfactory, but it had some weaknesses.

"This is very drastic," I said. "The hours of labor and wages are involved, and I think I ought to get the president of the American Federation of Labor to go over it."

I called in William Green. He liked some of it but said that no provision was made for collective bargaining. He thought the bill could be used as a method for putting the labor unions out of business. General Johnson took the bill and redrafted it, incorporating Section 7A, which was meant to assure labor's right to collective bargaining. Written in general terms, 7A was a problem in semantics. It was a set of words to suit labor leaders, William Green in particular. When they discovered later what could be done under 7A, they called it "labor's Magna Carta."

We were ready to go ahead. NRA seemed the answer to many problems as far as the new administration was concerned. The President had wanted something done to revive industry quickly and to introduce the practice of short hours and a method to prevent wage decline. I was a little disappointed that the NRA program was pictured as a government-industry co-operative enterprise, but otherwise I was impressed with it. I thought we had found a way out of the constitutional difficulty that impeded regulation of hours and wages.

The President was ready to ask Congress for the enacting legislation but there was a last minute fight for a change. One issue was a demand for a better public works clause, which I shall discuss in a later chapter.

The bill was introduced in the Senate by Robert Wagner and in the House by Robert L. Doughton. As Congress proceeded with the task of enacting the legislation, the President cast about for a man to head up NRA. Hugh Johnson seemed to be mentioned most often. He had done much to draft the program. He was considered a member of the President's so-called "brain trust" and had had experience in the industrial control program during World War I under Bernard Baruch. He was an extremely likable and dramatic personality.

During this period Baruch came to my house socially once and in the course of the conversation asked me, "What's this I hear about Hugh Johnson being considered for administrator of the Recovery Program?"

I replied that I thought it was likely.

Baruch went on, "He's been my number-three man for years. I think he's a good number-three man, maybe a number-two man, but he's not a number-one man. He's dangerous and unstable. He gets nervous and sometimes goes away for days without notice. I'm fond of him, but do tell the President to be careful. Hugh needs a firm hand."

Baruch wasn't seeing the President then. I forget why. Some disagreement about the fiscal and gold policy, I believe. I reported the conversation, but it was too late. Johnson had been told he was to be appointed.

The NRA bill was divided into two parts, Title I dealing with industrial codes and labor, and Title II embodying the public works program, which we had managed to salvage. There had been talk of a cabinet committee of three to administer the act, but most people on second consideration had agreed that, however much that might bring justice and accumulated wisdom into the picture, it would certainly not bring speed.

Roosevelt brought the bill into cabinet meeting one day, expressing gratification that it had been passed by Congress and saying that he meant to sign it that very afternoon in our presence and announce the appointment of Hugh Johnson as administrator. After discussing the problems of administration of Title I and the hazards of cartelization, which must be guarded against unremittingly, he said, "What do you think about the administration of Title II? As the bill is written it seems to be taken for granted that it will be administered by the administrator of Title I, but I suppose it could be separated. I have read the bill, and I see no reason why I should not appoint, under the law, another administrator. What do you think of it as a matter of policy?"

One cabinet member after another spoke up to say that they believed it highly desirable to separate the two. The administration of Title I itself would be an enormous job, it was agreed, challenging and difficult. It was pointed out that the administrative task of Title II would require close and constant timing. No chances could be taken with it. It could become a pork barrel; it could become corrupt; it could be extremely wasteful of the people's money. It must be administered with the utmost of careful controls, of integrity, and of cautious, businesslike legal procedures.

I knew that it would be a terrible blow to Hugh Johnson if he were not appointed administrator of both Titles. He had anticipated working them together, utilizing the public works program as bait to get people to go along on some of the stern realities of the codes he expected to propose. But I inclined to agree with my cabinet colleagues that for the welfare of the country and for the President's peace of mind, it would be wise to separate the two Titles in their administration.

The President said, "I think I agree with you. It will be hard on Johnson. He won't like it, but I think it is the best thing to do. Johnson is waiting outside to be brought in and told that the bill is signed and that he is administrator."

Harold Ickes was chosen rather suddenly to administer Title

II, and then the President sent for Hugh Johnson. All smiles, he told Johnson that he was about to sign the bill and was appointing him administrator. Johnson made a pleasant little speech of thanks and promised to devote his life to the great project. Then the President told him, as agreeably, I think, as it could have been told, that in talking it over with the cabinet it had seemed to them all that to ask any one man to administer both Title I and Title II was putting an inhuman burden upon that man; that to direct and develop industrial recovery under Title I was tough enough; and that he had come to the conclusion that he should lift the burden of the more pedestrian but difficult and time-consuming job of public works under Title II from his shoulders; and that he had just decided to appoint Ickes to administer Title II.

Johnson's smile was gone. The blood mounted to his face. He grew purpler and purpler as the President talked. When the President had finished, Johnson spoke in a strange, low voice that came from deep within him. "I don't see why. I don't see why," he said.

The President paid little attention. He dismissed the cabinet and beckoned to me.

As I came over to his chair he whispered, "Stick with Hugh. Keep him sweet. Don't let him explode."

I walked over to Johnson, who seemed to be in a daze. I linked my arm in his and we walked slowly toward the door. Hugh muttered, "He's ruined me." We made our way through the corridor. I tried to cheer him up, but he paid no attention to my words. "I've got to get out, I can't stay," he kept repeating.

I realized that, above all else, I had to keep Johnson away from the press. I led him out a side door and we got into my car. I told the chauffeur to drive down by the Tidal Basin. We drove all through that section, and when the chauffeur asked for further instructions, I told him, "Just keep driving—anywhere." We visited every green park in Washington that day, some of them many times, as I tried to "reason" with the General.

"Don't blow up," I pleaded. "Don't pull out."

And all he would say was, "It's terrible, it's terrible."

But the passage of time, as we traveled many miles of Washington's streets, calmed Johnson. I praised the great job he had done in inventing and planning NRA. I urged him to be a good soldier and go along with the President's wishes. Finally, Johnson promised that he would, and my longest automobile trip in Washington ended in peace, if in exhaustion.

In a day or so the President had Johnson in, gave him a pep talk, and the crisis was averted. For some reason Johnson got it into his head at that time that I was his only friend in the cabinet. I believe he thought that I had tried to prevent the President's decision, although I never, of course, claimed that. All I had done was ride the streets with him when he was in emotional distress and keep before his eyes the picture of himself as a soldier and a hero and as a great inventor of the method of saving the country.

He also heard from me that afternoon about the plan to have a cabinet advisory committee for Title I, and, while he was rather startled, he said, "I am glad you are on it. You will promise me, won't you, that you will stand by and save me from those harpies?"

Without debating the character of my colleagues, I promised to stand by.

The next day, I think, he told a group of people, "Frances Perkins is the best man in the cabinet." He was, of course, merely showing gratitude that I had been his friend in an hour of need. What he really meant was that I was the best woman in the cabinet. He was an emotional type.

It developed that Johnson's energy, imagination, and drive were invaluable. There was hardly anyone else in the United States who could and would have done just what he had to do at the time to stir frightened, lethargic people into action.

Roosevelt counted greatly on NRA to act as a shot in the arm for industry, and it did. At the President's request, and also at General Johnson's, I kept close to the NRA and made great efforts to promote its success. The President appointed a committee of cabinet officers to be general advisers to General Johnson and to insure that the NRA kept within bounds and did not take over all government functions, since Johnson had a tendency to think in large controlling terms.

General Johnson didn't like this advisory committee. It chafed him. He hated to explain himself. Most of the members stopped coming to meetings because it seemed futile. I stuck because the necessity of getting the country onto a program of short hours and wages above subsistence seemed paramount to any administrative difficulties.

Before the bill was through Congress and Johnson began operating, he and Mrs. Johnson used to come to see me often in the evenings, and I realized that his ideas included "codes of fair practice" for each industry. He planned to give his personal approval to each code. Then he would recommend it to the President, who would sign it. It would become the over-all pattern for that industry, entitling those who signed the agreement to be exempted from the more difficult sections of the anti-trust law. He expected to have his own legal counsel, economists, and statisticians, and to make up his mind and proceed to the President without advice or approval of the other, older government agencies and without public hearings or publication of proposed codes in advance.

When this was reported to the President, he saw the hazard of such procedure. He persuaded rather than directed General Johnson to utilize the economic and statistical bureaus of the Departments of Commerce and Labor and to consult the Attorney General systematically on the ground of economy and integration of government activities. Incidentally, this process gave two cabinet officers knowledge of what was going on before it was too late to check monopolistic or undemocratic trends and to inform the President of dangers and problems ahead. The President's final suggestion, which really appealed to Johnson, was that the publicity attendant upon public hearings would, in fact, be a great educational feature for securing understanding, confidence, and support of the people throughout the country. This proved to be true.

The President farmed out to me the problem of persuading the General to have a systematic method of getting advice and approval from the parties affected by the codes. The President approved the idea, which I hastily developed, of having advisory committees of labor and employers as an integral part of the code-making structure.

I was drawing heavily on New York State experience with which the President was familiar. There the Industrial Board has the power to adopt rules and regulations about the physical condition of the work places, which have the binding effect of law once adopted. But the law provides that the codes must be recommended and approved by an advisory committee consisting of equal numbers of employers and workers in the industry, together with representatives of the general public, who are usually experts on the subject matter of the code.

Drawing upon a familiar but tested system of delegation of authority with safeguards against abuse, Roosevelt said, "That's sound and we know how to work it."

It was no easy task to persuade General Johnson to agree to set up advisory committees. He didn't want to be bothered with them. A labor advisory committee seemed just an obstacle. An advisory committee of employers he thought unnecessary, since the employers would be in the group making the code. The larger competitive problems between industries he could settle himself. He had the interests of labor at heart too. That was what the NRA was all about. If he hadn't just given me a copy of *The Corporate State* by Raffaello Viglione, in which the neat Italian system of dictatorship for the benefit of the people was glowingly described, I might have felt easier about his counter-proposal to select a labor man to sit at his right and a businessman at his left, for whom he would outline the code and ask if they had any objections.

He recalled that in World War I he had had Hugh Frayne, an admirable but elderly and complacent retired labor leader, sit beside him on the Procurement Board, and he had been "fine—never made any objections or any trouble."

I finally persuaded him on the grounds that we might "have trouble" and many objections from labor if it was not consulted. He compromised to the extent that the Secretary of Labor should appoint the members of the Labor Advisory Committee and the Secretary of Commerce the Employer Advisory Committee.

He was afraid of committees selected by "these labor skates." He told me, "You appoint them, and you'll have to handle them." As a matter of fact, the advisory committees proved to be one of the strongest and most important parts of the NRA structure.

The Consumers' Advisory Committee was a last minute thought of my own to protect the community against a combination of labor and industry, which might have been adverse. Johnson probably agreed to it because Mary Rumsey, whom he liked and respected, promised to be chairman. Mrs. Rumsey was a public-spirited citizen of New York who had for years been a leader in civic and social reforms and was a Roosevelt supporter early in the campaign. She was E. H. Harriman's daughter and a convinced and advanced liberal. Every plan was considered on the basis of loyal friendship in General Johnson's mind. As a matter of fact, the Consumers' Committee never was able to do a great deal in the NRA except head off obviously bad economic practices like "the mark-up." But its existence established a new principle—that consumers must be considered in any economic plan—and it gave invaluable experience to government for future use in price and marketing regulations.

Many fine people representing management, labor, and the public were drawn into the government by the NRA. Averell Harriman, of the Union Pacific Railroad, recently Ambassador to Russia and now to England; John Winant, former Governor of New Hampshire and wartime Ambassador to England; Edward Stettinius, at that time member of the board and chairman of U. S. Steel; Max Gardner, former Governor of North Carolina; Frank Graham, president of the University of North Carolina; Alexander Sachs, economist to Lehman Brothers and chief economist in NRA; John Frey, chairman of the Metal Trades Department of the AF of L; Arthur Wharton, president, Machinists' Union; Thomas Kennedy, vice-president, United Mine Workers; Sidney Hillman, president, Amalgamated Clothing Workers; George Meany, secretary, New York State Federation of Labor; Martin P. Durkin, president of the Illinois State Federation of Labor and Labor Commissioner of Illinois; Emil Rieve, president, Hosiery Workers' Union; Clay Williams, counsel for the tobacco industries; Leon Henderson, economist of the Russell Sage Foundation; Harold Stephens,

Assistant Attorney General and brilliant leader of the Bar of Utah; William H. Davis, leading patent attorney of New York; Harriett Elliott, dean of women, University of North Carolina; Tom Blaisdell, economist and teacher at Amherst College. These and hundreds of others who could never have been brought into typical Civil Service jobs began to give enormous public service, which continued to be of benefit to the people even after the NRA was over.

For the first time in years young people—under forty-five and even under thirty—were used in government policy-making and administration. This was an advance where Roosevelt's daring gave a lift to the new generation. Responsibility and leadership developed among these younger groups, to our advantage in later war leadership, economic progress, and social justice.

The NRA became, in fact, one of the most vital causes of the revival of the American spirit, and signalized emergence from the industrial depression. Industry after industry, beginning with textiles—often regarded as a model code—set up codes of fair practice. These provided for fair competition and honorable practices in industry, and every code called for limitation of hours, minimum wage regulations, limitation or abolition of child labor, and other labor standards. The code proposed by the code authority of an industry was referred to the Labor, Employer, and Consumers' Advisory Committees, which discussed it and suggested changes. The administrator then held public hearings and, after considering the objections and support so brought out, recommended the amended code and took it to the President as the President's Re-employment Agreement. On signature it became effective.

After a few months of experience with NRA, it was evident that its operation had led to improvements in working conditions and the status of labor. Through NRA codes the regulation of hours of labor of men and women alike was undertaken for the first time in our history. Whereas state laws regulated only the hours of labor of women, some permitting women to work as many as ten hours a day, under NRA most of the codes prescribed forty hours a week as the standard, and about twenty-five per cent required a limit of eight hours or less as the hours to be worked any one day. Thus we came practically to a five-day, forty-hour week as standard in the United States.

This was accompanied by an increase rather than a decrease of hourly wages and weekly earnings. From June 1933 to June 1934 the average hourly earnings in manufacturing increased thirty-one per cent. The downward spiral of hourly earnings was checked and an upward spiral set in motion. The per capita weekly earnings in manufacturing increased fourteen per cent in the same period, while the cost of living increased less than seven per cent.

NRA gave us the opportunity to try many sorely needed social adjustments. The labor and employer advisory boards, for instance, were proving grounds for a technique of employer and employee conferences for the settlement of problems by mutual agreement.

From the beginning, all codes were referred before adoption to the Labor Department for analysis of labor provisions and for technical comment upon their practicability and enforceability. In many cases the staffs of the Children's Bureau, Women's Bureau, and the Bureau of Labor Statistics proved the only resources of the government for getting these codes on a sound, workable basis. The Women's Bureau, under Mary Anderson, obtained and compiled for NRA code use specific data on more than a hundred and twenty industries employing women during the fiscal year ended June 30, 1934. The methods of determining who were substandard workers and how hours might be averaged over weeks or months were worked out by people in the Department of Labor and submitted to NRA for adoption. The safety standards for the prevention of industrial accidents were prepared by the Department and recommended to NRA for inclusion in the codes. Methods of enforcement and compliance based on the long experience of the states in enforcing labor laws were worked out in the Department to guide the NRA. The President continued to insist on the use of existing government agencies to the advantage of all concerned.

NRA proved to be an education to the American people and government in the relationship among different elements in business. The idea of fair competition codes, implying that there had been unfair competition, was in itself educative. The vigorous fights in the NRA between small and large businesses and between different types of enterprises to get into the codes terms more favorable to themselves were an eye-opener to those who had not known the extent to which American business had been dominated, in its price, production, and labor policies, by certain great industrial enterprises, so few in number and yet so powerful.

Another lesson for the American people was education in trade unionism. Under the protection of Section 7A the trade unions started to organize in earnest. The rapid growth of membership when workers were relieved of the fear of being fired if they joined a union was evidence that there was a real trade union movement in the making in the United States. It was evidence too that trade unions could function effectively in determining some economic factors for the protection of their members and for the general welfare of their industries.

NRA was enormously popular. The Blue Eagle spread everywhere, and in some people's minds the New Deal and NRA were almost the same thing. As a matter of fact, other programs which had been inaugurated were also operating to improve conditions. But there was a great lift in the spirit of the people as they marched in parades, proudly displayed the Blue Eagle in their windows, and listened to Roosevelt explaining it on the radio. They began to have faith in themselves, and they determined to make it work.

Roosevelt's cabinet advisory committee was perhaps an example of the administrative duplication we were to see so many times in the future. I had never noticed this characteristic in the Albany days. My own duties had been well defined and segregated, and I had never heard complaints from heads of other departments that Roosevelt mixed up their work with other people's and caused confusion. That became a constant complaint in Washington. In Albany, however, he had had a much smaller administrative group and a much smaller problem and population to deal with.

Roosevelt always thought in terms of co-operation among

different elements in his government, and it never occurred to him that they would not co-operate but compete. In Albany he had had co-operation between departments merely by indicating that it would be a good idea. When I had talked to him in New York about industrial hygiene and had offered suggestions for its extension and improvement, he had replied, "Why don't you talk to the Health Commissioner about that, and then both of you come and tell me what you think." When I had raised a question of vocational education, particularly for the rehabilitation of injured and crippled people whom I had seen going through the workmen's compensation procedure, he had said, "Why don't you talk that over with the head of the Department of Education?" Such conferences of department heads had brought joint conclusions. Roosevelt had always been satisfied with these and had felt that if we agreed the answer must be pretty nearly right.

This background, I think, was always in the back of his mind when he brought in someone from another department in the Federal Government to participate in a program which a public official felt was his sole responsibility. This technique was also a kind of pipeline, not for a spy's report but to give him the vicarious experience of what was going on in an enterprise in which he was interested.

I know this was true in the NRA. He wanted to get from his cabinet officers continuous appraisal of the work of NRA. Hugh Johnson saw Roosevelt often enough, but his method of presenting what he had to say was so dramatic that the President sometimes got only the personality and the immediate battle in which Johnson was engaged, and failed completely to learn the underlying problems and policies.

As I studied the operation of the NRA, I saw certain dangers in its structure and in its purposes and policy. It occurred to me that we must bend every nerve to make the administration of the NRA a truly democratic process. This was always Roosevelt's instinctive direction, and in spite of confusions in operation and perhaps some people's drift to ideas of total controls, he managed to extract the good from the plan.

The President regarded the NRA purely as an emergency

agency. He hoped that out of this experience would come a pattern of hours and wages and operating practices and fair competition which might be embodied in law when the emergency was past, or adopted, without law, as part of the permanent way of our industrial life. He conceived of less administrative improvisations and more reliance on simple statute and administration lodged in the regular already established agencies of government.

Looking back on those days, I wonder how we ever lived through them. I cannot, even now, evaluate the situation. One thing I do see—it was dynamic. It was as though the community rose from the dead; despair was replaced by hope. Certainly an enormous number of good enterprises grew out of NRA whether or not it was itself successful. They were not only new enterprises in governing but new attitudes among businessmen. The laissez-faire and stick-in-the-mud type began to disappear from the leadership of business thinking, and younger, better educated, and more informed men came to have influence. Organized labor took a new lease on life. And what is perhaps of most importance to the future, business and labor began to participate with public officers in developing a sound, socially just economic and industrial pattern.

18.

LABOR AND THE CODES

The NRA was a seed bed out of which many other activities and experiments grew. It was not only an administrative enterprise, but also a forum in which employers and workers, the government and the public, met and debated ideas and issues.

I doubt that it had crossed the President's mind that NRA would raise problems of industrial relationships. The depression had been marked by few strikes or industrial disputes. Workmen had been frightened, and unions enfeebled by loss of jobs and of members. In 1933 American Federation of Labor membership had fallen to about two million. That embraced all the craft and industrial unions of the country, with the exception of the Railroad Brotherhoods, which had a membership of about 270,000, and the Amalgamated Clothing Workers, which had been separated from the AF of L for many years and had a small but effective membership.

The NRA Labor Advisory Board was not in a strong position when it came to pressing the point of view of the workers in the consideration of codes. There was relatively little organization in the large manufacturing and distributive industries where codes were needed most and were being drawn up first. The Labor Committee, when consulted about a code, was obliged to rely largely upon the Department of Labor for information about working conditions in an industry, an industry's earnings, the cost of living in the area, and so on. In many industries the Labor Department was the only spokesman for the workers' needs.

There were eight or ten employees in the Department in this period who did little but serve on code committees, recommending wages, hours, and other working conditions based on Departmental and Bureau research and judgment. The advice of the Labor Advisory Board was good and, on the whole, sound, because of the experience of its members. However, one could not escape the fact that representation of working people through their own organizations was pathetically limited.

Consider the case of the steel code, one of the first proposed under the NRA. The way it was handled was typical of the problems of the day.

The depression had dried up the demand for steel, and it is doubtful whether any steel company was making money. Some were losing badly. United States Steel, for example, was in a difficult situation. It had relied largely on structural and heavy steel and had not been driven to put in new rolling mills and blast furnaces or equip itself to produce the small items which, in the depth of the depression, had almost the only market. United States Steel was pressing for a steel code, and Bethlehem and the other large companies were also willing, though doubtful on some points.

It is possible, as has often been charged, that the great industrialists of the steel corporations were mostly concerned with reaching agreements, with the blessing of the NRA, which would be legal under the anti-trust act—agreements on pricing, marketing practices, and other matters. Certainly, however, those who voted for the NRA, and, to a large extent, steel employers themselves, had learned from the depression that prosperity was a two-faced goddess and that no one would be prosperous unless the workers had a modest prosperity. Their wages must enable them to be a continuous market for consumer goods, and in turn the makers and distributors of consumer goods would be a continuous market for steel and durable goods.

The co-operation of the steel industry, basic in America to so many other activities, was essential to the success of the NRA. General Johnson, working through his friendship with Bernard Baruch and others in the group of industrialists whom the President had persuaded to agree to this experiment in planned recovery, made consistent efforts to get early agreements from the steel industry to enter into a code.

Consulting with General Johnson, I agreed that the Depart-

ment of Labor would represent the steel workers in the preparation and development of this code. Since the workers in steel
were almost totally unorganized and no one on the Labor Advisory Committee had any authority to speak in their interests,
it was agreed that at the public hearing, the Secretary of Labor
should present the steel workers' case. It was the best we could
do under the circumstances.

I talked to the President, pointing out that it was unorthodox for a government official to submit a case for a partisan
position.

"It is no more unorthodox than the NRA itself," he said.
"After all, we are trying to do something. It is like a war. We
are dealing with unusual factors. The codes have to be adopted.
Otherwise we can't get recovery and purchasing power. Neither
can we get the support of all the people unless they know that
the real interests of labor have been considered.

"I think," he added, "the Secretary of Labor ought to be the
Secretary *for* labor. Go ahead. Do the best you can. And," he
went on with his big, hearty laugh, "if anybody says that's unorthodox, lay it onto me. They already have me tagged. But it's
doing the country good."

The economic material and the arguments I presented were
carefully prepared with the co-operation of my colleagues in
the Department of Labor and particularly of Alexander Sachs,
who contributed enormous economic knowledge to all NRA
problems. To the steel workers hidden away in remote communities, with access to the news only through local newspapers controlled largely by their employers, we wanted to make
clear the true interest of the government in them and their
problems. We wanted to make this clear to the public and to
the employers. We wanted it plain that there would not be a
complacent agreement between the government and the employers, but that the workers' interests would be realistically
and vigorously considered. To promote this I decided to visit
some steel producing areas. I wanted to seek out the workers
themselves, asking their views and complaints.

I telephoned the President. "Ostensibly, I am going to get
some information for my appearance in the public hearing on
the steel code," I told him. "Actually we probably know right

now the best level of wages, hours, and general working conditions to recommend. But I want you to know that I am going,
among other places, to Homestead, Pennsylvania, which has
such a bad historical record, and to other towns in that valley,
and down by Sparrow's Point where Bethlehem has its new-
est and, theoretically, most efficient plant. All the old-fashioned
steel companies are afraid of it. I don't know the labor situation
there."

"That's a good idea," he said, and chuckled. "But don't get
yourself arrested."

I took Father Francis Haas with me. I chose him because he
was a friend of labor, because the cloth of his profession, I felt,
would give us standing, and because I needed at least one other
individual to go along as aide and observer and helper. I did not
want to go "in state" with a battery of economic advisers, publicity men, minor public officials, and obsequious secretaries.

Later, when I told the President that I had been rebuked for
not taking an entourage, he said, "You and I have the instinct
for freedom of association. Unfortunately, I can't practice it
any more. What with the Secret Service and the politicians, I
never get the opportunity to get close to anybody." He spoke
with a touch of sadness. "But keep it up as long as you can,
don't let them get you down. The common people don't care
about all that style, Frances, and, after all, you and I are engaged in trying to bring them into things.

"You know, that is one of the great things about Eleanor,"
(Mrs. Roosevelt) he added, "she has already thrown off the
Secret Service. They can't keep up with her. The result is that
she goes where she wants to, talks to everybody, and does she
learn something!"

Before going on this trip I telephoned Myron Taylor, president
of United States Steel, and Eugene Grace, president of Bethlehem Steel. I asked for their co-operation and told them that I
wanted, above all, to talk with the workmen privately. Both
gentlemen politely agreed, whether reluctantly or not I shall
never know. The result was that plant managers were informed
by the top officers that I was to have complete co-operation.

It was in one of these towns, I think McKeesport, that I met

William Irwin, who later became president of United States Steel. He had concluded in his own mind that I should be given assistance. He was courteous, frank, and vigorous in his co-operation. I felt that he had a better appreciation of the steel workers and their problems than anyone I met in the steel industry. I felt there was a human exchange between him and them. They were not as sour and secretive about him as they were about other officers of the local mills.

I visited several big steel plants, and every courtesy was shown me by the superintendents. I talked with a good many steel workers on the job. Perhaps they did not speak freely because they were on the premises of their employer. I even visited some of their homes. I also escorted reporters from Pittsburgh newspapers and the wire services inside steel mills they had never been allowed to enter before.

The workers and their wives were quite uncritical. The idea that the government wanted to put a floor under wages was "wonderful." Everything we said was "just fine."

"You tell the President," many told me, "we are with him. Tell him we thank him."

My trip to the steel areas was made dramatically successful by the bad judgment of the Burgess of Homestead. Otherwise it would hardly have been noticed by anyone except the workers with whom I had conversations.

The Burgess, as the local executive officer is called somewhat archaically in these Pennsylvania communities, had consented to let me hold a meeting in the Hall of Burgesses.

The Burgess and all his officers were in the hall when the meeting started, which was proper and added a touch of official courtesy. The local newspaper editors were there, and many workingmen from the mills. These men were not too articulate, but they asked questions and stated points of view on what was the matter with the steel industry—usually specialized local complaints.

At the end of the meeting, as I was saying good-by to the Burgess, there was a disturbance downstairs. A newspaperman whispered that a lot of men were in the lower hall and on the sidewalk because the Burgess had not allowed them to come in.

With naïve simplicity, because I believed that the Burgess was a public officer to whom all citizens of his community were equally important, I told him I was sorry these men had not been able to attend. Could we not have the hall for a few moments more?

The Burgess, red in the face, puffed and stormed. "No, no, you've had enough. These men are not any good. They're undesirable Reds. I know them well. They just want to make trouble."

Perhaps they did want to make trouble, but if I didn't hear them they would make more trouble. Perhaps they might have something constructive to suggest about the code. If I did not hear these people the public reaction would be bad—"steel workers have no voice, steel trust controls the code." I could imagine the words and the headlines! Nor did I think it would be good for the steel industry. I had met good men in it, and not all of them were determined to "suppress their workers." At any rate, I had been brought up in the tradition of free speech. I took it for granted that it was the "duty of public officers," as Plato says, "to listen patiently to all citizens."

I said good-by to the Burgess and went downstairs. I found a couple of hundred people, many of them angry. They had been pushed out of the building onto the sidewalk by the local police. I tried to be as pleasant and polite as possible. The last thing I wanted was a difference with the local authorities. I stood on the steps of the Burgesses' Hall and started to make a little speech.

"My friends, I am so sorry that you were not able to get into the hall," I began. "It was very crowded, but perhaps we can hear what you have to say right here."

By this time the Burgess, two secretaries, and the police appeared, shouting, "You can't talk here! You are not permitted to make a speech here—there is a rule against making a speech here."

The men on the sidewalk were tense with interest, wondering what I would do next.

There was a park across the way. "All right—I am sorry. We will go over to the public park."

Immediately the red-faced Burgess and his police were at my side. "You can't do that, there is an ordinance against holding meetings in a public park."

I protested, "This is just a hearing, not a meeting; it won't be long, only a few minutes."

The Burgess kept reiterating that they were "undesirable Reds," although they looked like everybody else to me.

As I hesitated, my eye caught sight of the American flag flying over a building on the opposite side of the square. Ah, I thought, that must be the post office, and I remembered that federal buildings in any locality are under the jurisdiction of the Federal Government. I did not know the politics of the postmaster, but I was an officer of the Federal Government and I must have some rights there.

To the crowd I said, "We will go to the post office, there is the American flag."

It was almost closing time. I have never forgotten that postmaster and his assistance. I had only a moment to explain matters to him. Nothing very dramatic happened. The people filed in, and the employees hung around to enjoy the meeting. We stood in the long corridor lined with postal cages. Somebody got me a chair, and I stood on it and made a brief speech about the steel code. I asked if anybody wanted to speak. Twenty or thirty men did. They said they were greatly pleased with the idea. They said they wished the government would free them from the domination of the steel trust. One man spoke about philosophic and economic principles. A few denounced the community. I invited the most vocal and obstreperous of the speakers to come to Washington and promised that he would have an opportunity to appear at the public hearing. We ended the meeting with handshaking and expressions of rejoicing that the New Deal wasn't afraid of the steel trust.

That evening in Homestead, McKeesport, and in one or two other communities we held meetings in the parish hall of local churches. Father Haas had been busy arranging for these during the day, and the local pastors had sent word to steel-worker parishioners. One pastor in particular I remember—a Polish priest who spoke almost no English. His parishioners came scrubbed within an inch of their lives, with hair slicked down and with clean overalls or coats on. They understood no English either. The priest brought along an interpreter. First, under the pastor's direction, we said a few prayers, including a prayer for the President, which the people recited in unison and with great feeling. I was handed a translation; they were asking the blessing of Almighty God upon the President. I spoke, and many of them spoke briefly, and with confidence in this protected place. I learned as much about the hopes and needs of the steel workers through those half-dozen meetings in the parish halls as from the economic studies which the learned people in the Labor Department had prepared.

My own lamentable lack of instinct for publicity prevented me from making effective use of that visit. But a smart local newspaperman wired the story of the Burgess of Homestead turning me out of the hall and of the meeting we held in the federal building. On my return to Washington the press was at my door wanting to know what had happened. When one reporter asked me why the Burgess had acted like that, I replied, "Why, he seemed a little nervous."

The President read about the "nervous Burgess of Homestead" and telephoned me, laughing and saying, "You did just the right thing and you gave the post office free advertising. That's priceless." And he began expounding one of his favorite themes. "You know, the post office in every community ought to be the people's contact with the government. We ought to make more of it. The post office is a natural for co-operation between the people and the Federal Government."

A number of weeks later we were preparing for final adoption of the code, and I wanted to get what had become common in all NRA codes: a statement from employers, workers, and the government that the code met with their approval, and that they would agree to operate in accordance with its terms. Since there were no organized steel workers, it occurred to me that if the operators of all steel companies would meet in my office with officials of the Department of Labor, and if we could have William Green, president of the AF of L, as a general representative of workers in the steel industry, although of course in no sense their true representative, we could give agreement to the code in a few minutes.

Green was entirely willing. When the heads of the big steel companies—Eugene Grace, Myron Taylor, William Irwin, Ernest Weir, Thomas Girdler—and executives of smaller steel companies, came into my office, Green was sitting there. I started the introductions.

Most of them did not permit themselves to be introduced to Mr. Green. They backed away into a corner, like frightened boys. It was the most embarrassing social experience of my life. I had never met people who did not know how, with hypocrisy perhaps but with an outward surface of correct politeness, to say how-do-you-do even to people they detested. I had been engaged in conversation with Green and went right back to him, thinking perhaps he would not notice the coldness. After a while, at the invitation of the steel executives' lawyers, I went over to the corner where they were having their huddle to see what ailed them. I found that they had expected to see only me and economists of the Department of Labor. They did not see how they could meet with the president of the AF of L. I was a little shocked, unable to believe that grown men could be so timid. But their faces were long, their eyes were solemn, and they were the picture of men with no self-assurance whatsoever.

Only William Irwin did not join the huddle. He pulled up a chair next to William Green and in an entirely personal and jolly way they chatted, not about the steel industry, of course, but about politics, public affairs, the NRA, and the weather.

I still could not see why anybody should be afraid of William Green, mildest and most polite of men. The steel executives explained to me privately that if it were known that they had sat down in the same room with William Green and talked with him, it would ruin their long-time position against labor organization in their industry.

"But," I argued with them, "Mr. Green doesn't represent the steel workers. He is not a steel worker. I will tell you what he is going to say."

I gave them a copy of his prepared remarks. He was to make a laudatory statement regarding the NRA and to give his full approval to the proposed steel code.

No, that would not do. They were still afraid that it would become known in the steel industry towns that they had spoken to Mr. Green of the AF of L. This backing and filling went on for almost three quarters of an hour. The difficulty penetrated to Green. I apologized to him. He was courtesy itself. In the end, however, he left in a huff.

As the great barons of steel filed out, still looking solemn and sorrowful, I could not resist the temptation to tell them that their behavior had surprised me and that I felt as though I had entertained eleven-year-old boys at their first party rather than men to whom the most important industry in the United States had been committed.

I told the story to the President. By the time I spoke to him I had recovered my sense of proportion and could join him in a good laugh. This episode he never forgot. He often referred to it years later, and even after Myron Taylor had become one of his best friends he would say, "You know, Myron has learned a lot from us. He is a better man than he was that day he wouldn't talk with William Green. And I think he is happier."

Taylor, of course, eventually got to the point where he talked easily not only with Green but with Philip Murray and John L. Lewis and took a constructive and active interest in labor relations.

A few weeks later I was having a dinner party of twelve or fifteen guests and Green was among them. During the dinner a member of my family was called to the telephone and I heard her say, "Oh, how nice! Do come over. We're having a few people in to dinner. Do join us for coffee."

I didn't think to ask who it might be. But we had no sooner left the dining-room and I was standing with Green near the door of the living-room when the door opened and in came Mr. and Mrs. Myron Taylor. This time everyone's manners were equal to the occasion. After a little chat about nothing Taylor and Green sat down on a small sofa and with one other gentleman engaged in a long and apparently absorbing conversation.

It was broken up only when Mrs. Taylor went over and said, "Myron, can't I talk to Mr. Green too?"

Our experience with the textile code was also revealing.

When the code, one of the earliest adopted, was in preparation, we had the same problem of inadequate union representation, but there was a union, known as the United Textile Workers of America. Thomas McMahan was president. A plump, jolly, elderly man, he had years ago resigned himself to the idea of a small union in a few factories. Now and then they had tried to organize in the South. Unionizing programs often turned out badly.

When our economists had worked out what would probably be the general requirements of the textile industry, I sent for McMahan. I found he had not formulated an idea of what the workers would like in the code.

"We have always struggled," he said, "to get the eight-hour day, so I thought I would say, if you want me to appear at the public hearing on the code, that we want the eight-hour day."

"This code stipulates a forty-hour week," I said. "Don't for pity's sake talk about forty-eight-hour demands. Haven't you been reading the paper? The forty-hour week is to be recommended by the Department of Labor and the employers' group. Surely labor can't be behind on that."

With a startled expression he said, "All right, if you say so, Miss Perkins." So much progress was a surprise to some parts of the labor movement.

Some industries had labor well organized. If they did not have large membership, at least they had a corps of thoughtful, competent people able to see better than any government economist what the terms of a code ought to be. The clothing workers, represented by David Dubinsky and Sidney Hillman; the machinists and metal trades workers, represented by John Frey; the printers, adequately represented by many of their officers; the building trades, whose industries for the most part were not being put under codes, were organized and understood the contributions labor was being asked to make. The United Mine Workers, although far from peak membership, had sufficient strength to be effective and were prepared to represent the workers of that industry intelligently.

On the whole, the gains made for labor were greater than could possibly have been made by waiting for the longer and slower process of organization. The gains, of course, were not aimed exclusively at making things better for labor. Without an internal market supported by the wages of millions of working people, there would be a further decline of our economy and a deeper depression. That was the theory. The setting of minimum wage rates, sometimes even rates above the minimum, by the code process had a revivifying effect. It gave to working people a little money in their pockets to spend of a Saturday night, and the results affected all industry.

Combined with the relief program and with public works, it constituted an effective demonstration of the theories which John Maynard Keynes had been preaching and urging upon the English government.

Roosevelt himself was unfamiliar with the economics of Keynes. Others in the administration had read his works, but he had not yet attained popular acceptance. His was the formula that public expenditures should be increased when private expenditures fall off.

Keynes came to this country in June 1934 and again later on. He was liberally consulted, not, I think, by Hugh Johnson, but by a number of other people in the government who were anxious to have his comment. He pointed out that the combination of relief, public works, raising wages by NRA codes, distributing moneys to farmers under agricultural adjustment, was doing exactly what his theory would indicate as correct procedure. He was full of faith that we in the United States would prove to the world that this was the answer.

When we began to draw in our horns on public works and relief expenditures in 1937, he predicted what turned out to be true, that we would have another decline.

Keynes visited Roosevelt in 1934 rather briefly, and talked lofty economic theory.

Roosevelt told me afterward, "I saw your friend Keynes. He left a whole rigmarole of figures. He must be a mathematician rather than a political economist."

It was true that Keynes had delivered himself of a mathematical approach to the problems of national income, public and private expenditure, purchasing power, and the fine points of his formula. Coming to my office after his interview with Roosevelt, Keynes repeated his admiration for the actions Roosevelt had taken, but said cautiously that he had "supposed the President was more literate, economically speaking." He pointed out once more that a dollar spent on relief by the government was a dollar given to the grocer, by the grocer to the wholesaler, and by the wholesaler to the farmer, in payment of supplies. With one dollar paid out for relief or public works or anything else, you have created four dollars' worth of national income.

I wish he had been as concrete when he talked to Roosevelt, instead of treating him as though he belonged to the higher echelons of economic knowledge.

19.

TROUBLE IN COAL

Most industries were anxious to be put under a code. Large industrialists and small businessmen, labor and the public, were glad and eager to try this method. All sorts of people and industries, which ought never to have been under a code, came clamoring to Washington, to Johnson, to the President, to all of us, to say through their representatives, "We want a code, we must have a code."

It is unfortunate that General Johnson fell for the popular demand. Time and energy were spent holding long-drawn-out sessions and looking up economic data for the fishhook or collar-button industries and other such small specialized divisions of economic activity, which did not need to be treated so specifically, but which could have naturally followed the principles of the codes in the basic industries. Local retail trades codes, in particular, were unnecessary and unfortunate. Johnson was advised that we would do well to stick to fifteen or twenty basic industries and be sure that the codes for those industries were sound and practical, based on solid economic information. The administrative and enforcement problems would have been infinitely ameliorated.

Johnson, however, liked the excitement, and I am not sure that the President didn't like it too. It gave him that sense of self-verification he found so necessary to keep his mind fresh and alert about the needs of the people. When I protested that the NRA would bog down under the terrific load of unimportant codes it was setting up, he commented, "Oh, they will work out of it. But it is important to let people find this form of expression. It is in the right direction, and we have to let them participate even though their participation is not very significant."

There were some basic industries, however, which held back from the adoption of codes. A case in point was the coal industry.

At one time the coal industry was the sickest in the United States. By confession of the coal operators, they were in despair over their capacity ever to revive it. The decline of purchasing power had affected the market for transportation, the market for steel, and the market for manufactured goods, which coal supplied. Always two or three steps removed from consumer goods, except for the coal which went to householders, this basic industry was perishing for lack of markets.

One of the most vivid memories of my first week in Washington was the visit of a large group of coal operators to the President. It was a visit in which they expressed their sense of defeat.

The President was extremely preoccupied with the bank closing and fiscal policy. He had hundreds of appointments, and a host of projects, later developed into an administrative program on the domestic front, was under consideration. He heard them courteously, but he could not take the time to hear all they had to say. He made a quick decision to get them off his hands and, at the same time, get some thoughtful attention for their problem. He remembered that the Secretary of the Interior had the Bureau of Mines in his Department as well as responsibility for the natural resources of the country. He realized that if the mines were shut down permanently there would be problems of unemployment, and he thought of the Labor Department. Without consulting us he turned the coal operators over to the Secretary of the Interior and the Secretary of Labor.

We had no preliminary preparation. We had been at work only a few days and were still getting our Departments organized and trying to find our bearings. But we held two days of the strangest hearings that it has ever been my duty to sit in on. Absolutely new in the government, Harold Ickes and I sat behind a table, looking solemn as owls and representing the Government of the United States. We were so new at being "the Government" that it was really only the externals of representation.

But I suddenly got the sense of responsibility to a whole industry and to a whole nation and not merely to the President or to my special field. I had a sense of what "the Government of the United States," put into just those words, means in its influence, leadership, and conscience for all the people of the United States. In a democracy this responsibility of being "the Government," of being the individuals who, for the moment, are trusted with the duty of saying "yes" or "no" within the constitutional guarantees, is something scarcely faced by most people in advance of assuming office.

I did not ask Ickes about what went on in his mind, but certainly these ideas went through mine, and I said to myself, "Lord, I am not worthy, but I must do these things. I must give them my best thought and attention." A newly realized sense of authority is sobering.

We heard their stories. They were catastrophic stories: whole communities were practically down; local grocery stores could not operate; local schoolteachers were not being paid; local merchants and transportation systems were nearly bankrupt; everybody was in debt to somebody; soon the time would be at hand when wholesale grocers, clothing supply people, and others would no longer send goods to local merchants because their credit was almost exhausted; and all this misfortune came because the mines were down.

The miners, prime source of business in the small communities, had nothing to spend when the week was out. A whole community of middle-class folk, living out of serving the needs of the productive workers in the mines, was almost in collapse in some towns. There was practically total unemployment. The operators laid before us their reports of earnings for the last ten years. It was a story of constant decline. Surpluses were gone and stockholders hadn't been paid. Salaries to absolutely essential executives were in arrears. The operators described the plight of mine workers in terms of sympathy, which made one realize that when it comes to the facts of life there can be real understanding between owners and workers in particular industries.

The only exceptions were a few highly productive mines in the smokeless field where, because of the physical configuration of the coal seam and a favorable transportation situation, coal could be mined and go to the seaboard with a minimum of expenditure for power and transportation.

The burden of recommendations from coal operator after coal operator was that the government must take over the mines. "Will the government please take them?" they pleaded. "The operators will sell the mines to the government at any price fixed by the government. Anything so we can get out of it."

I found myself at the noon recess saying to one operator after another, "Now take courage, Mr. X. You can do it. You'll be able to run these mines. It isn't so bad as you think. I don't think you should give up. Just have courage. It's your work in the world. The government's going to do the things necessary to relieve the financial strain."

I didn't know exactly what the government was going to do, but the government had a platform pledged to do something to make it possible for the people to buy once more and for the wheels of industry to turn again. We were unable to give them any outline of what the government would do, but Mr. Ickes and I strove to encourage them to hold out a little while longer. We assured them that the government did not want to take or buy the mines; that it believed that the mines had better be operated by private ownership.

Ickes whispered to me, "What in the world would we do with the mines if we took them over? How could the Government operate them? Nobody in this Government knows how to run a coal mine. This isn't a nationalization program we have undertaken with Roosevelt."

The coal operators felt a little better at the end of the day. We had established a cordial relationship with them. Secretary Ickes began to study, through the Bureau of Mines and other agencies, the economy of the coal industry. I put Labor Department people to work examining the labor situation in the industry. I found that it was just as desperate as the coal operators had indicated. A larger proportion of employable people who had worked regularly were out of work than in any other occupa-

tion. Because of the very nature of the coal industry, these people were, for the most part, stuck in remote hamlets where, if
there was no work in the coal mines, there was no work at anything else. The young people had no way to get out of the valley,
nor any hope of a job elsewhere.

Soon the NRA was going strong with codes in textile, steel,
some of the machinery industries, and other basic industries.
Soon there were beginnings of a revival of work. Opportunity
opened and hope once more smiled all over the country.

The coal operators began to feel better. They began to find a
market for their coal. The steel mills were buying again. The
railroad systems were buying. People were moving. Goods were
moving. Now the coal operators not only thought it unnecessary to give or sell their mines to the government, but thought
that perhaps they could avoid all the regulations that came
with a code.

It was at this point that the workers in the mines began to
get angry. John L. Lewis had made a big drive for organization
in the first weeks of the NRA, and thousands of new members
had joined the United Mine Workers. The literature sent out in
the organizing campaign had told the miners, with more drama
than truth, that "the President wanted them to join the United
Mine Workers" so that they might work with the Blue Eagle
and have a code which would spell liberty and better times
in the coal industry. They had wanted to help the President
revive the country and had responded to this appeal. Now they
wanted to know where the code was.

The coal operators were divided into three or four separate
groups. They had never co-operated among themselves. The
Southern Appalachian area, the western area, the Pennsylvania
or Northern Appalachian area, and the deep southern area
had separate organizations and divergent ideas. In addition,
the mines which had been able to operate at a profit even in the
depression saw no reason why they should be asked to co-
operate in building a code which would keep the marginal
mines alive and in competition with big-scale, profitable coal
operation. There was delay, more delay, and still more delay in
the preparation of a code.

The economists and the NRA worked on it. Tentative codes were drawn. They were passed around by various officers of the NRA to different groups of coal operators, corrected, and taken back again. Labor began to growl. The miners held meetings and passed resolutions demanding a code.

John L. Lewis, who sat on the Labor Advisory Board, was well aware of this demand and expressed labor's need for a code. But no one thought John L. Lewis "a menace" in those days. He was regarded as an intelligent, capable labor leader who was famous for living up to his contracts. He became quite a personal friend of Hugh Johnson's. They "got on" well and even sang sad songs in harmony coming home from NRA meetings. This was 1933.

At this point General Johnson asked the President to invite some individual coal operators to the White House and to try personally to persuade them to agree to a code. This was an illustration of General Johnson's almost touching but naïve feeling that the President was all-wise and all-persuasive and that anybody would do anything the President asked him to do. Johnson had developed a kind of simple adoration which he believed everybody ought to share, and it was always a shock to him when they didn't. If the President asked him to do something, he felt sure that he would have no alternative but to say yes. I once tried to tell him that his own approach came from the combination of his emotional nature and his training as a soldier and that he mustn't expect other people to give up their right to differ with any President, even Roosevelt, but he persisted to the end in condemning those few who wouldn't go along with the Blue Eagle and President Roosevelt.

Some of the coal operators were invited to spend an evening at the White House. At the last minute I suggested that we get at least one or two whom we knew to be well disposed, so that there might be in the conference a nucleus of people who would like to say "yes." We added a few names, among them Josephine Roche. She was a bona fide owner of a coal mine, operating it herself in the Rocky Mountain area. Miss Roche came, co-operated, handled herself with skill, and gathered around herself a little group of coal operators who saw the advantage of having a code to protect them against the unfair competition of the large coal operators.

At last it was agreed that a code should be put into operation. Even then there were innumerable delays, and labor grew more restive. In looking back, I feel quite sure now that the officers of the United Mine Workers promoted the restiveness, or at least did not attempt to allay it. There were meetings and resolutions and threats of strike. Johnson grew nervous. He could not endure the thought of an interruption in the stream of activity out of which industrial recovery was to grow. A strike, particularly in coal, would affect every industrial activity adversely; it would be, he thought, intolerable.

But there came a day in the Pennsylvania area when the men were to go out. It was a Saturday—a day off—and the next day was Sunday; there was time to move. Johnson, moving with the speed which was one of his talents, asked Edward F. McGrady, Assistant Secretary of Labor, whom I had lent him as a general aide and liaison officer, to go and make speeches all through the troubled area and to promise that Hugh Johnson would appoint a labor mediation board which would assist the coal miners to settle their differences. By this time many grievances were being voiced, but the principal grievance was that there was no code.

Such a board was hastily selected. The board held conferences, brought people together, and the strike was soon over. This was really the genesis of the National Labor Relations Act.

In the course of time a coal code was adopted but, more important than the code for the coal industry, a basis was laid in the conferences for an act known as the Guffey Coal Act, which was regulatory over the price and marketing structure of the coal industry and had the endorsement of both labor and employers.

20.

MEDIATION

By late summer of 1933 there was restiveness in other places. Workers in some plants were complaining to the NRA that codes were not being complied with and that employers were refusing to meet with committees of workers as the latter believed they should under Section 7A. There were grievances that foremen were requiring tasks beyond the capacity of an individual to perform. The stretch-out, this was called.

The conciliators of the Department of Labor hurried here and there. The Labor Department set up special boards to deal with worker-employer relationships in particular industries; we were gradually thrashing out the threatened disputes and making adjustments. There were not many difficult strikes, but strike talk was everywhere. I suppose this is characteristic of a period after depression when times are, or look, better. Labor then seeks to correct in one drive all abuses and difficulties that have grown up in depression times. No doubt an enormous number of grievances had accumulated during the depression.

At times the local labor pressure was beyond the capacity of labor union officers to handle. It was difficult to know how much of it was a spontaneous movement of the workers; how much was an expression of grievance against union leaders who, the rank and file thought, had been negligent of their interest; how much was stirred up from the outside; and how much was an actual demand of the rank and file for immediate improvement of working conditions.

It must be remembered that the NRA itself created grievances between labor and employers which had not existed previously. Publicity led working people to believe that a code was their salvation if they were to have the protection and advantages everyone else was getting. While the terms of the code, particularly for minimum wages and maximum hours, might be more favorable than anything the union had been able to achieve in an industry, workers were aggrieved if their wage rates did not match those of some other industry.

Section 7A was subject to excited interpretation by organizers, who gave working people an exaggerated notion of their rights. I do not question that, in the light of later court decisions, those rights were inherent in the NRA legislation. But, pending such court decisions, there was ample dispute over the scope of the rights. And this made for grievances in threatened strikes, and sometimes strikes.

In factories never before organized, the workers suddenly joined a union. Managers were amazed when newly elected union officers—men who had been working for them for ten years—came in and demanded collective bargaining and a contract. That wasn't what the management of the factory had anticipated. It was contrary to practice and custom, and the workers were swift rather than gradual in their demands for collective bargaining contracts. If demands were not immediately granted, there was a grievance.

Employers banged the table and said they would not meet with their workers. They would abide by the code they had signed, but they would be hanged if they would meet with a committee of their workers. They never had done that. What business was it of the workers'? They were paying the code wages, working the code hours, and whatever else the workers wanted was out!

Other employers had consulted their lawyers and had never signed the code. Now they insisted it did not bind them. More labor trouble!

General Johnson and his office were besieged by people threatening strikes. Johnson's idea was that the Labor Advisory Board ought to rush out and give orders that no one was to strike. Members of the board often tried this, out of sheer good will for the General and out of a desire that there should be no interruptions in the NRA recovery program. It was hardly successful, and added to confusion.

Johnson thought that the Department of Labor ought to

"rule" labor. He would draw himself up, scowling and throwing out his chest, and say to protesters, "Why, you should see the Secretary of Labor. The Secretary of Labor will issue the necessary orders, tell you what you are to do and what the employer is to do."

There was no such power in the office of the Secretary of Labor, nor should there be.

One day General Johnson telephoned that he was thinking of appointing a mediation board inside the NRA. I protested that the facilities of the Department of Labor might better be used and developed for this special service. He argued that it would be impossible to wait for the slow process of conciliation. Moreover, he said the recalcitrant employers who, he thought, were the chief promoters of labor disputes, would never respond to Labor Department conciliators. I agreed to help him build up a labor mediation board in the NRA.

He wanted Robert Wagner as chairman for several reasons. Wagner was a Senator of the United States and as such represented congressional authority and stability. He was known throughout the country as a friend of labor and had been the author of many bills which labor favored. Moreover, he was honestly interested in the NRA.

Johnson's idea was that the Board should have labor and employer members. We got hold of a good group: Senator Wagner, chairman; Leo Wolman, economist; Walter C. Teagle of Standard Oil; William Green; John L. Lewis; Gerard Swope, president of General Electric Company; and Louis E. Kirstein, president of Filene & Company in Boston.

The Board was later augmented by the appointment of Pierre S. DuPont of the DuPont Corporation; Henry S. Dennison, the Massachusetts paper manufacturer; Ernest Draper, vice-president of Hills Brothers; George L. Berry, president of the International Pressmen's Union; the Reverend Francis J. Haas of the Catholic University of America; S. Clay Williams, attorney; and Leon C. Marshall of Johns Hopkins.

The Board, set up in late August 1933, started out to deal with every labor dispute that came to the attention of the NRA. It did a good job. It settled a lot of disputes by common sense, persuasion, and resourcefulness in finding compromises. It learned a lot, which was reflected in its reports. I tried to see that these got to the President. He was also learning a lot about industrial life and tension in the United States. He hadn't expected so much trouble.

The Board found a frequent trouble was that many employers refused to permit trade union membership or to meet with their workers. Senator Wagner did his best to be persuasive. Finally he became angry with resistance to what he thought, out of his New York experience, was simple fairness. Something must be done to protect a man from being "fired" for union activity or membership and to insist on the right of workers to collective bargaining through representatives of their own choosing.

Other members of the Board in part shared Senator Wagner's resentment. But the only penalty they could apply was to take away the Blue Eagle, sign of full compliance with the National Recovery Administration.

There was a particularly stubborn owner of a hosiery mill who, code or no code, Blue Eagle or no, would not deal with the union. He asserted that the workers in his mill did not belong to the union and did not want it, and that the union was trying to "horn in." He had been persuaded to come for a conference to Washington. Gerard Swope dealt with him in my office. Swope, a patient mediator, tried to reason with him. This tough operator was a German and looked like a Nazi. But that day he merely would not agree to meet the union.

"I have a suggestion," Swope said. "Let them vote on it. We'll have a free election by secret ballot and every employee of yours can vote whether he wants to be represented by the union or not. That's fair, isn't it? Then you'll know."

"Vy," replied the mill owner in a thick accent, "vy should they vote?"

"Because," said Swope quietly, though he was boiling and furious by this time, "this is America and that's the way we do things here."

The employer refused, but the next week we took the vote anyhow, under the supervision of the local election authorities,

with the Conciliation Board of the Department of Labor checking the voting lists. The workers voted overwhelmingly for the
union.

This, I think, was the first instance of such a vote, which later
became a routine matter required by the law Senator Wagner
was then at work upon. It grew out of the necessities and accommodations of the situation.

I was sure General Johnson would not want Wagner's proposal to become a permanent law, and he didn't. But he never
told Wagner openly that he did not approve.

Wagner was powerful in the Senate at the time because he
had foresight and had been successful. The measures he had
stood for through the years, sometimes unsuccessfully, were
now the most popular the country had seen. A movement grew
in the Senate to support his bill.

It ought to be on the record that the President did not take
part in developing the National Labor Relations Act and, in
fact, was hardly consulted about it. It was not a part of the
President's program. It did not particularly appeal to him when
it was described to him. All the credit for it belongs to Wagner.

The proposed bill, it must be remembered, was remedial.
Certain unfair practices which employers had used against
workers to prevent unionization and to cripple their economic
strength had been uncovered by Wagner in the administration
of Section 7A of NRA. The bill sought to correct these specific,
known abuses, and did not attempt to draw up a comprehensive
code of ethical behavior in labor relations. Such a comprehensive code, however, was needed. Roosevelt supported my suggestion that labor leaders who wanted to distinguish themselves
should draw up such a code and let us take a look at it. A code
developed by labor itself even now might be both knowing and
practical and might evoke the adherence of the great body of
labor people. Principles so arrived at might be added to the
National Labor Relations Act in the future.

Since Senator Wagner was going to introduce a bill anyhow,
we wanted it to be a good practical bill.

I was frank in my judgment that if the bill were to become
law the National Labor Relations Board should be set up in the

Department of Labor rather than as an independent agency. I had sound reasons; they seem just as sound now.

An independent agency makes too much demand upon the time and attention of the President, or else it ignores the general policies of the administration and becomes doctrinaire. Moreover, there had long existed in the Department of Labor a Division of Conciliation. Its job was to adjust industrial disputes, and its mediation rested strongly upon a basis of voluntary cooperation. If the new activity were lodged in the Department of Labor we should be able, by the conference method, to get agreement in most disputes. I argued also that it would be wise to concentrate in the Labor Department, a going concern, all problems concerned with labor. The selection and training of subordinate personnel would be likely to be more practical in an established experienced agency.

General Johnson was equally determined that the new enterprise should be within the NRA. He actually conceived of the NRA not as an emergency agency, but as a permanent regulatory function of government.

He once confided, "When this crisis is over and we have the recovery program started, there won't be any need for a Department of Labor or a Department of Commerce, and perhaps some other departments. The NRA will embrace all those functions and carry them out effectively.

"Oh, yes," he added, as if fearing to hurt my feelings, "the Department of Labor can be a research unit within the NRA."

When I explored Johnson's determination to keep everything within the NRA, I found myself beginning to be doubtful of him. I wondered whether he knew what he was about, whether he had a clear conception of public policy in the United States, whether he understood the democratic process and the representative form of government, and whether he might be moving by emotion and indirection toward a dangerous pattern.

By this time Johnson was a sick man. Perhaps he was not well when the NRA began. Often he was obliged to be away for days and weeks at a time, without communicating with his office. It was difficult to deal with him and he didn't like to admit he was ill. He wanted to believe that everybody would do what he wanted done whether he was there or not. His administrative rule was very personal, and personal loyalties of an extreme kind were the principal test for associates and subordinates. It became increasingly difficult to come to any decisions involving him.

Senator Wagner, Simon Rifkind, his assistant, Charles E. Wyzanski, solicitor of the Department of Labor, Donald Richberg, counsel of NRA, and others had agreed that the NRA was no place for a permanent National Labor Relations Board. Whether it should be in the Department of Labor we had not yet decided. The discussion never ended because Johnson never stayed with it long enough to come to conclusions. Finally I insisted that we take an entire morning and reach a decision. Johnson pleaded that he was too busy, but he came to my office, bringing Richberg with him. We had agreed in advance that at this meeting we would decide the final location of the National Labor Relations Board.

We went over the same old arguments. Johnson got restless and fatigued; he digressed from time to time. We could make no progress.

Suddenly he rose and said, "I can't stand this any longer. I have too much to do. I can't stay here and fiddle around about a thing like this. I don't know what you are talking about. I don't know what your objections are."

In some consternation, I said, "But, General Johnson, we must settle this. We agreed we would settle this today. Senator Wagner has just stated why he does not think this Board should be in the NRA. We haven't got your assent to his position or anything else. You must agree today to something or we can't make any headway. The Senator is going to introduce this bill at once."

Johnson spoke explosively, "Well, I'll leave my counsel here. Don Richberg has my power of attorney. Whatever he says is all right."

I went over to Johnson, took him by the coat lapels, and said emphatically, "General Johnson, do we understand you and will you stick by this? Don Richberg will represent you. He will stay in this conference as long as we need him. Is that correct?"

"Yes," said Johnson.

"Do you promise that you will be bound by it?"

"Yes," he said. "Whatever Richberg says, I agree to."

"All right," I said, "I can release you from your promise to stay here all day."

We agreed that the Board should not be put into the NRA.

I made a strong argument for its inclusion in the Department of Labor, but Wagner was opposed for reasons which, when viewed in retrospect, seem slightly humorous.

"With all respect to you," he said, "I want to say that the people of this country think that the Department of Labor is pro-labor. If the NLRB were in the Department of Labor, I could never make them believe that the decisions of the Board would not be pro-labor."

One sometimes wonders a little ruefully whether or not this Board would not have been better off under the more pedestrian supervision of the Department of Labor. One does not know. However, the Labor Department was never accused of being more pro-labor than the National Labor Relations Board, and those accusations grew more extreme and exaggerated as time went on.

In any case, Wagner held firmly to his view that the Board should be set up as an independent agency. The bill was prepared that way. Wagner, Richberg, and I examined it and we thought it was within the limits of our agreement. Wagner prepared to introduce it.

About two weeks later I had a telephone message one Saturday morning from General Johnson's secretary. Johnson had been in Walter Reed Hospital for several weeks, but he wanted to see me that afternoon at two. He was also asking Senator Wagner to come. Neither Senator Wagner nor I had the slightest idea why he wanted to see us. But he was sick; we were fond of him; we had all been in this NRA enterprise together; we went.

We found him in bed, quite ill, somewhat confused in expression. He didn't talk about the National Labor Relations Act. He talked about loyalty; he talked about co-operation; he talked about how he had trusted us. I realized that he thought we had sold him down the river about something.

"General Johnson," I said, "we followed Richberg's views on

the final draft of the National Labor Relations Act. You remember, don't you, that you told me Richberg could speak on your behalf?"

"Richberg is not my friend," he replied. "Richberg is not loyal to me."

This was a new one. Poor Senator Wagner was distressed. We stayed for two hours. When we left the Senator said to me, "Do you know what Johnson wanted to talk to us about?"

I had thought originally, and so reported to the President, that the National Labor Relations bill was unlikely to become law. I felt sure that labor would object, for the recognition of a union under the NLRA would depend upon the counting of noses. A labor union would have to prove it had the backing of a majority of the workers in a plant. This was certainly new doctrine in 1934.

It had not been AF of L policy in the past to count noses before a committee went in to see the boss to demand better wages, hours, working conditions. No labor union had ever asked a government board to tell it whether they could represent a whole factory or one department or one craft. That was the union leader's judgment. Closed shops had been gained by bold methods at times. This bill would make that impossible. A union would have to prove majority support.

I expected Matthew Woll and William Green of the AF of L to tell me that they were opposed to the Wagner bill. They were enthusiastically in favor of it. I remember Woll saying with a superior smile, "My dear Miss Perkins, times have changed and we must change with them."

The thinkers of the AF of L were blind to future problems. The men who had told me that times had changed were among the first, after the CIO had made its appearance, to demand that NLRA be amended or even repealed.

The bill was passed in the form Wagner desired on June 19, 1935. Roosevelt signed it on July 5 and turned to me, as he always did in matters relating to the labor field, for assistance in finding proper people to be appointed.

Lloyd Garrison, dean of the University of Wisconsin Law School, and Francis Biddle, Philadelphia attorney, both served brief terms as chairman of the Board. In the autumn of 1935

Warren Madden, dean of the University of Pittsburgh Law School, became chairman after much canvassing and many refusals.

After the Board was appointed the President said with a sigh, "Since this Board is not in the Department of Labor, as I think it ought to be, how am I going to manage? How am I going to know what goes on in this entirely new independent agency?"

He turned to me. "I'll tell you what. You set up a kind of watch tower in the Department of Labor. Keep in touch with the Board and tell me what they are doing, so that if they do anything wrong I can reprove them."

He was amused at my expostulation that you couldn't control a judicial body that way. He directed the NLRB to make a monthly report through me, and he told the chairman to keep in close touch with the Department of Labor. This was all right for purposes of general contact, and it was suitable for me to be the medium whereby the President learned about the number and classes of cases coming before the NLRB. But it was no way to control appointments to subordinate posts and to the regional offices. Certainly it was not an effective way of introducing the President's point of view into the formulation of the Board's policies. The President, for instance, was startled when he discovered that the Board had ruled that no employer had standing before the Board to file a petition for an election or to ask the Board to solve a jurisdictional dispute for him. (Rules have since been modified.)

The NLRB became extremely important in the labor history of the United States. Undoubtedly big-scale unionization of labor was made possible under its protection. In 1933 there were about 2,225,000 union members in the country. In 1945 there were about 14,000,000. In some industries and localities the unions have won strength not only equal but sometimes superior to that of employers. In some places excesses have been practiced by labor unions. Such practices were not anticipated by those who drew or passed the act. Experience undoubtedly will see them corrected. On the other hand, excellent relations and co-operation between employers and workers have developed in many areas.

There have been many crises in the life of the NLRB, and

two or three reorganizations. It has always been hard to find just the right people willing to serve, for they must be judicial in temperament and yet have plenty of firmness. It is a grueling job. Board members are constantly exposed to condemnation for following what they believe to be the meaning of the law.

The President sought, by varied appointments, to establish more statesmanship and more stable attitudes in the Board. It remained wholly independent, and from President Roosevelt's point of view it was wholly unpredictable.

If there had been no split in the labor movement and no creation of a rival organization in the CIO, the Board might long ago have passed its controversial period and settled down to peaceful life with a small routine calendar. The implications of that split in the ranks of labor must be left for a later chapter.

21

WAGES AND HOURS

Although the Fair Labor Standards Act, popularly known as the Wage and Hour Act, was a late piece of New Deal legislation (it was not passed until the summer of 1938), President Roosevelt had come to Washington in 1933 prepared to devise a method of placing limitations upon hours of labor and a floor under wages, to guarantee at least a subsistence wage. The NRA seemed to be an approach to that objective which was thought to be quite safe on the grounds of constitutionality.

While the NRA codes were being formulated in 1933, the President promulgated under NRA a document called the President's Re-employment Agreement which generated great enthusiasm throughout the country. Employers signing this agreement stipulated that they would pay not less than fifteen dollars for a forty-hour week, pending the issuance of the appropriate code of fair competition for their industry. The general acceptance of these standards was strengthened by an Executive Order requiring all contractors receiving PWA or Emergency Relief funds to adhere to them.

The codes were so hastily drafted, however, that many of them contained very low minimum standards. This caused great dissatisfaction in labor circles, and heavy pressure was brought to bear upon the administrator for upward revision. Moreover, the internal situation in the NRA was becoming confused and explosive.

The administrator, instead of making a few codes for the basic industries, had been lured, as I indicated earlier, into involvement with insignificant industries which trooped into Washington "to get a code." In enforcing these codes, the Compliance Section, as it was called for polite purposes, had developed the habit of instituting civil or judicial proceedings against small businessmen. This was understandable. It was relatively easy to discover violations among small employers. Many of them were ignorant of the law and carried much of their bookkeeping in their heads. Public reaction to these prosecutions was unfavorable.

As the Labor Advisory Committee grew more experienced and as the country's economy began to improve, it became obvious that a higher level of wages was needed. There was controversy as to how this should be accomplished. The appropriate way, of course, was to call the code committees, debate the matter, conduct hearings, and revise the minimum in the same way that it had been originally determined.

But by that time General Johnson was exhausted and apparently could not stand the nervous strain of facing the code committees again. He had always had a tendency to decide matters by decree, and he felt that his views should be accepted without further correction, not only by the advisory committees but by the code committees themselves. His health was suffering and he had to be away from his office at frequent intervals. Decisions were often in the hands of his secretary, Miss Robinson, a very competent girl in whose judgment he had great confidence; but as a result there was often an undercurrent of rebellion in the NRA.

Finally, General Johnson decided to go ahead and raise the minimum rates in a spectacular and flamboyant fashion. His plan was to convene all the code committees at Constitution Hall, where they were to be addressed by the President, who was to announce what was to be done. I and many others opposed this idea vigorously, since it meant using the prestige of the White House to cover up shortcomings of the NRA. But General Johnson held the notion that it was enough that the President should issue orders as Commander-in-Chief.

Johnson and I had a battle over this speech. I persuaded the President to take out the proclamation and make only a speech of good will and good wishes, recommending that they consider the wage question and saying why. The President was inclined to agree with me until Johnson had one of his emotional explosions. The President said, "Oh, anything to satisfy Hugh," and put the passage back. I carved the demand out of the speech three separate times and each time Johnson got it back in. He was terrific in his emotional moods. I got it out a last time, thinking it was now too late for Johnson to get at it. But when the President delivered the speech, the demand was in again. The reaction on the assembled code committees was terrible. The President had received a fine ovation when he came in. When he went out, he got respectful applause and puzzled looks.

Ralph Flanders, an intelligent, liberal-minded Vermont businessman, something of an economist in his own right, got up at the afternoon session and tore the whole argument to pieces. He received thunderous applause. Those of us who had been asked by Johnson to make minor reports played our parts that afternoon, but we knew that the NRA was now in very hot water.

I often thought that the NRA would blow up by internal combustion. I feared that key people would resign in a body with a denunciation of Johnson and the whole works, and that Johnson would make a counterblast and offer his resignation to the President, with his followers doing likewise. Finally, I thought, the President, tired of the mess, would accept the resignations and say, "All right, the NRA is over."

During this period of doubt over NRA's future, I began to explore means to save what I thought was basic and important—the limitation of hours of labor and the establishment of a floor under wages. I persuaded the solicitor of the Department of Labor to draw up two bills. One, a public contracts bill, employed the conception Felix Frankfurter had given us in 1932 that the Federal Government had power under the Constitution to determine the labor conditions under which goods purchased by the Government should be manufactured. The other, assuming the constitutionality of federal legislation, called for general wage and hour standards and embodied the ideas that the Black thirty-hour bill of 1932 and 1933 had lacked.

In one of our conferences on the impending fate of the NRA,

I said to the President, "Never mind, I have something up my sleeve."

"What have you got?" he said, with the ready curiosity which so often lifted him out of gloomy moments.

"I've got two bills which will do everything you and I think important under NRA," I said. "I have them locked up in the lower left-hand drawer of my desk against an emergency."

He threw his head back and laughed. "There's New England caution for you, I declare."

"But you and I agreed in February 1933," I reminded him, "that putting a floor under wages and a ceiling over hours was essential and that it would be a wise and necessary program to be carried out on the federal level, if possible. We've explored the NRA. It is fine, but if it doesn't work or breaks down, we have to be prepared for something else."

"You're pretty unconstitutional, aren't you?" he said. "Are you trying to say that the Constitution doesn't matter between friends, the way Theodore did?

"You know," he went on, "I have been in office for two years and haven't had an appointment for the Supreme Court. That is most unusual, I am told. What that Court needs is some Roosevelt appointments. Then we might get a good decision out of them."

He spoke pleasantly, without rancor. I am sure that his mind at that time held no idea of what was later called the "Court packing plan." He merely thought that nature would soon provide for the retirement of one or more of the older conservative justices who always voted against the constitutionality of "New Deal" laws. There were still four Justices on the Bench who since World War I had handed down decisions against federal attempts to change conditions in the mining and manufacturing industries.

One such case had been *Hammer* v. *Dagenhart* in 1918. Here the Court had considered the Child Labor Act, passed during the Wilson administration, in which Congress had forbidden entry into interstate commerce of goods manufactured in plants which employed minors under the specified age. Although the Court had previously upheld the acts of Congress regulating labor conditions in the railroads, a majority of the Court in this case held that the power to regulate commerce did not extend to the production of goods as distinguished from their movement across state lines. This was a very narrow construction of the commerce clause. But it was controlling in 1934-35 in regard to the New Deal legislation.

This same Court took a very broad view of the "due process" clause when confronted with legislation passed by the states to provide for a minimum living wage for women and minors. In *Adkins* v. *Children's Hospital* in 1923 the Court struck down a minimum wage statute affecting the District of Columbia on the ground that the due process clause in the Fifth Amendment guaranteed freedom of contract and that minimum wages based upon the cost of living destroyed such freedom. Since the due process clause also appears in the Fourteenth Amendment as a limit upon the police powers of the states, the effect of the Court's decision was to render state minimum wage legislation unenforceable.

During the late twenties New York and several other industrial states passed a new kind of minimum wage legislation which, it was hoped, might fare more favorably in the Supreme Court. Minimum wages were to be based upon reasonable value of the services rendered rather than on cost of living. These statutes, however, had not in 1935-36 been passed upon by the courts.

The shadow of the decisions in *Hammer* v. *Dagenhart* and *Adkins* v. *Children's Hospital* hung over the labor provisions in the NRA fair competition codes. These fears were well grounded, for the codes were doomed in 1935 by the Court's decision in the famous Schechter case, which resulted from an attempt to enforce the labor provisions of a poultry code upon a small company of butchers.

Moreover, the Court in 1935 also decided unfavorably against another aspect of NRA. In the so-called "hot-oil" cases, arising under the application of the petroleum regulations in Section 9 of the National Industrial Recovery Act to several oil companies, conservative and liberal members joined in a scorching opinion which held the regulations invalid. During the government's argument before the Court, it was revealed that there was no public repository of the provisions of the codes and that amendments were known only to a few divisional administrators who kept them in their desks. The Court insisted that when Congress delegated discretion to an administrative official or agency, definite standards and conditions under which that discretion should be exercised must be established.

Another dubious feature of the code system was that the police power granted to the NRA had been redelegated to the code authorities, which were institutions composed of individuals who had taken no oath of office.

In the Schechter case, the Court held that the failure of Congress to define in more precise terms the substance of the standards in the codes, and the lack of safeguards for due process in the code-making procedure, were sufficient to invalidate all the codes issued under Section 3. The Court went further. It found that the application of the NRA to a company which had only a local market, even though the goods for processing were received from outside the state, was beyond the power of Congress to regulate.

The sweeping character of the Court's opinion produced immediate confusion, and after it was handed down, the President by executive order suspended all the codes. There was a bill pending before Congress at that time to extend the NRA for another two years, and considerable legal debate ensued in Government circles as to whether it would be wise to seek to amend it in the hope that the worth-while features of the codes might be preserved. The day after the decision I called a conference of some of the leading legal figures in the administration, including Harold Stephens, Assistant Attorney General; John Dickinson of the Department of Commerce; John Burns, general counsel of the Securities and Exchange Commission, and Blackwell Smith, counsel for NRA. It was the consensus that although the majority opinion had cited *Hammer* v. *Dagenhart* with approval, the decision was not to be taken as meaning that industries producing goods for interstate commerce rather than for local markets were beyond the pale of congressional regulation so far as labor conditions were concerned. The Labor

Department solicitor, Charles Wyzanski (now a federal judge in Massachusetts), cabled me from Geneva, where he had gone on ILO business for the Department, that the text of Chief Justice Hughes's opinion led him to conclude that a great deal of the NRA could be salvaged, including the labor standards.

I carried the view of these lawyers to the President and urged that consideration be given to such a step before dropping the bill to extend the life of the NRA. But Attorney General Homer S. Cummings, who had also been in conference with him, was certain that the Court's opinion had destroyed further congressional action along that line. Cummings was angry and believed the Court had exceeded its powers in this and other recent cases. He was convinced that the Court majority meant to destroy the whole New Deal program. He recommended that the President abandon anything like the NRA and that he tell the country that the Supreme Court made it impossible to have this kind of legislation. The President acquiesced.

"You know the whole thing is a mess," Roosevelt told me. "It has been an awful headache. Some of the things they have done in NRA are pretty wrong, though I think it is going better now. We have got the best out of it anyhow. Industry got a shot in the arm. Everything has started up. I don't believe they will go back to their old wage levels. I think the forty-hour week will stick, except in a few instances. I think perhaps NRA has done all it can do. I don't want to impose a system on this country that will set aside the anti-trust laws on any permanent basis.

"I have been talking to other lawyers besides Homer Cummings, and they are pretty certain that the whole process is unconstitutional and that we have to restudy and revise our whole program. Perhaps we had better do it now. So let's give the NRA a certain amount of time to liquidate. Have a history of it written, and then it will be over."

The President, however, asked Congress to remain in session during the summer and to study other approaches to its problem. The bill establishing the National Labor Relations Board had passed the Senate, but both this measure and Senator Guffey's bituminous coal bill—the bill regulating the price and marketing structure of the coal industry and agreed upon by employers and workers earlier—had bogged down in the House, as it was generally believed that such legislation was inconsistent with the codes. The President now gave these measures his blessing and asked me to get Representative O'Connor, chairman of the Rules Committee, to bring the Labor Relations bill to the floor of the House, where it was duly passed.

I instructed the assistant solicitors, Thomas Eliot and Gerard Reilly, who were working with Robert Stern of the Department of Justice, to recast the Public Contracts bill into acceptable form.

The Public Contracts bill was introduced in the Senate by Senator Walsh of Massachusetts, then chairman of the Committee on Education and Labor, who was able to bring it out of committee in acceptable form. Before the end of July it was approved in the Senate, after a spirited debate in which the bill ran the gauntlet of hostile amendments proposed by the more implacable critics of the NRA.

In the House, where it was sponsored by Representative Arthur D. Healey of Massachusetts, it met with more opposition and obstruction, but was finally passed, in diluted form, on the last night of the 1935 session. This Walsh-Healey Public Contracts Act was an important forerunner of the Fair Labor Standards Act, since it established the forty-hour week for contractors manufacturing supplies for the government, directed the Secretary of Labor to determine minimum rates for the manufacture of such commodities, forbade the employment of children in the performance of government contracts, and established an administrative procedure in the Department of Labor for detecting violations and enforcing the labor provisions in the contract.

I was still not convinced that a more comprehensive measure was not feasible. Some time earlier, I had asked Charles Gregory, Labor Department solicitor, to prepare a bill embodying principles I felt might satisfy the Supreme Court. This bill contemplated a procedure under which minimum wage boards could be appointed by the Secretary of Labor when, after investigation, it was determined that wages below subsistence levels

were being paid in a particular industry. The cost of living figures of the Bureau of Labor Statistics were to be taken as an
index. The bill provided that these boards should have power
to conduct public hearings, and to recommend to the Secretary
of Labor an appropriate minimum wage for the industry. These
boards might, after investigation, make recommendations for
the maximum work-week, but in no event should the maximum hours be fixed at more than forty-eight hours a week. The
tentative bill also provided for administrative discretion in
fixing the amount of overtime payment. This was one of the
bills that I had told the President I was keeping in my bottom
drawer.

At the President's urging, I canvassed the constitutional approach with a number of good lawyers outside my own Department: Robert Jackson, Solicitor General, Joseph Chamberlain, a
constitutional lawyer in New York with wide experience in
drafting labor legislation, Felix Frankfurter, Charles Burling-
ham of New York, a friend of the President, in whose views
he had great confidence, as did I. I also consulted John Lord
O'Brian, the Buffalo attorney, who had been in and out of
Washington on a variety of matters. Practically everyone was
doubtful about the constitutional approach, but felt that a
bill ought to be tried with the formula of "affecting interstate
commerce."

During 1936, however, the Supreme Court, in the Carter
Coal case, revived beyond any doubt the doctrine of *Hammer*
v. *Dagenhart* and, in the Tipaldo case, invalidated the new
kind of minimum wage legislation in effect in New York State,
thus giving broad effect to the rule of the Adkins case.

The President delayed in giving the go-ahead sign. He was
sensitive to the charge that he had no respect for the Constitution. He was facing the 1936 campaign, and he did not wish to
be burdened with that charge. Nor did he want to go into the
campaign with labor people badly disappointed. But his labor
record was good, he figured. He had done his best. It wasn't his
fault, but the Supreme Court's, that the protection on hours
and wages was out. Moreover, the Walsh-Healey Act was an
earnest of good faith. The National Labor Relations Act had

been passed and trade union members and leaders felt that they had protection in collective bargaining. There was a growing disposition among the more conservative element in the AF of L to think that that was perhaps enough.

Roosevelt entered the campaign, therefore, with a description of the benefits to working people in the short hours and minimum wage protection effected by the NRA. He regretted that the NRA had been canceled out by the Supreme Court, but promised that, if elected, his administration would try to find something to replace NRA's regulation of hours and wages.

Shortly after his re-election, the President said to me, "What happened to that nice unconstitutional bill you had tucked away?"

I sent it to the White House for study and was given to understand that it would be one of the principal bills on the administration's calendar for the new Congress. The Democratic platform had contained a plank in favor of legislation improving labor conditions and outlawing child labor, and in view of the overwhelming vote he had received, the President felt that the country was strongly behind such measures. The Supreme Court was still the big question mark. The reactionary trend in the most recent term of the Court seemed to doom any new social legislation and one feared that the principal legislative efforts of 1935 would suffer NRA's fate. The broad holdings in the Carter Coal and Tipaldo cases not only stood as a barrier to legislation regulating labor conditions but threw into jeopardy many of the statutes already being administered. The Agricultural Adjustment Act had been declared unconstitutional in a six-to-three decision, which cast doubt upon the validity of the unemployment and old-age-insurance sections of the Social Security Act.

On the advice of Attorney General Cummings, the President embarked upon the ill-fated Court plan and notified me that the wage-hour legislation would have to wait. By late spring of 1937 the President's Court plan was encountering hard sledding. Much of its support faded when the Court reversed itself on the minimum wage question in the Parrish decision of

March 29, and again, two weeks later, when it upheld by a 5 to 4 vote the power of Congress to regulate labor conditions in manufacturing industries in interstate commerce by sustaining an order of the National Labor Relations Board applying to the Jones & Laughlin Steel Company. An informal poll of the Senate disclosed that a majority would probably vote against the Court bill. This drastic change in the minority lineup in the Court which made it possible for the Court to sustain modern social legislation was due to many factors undoubtedly, but the discreet management of Chief Justice Hughes greatly contributed to the change. The President persisted in his support of the plan, however, and a serious rift began to develop within the Democratic majority.

At this stage the President decided upon a comprehensive minimum wage and maximum hour bill, partly as a measure for reuniting the party. His approval was given to a draft which included the principles of the bill Gregory had prepared for me plus various theories suggested by other persons. All were in a lengthy measure drafted by Tom Corcoran and Ben Cohen. The clause "affecting interstate commerce" was thought to be a new constitutional approach.

One last minute change was the insertion of a clause prohibiting the labor of youngsters under sixteen in industries engaged in interstate commerce or affecting interstate commerce, and providing for not more than eight hours of work a day for children over sixteen. As Grace Abbott, Chief of the Children's Bureau, so eloquently pleaded, "You are hoping that you have found a way around the Supreme Court. If you have, why not give the children the benefit by attaching a child labor clause to this bill?" The President readily agreed and was delighted that we might make this bill cover child labor as well as low wages and long hours.

On May 24, 1937, the President sent a message to Congress urging favorable consideration of the legislation, and on that day bills were introduced in both the House and Senate, and referred to their Labor Committees. Senator Hugo Black, who sponsored the legislation in the Senate, said he felt he could accept it as a substitute for his thirty-hour bill, although privately he still regretted the NRA episode. I think he never sufficiently recognized the degree to which that act had educated the country to the feasibility of wage and hour regulation.

In the House the bill was sponsored by William P. Connery of Massachusetts, chairman of the Committee on Labor. He was enthusiastic for the legislation, since his experience in Massachusetts, which had suffered from the exodus of textile and shoe industries to lower wage areas, had convinced him that national legislation was necessary to eliminate this destructive competition. He readily agreed with Senator Black, chairman of the corresponding committee in the Senate, to expedite consideration of the bill by the unprecedented step of conducting joint hearings.

At this time the political climate for the bill was so favorable that most industrialists who appeared before the committees confined their criticism to technical defects and to the possibility that it might undermine some industries by admission of foreign goods manufactured at lower labor costs.

Cold water was thrown upon the prospects of the bill, however, from an unexpected source. Neither William Green, president of the AF of L, nor John L. Lewis, then president of the CIO, gave unequivocal support at the hearings. Many AF of L officials privately expressed the traditional Gompers doctrine against minimum wages, repeating the old adage that "the minimum tends to become the maximum." In fact, representatives of the AF of L even went so far as to suggest that the regulatory provisions of the bill should not apply to any industry which had collective bargaining agreements. Lewis professed much more interest in a bill then under consideration for taking Government contracts away from firms which violated the National Labor Relations Act.

By the time the bill reached the floor of the Senate, its scope had been greatly reduced. The forty cents an hour provision in the original draft became the highest wage which could be set by the administrative agency rather than the floor. In my opinion, the forty-cent provision, in the original draft and in the one reported, was fundamentally unsound. The amount of the wage should have been left for the consideration of wage boards which could scrutinize the economic problems of an industry and fix a minimum wage for each industry as the evidence indicated.

While the bill was under consideration in the Senate, several of the more conservative AF of L officials, including Matthew Woll, a vice-president, William Hutcheson, who spoke for the building trades, and John Frey of the metal trades, came out openly against the measure. There was also considerable sectional division, with some senators contending that the bill was aimed against the South. Nevertheless, it passed the Senate.

Meanwhile, Congressman Connery died and was succeeded as chairman of the House Committee on Labor by Mrs. Mary Norton of New Jersey. She sympathized with the objectives of the legislation and was co-operative in expediting its consideration. The measure was reported by the House Committee on August 6, 1937, with some last minute amendments to placate the opposition of the AF of L. But the Rules Committee showed no disposition to bring the bill to the floor. It had been a hot summer and a hard one. Senators and representatives were eager to get home, and Congress finally adjourned with the bill still pending on the House calendar.

The President called a special session for November 15, 1937. In his message he said, "I believe that the country as a whole recognizes the need for immediate congressional action if we are to maintain wage increases and the purchasing power of the nation against recessive factors in the general industrial situation. The exploitation of child labor and the undercutting of wages and the stretching of the hours of the poorest paid workers in periods of business recession has a serious effect on buying power. In the interest of the national economy such adjustments as must be made should not be made at the expense of those least able to bear them.

"I further believe that the country as a whole realizes the necessary connection between encouraging businessmen to make capital expenditures for new plants and raising the total wage income of our working population. New plants today mean labor-saving machinery. What does the country ultimately gain if we encourage businessmen to enlarge the capacity of American industry to produce unless we see to it that the income of our working population actually expands sufficiently to create markets to absorb that increased production?

"I further believe that the country as a whole recognizes the need of seeking a more uniformly adequate standard of living and purchasing power everywhere, if every part is to live happily with every other part. We do not recognize the destiny of any state or any county to be permanently backward. Political and social harmony requires that every state and every county not only produce goods for the nation's markets but furnish markets for the nation's goods."

I quote from this message of November 1937 because it was a preview of the ideas involved in the struggle for a full employment policy in 1945. In November 1937, however, we were not thinking of full employment in terms of sixty million jobs. The President was thinking merely of getting the country back on the pre-depression level. It had been his hope that the upward swing begun in the summer of 1933 would continue, and that, as the older economists contended, business would restore itself once it had had a shot in the arm. But we had suffered a recession in 1937.

Faced with this, the President recommended the immediate passage of the Black-Connery bill. The struggle to get the bill through became intensive.

A coalition of Republicans and Southern Democrats in the Rules Committee continued to block the House from taking up the measure realistically. The President took a hand himself and suggested that an informal committee undertake a petition for signatures for discharge of the Rules Committee. Such a committee was organized and was informally headed by Representative Arthur D. Healey of Massachusetts. On November 17 a petition was placed on the Speaker's desk to force the House to consider the bill, and on December 2, as a result of the vigorous efforts of Healey and Mrs. Norton, 218 members had signed the discharge petition.

Meanwhile, prominent figures in the AF of L began to campaign publicly against the measure. They charged that the proposed independent five-member board would be given a blank check to regulate all hours and wages. This led the House

Labor Committee to offer a substitute bill changing the method of administration and providing for a single administrator in the Labor Department. On December 13 the House, by a vote of 258 to 113, discharged the Rules Committee from further consideration, and it appeared that the bill would have fairly smooth sailing. While it was under consideration on the floor, however, President Green of the AF of L, although he had been privately apologetic for the position taken by some of his colleagues, now threw the whole weight of his organization against the bill. Representative Lawrence Connery of Massachusetts, who had succeeded his brother, made a speech in opposition which resulted in several Democrats from the North and West joining the Southern Democratic-Republican coalition. Numerous amendments were adopted on the fifth day of the debate, and finally the bill was recommitted to the Committee on Labor by a vote of 216 to 198.

This was the first time that a major administration bill had been defeated on the floor of the House. The press took the view that this was the death knell of wage-hour legislation as well as a decisive blow to the President's prestige.

The President was not convinced. When Congress reconvened on January 3, 1938, his message on the state of the Union again urged suitable legislation, saying, "We are seeking only, of course, to end starvation wages and intolerable hours. More desirable wages are, and should continue to be, the product of collective bargaining."

He told me privately that he thought the bill had encountered such difficulties because of its length and complicated provisions. It was about forty printed pages long.

"Can't it be boiled down to two pages?" he asked me.

I had to remind him that it had been written more for the Supreme Court's scrutiny than for the average layman.

The Labor Department solicitor, Gerard Reilly, tried his hand at a new draft, and one Saturday afternoon late in January we brought it over to the President. This version was down to about ten typewritten pages, not two. The President expressed his satisfaction with it, and it was put into the hands of Mrs. Norton.

Since I foresaw that it was going to be a difficult and complicated process to get the legislation through, I took on my staff a young lawyer who was to do nothing else but know the bill and its daily progress, keep close to it, foresee difficulties, and forestall objections. This was Rufus Poole, who had been assistant solicitor in the Interior Department, and he was assigned to our solicitor's office. His resourcefulness and adaptability had a great deal to do with getting the wage-hour law upon the books. He started a one-man hunt to find out the precise objections to the bill and by whom they were held. By canvassing scores of congressmen he ascertained specific objections, and eventually he knew a large, dependable body who would be favorable. Ultimately he could predict with reasonable accuracy the vote for or against any amendment.

The AF of L finally stated the form of a bill it would stand for. Congressman Griswold of Indiana drafted a bill which was said to have originated in the AF of L Council. This simply established a forty-hour work-week and a forty-cent minimum wage in all industries. It omitted provisions for administrative investigation. The only method of enforcement was a section which made violations a criminal offense and left action to the courts.

On March 1, 1938, Mrs. Norton appointed a subcommittee of the House Labor Committee, composed of seven members, with Representative Robert Ramspeck of Georgia as chairman. Numerous people conferred with him, and he made heroic efforts to formulate a practical piece of legislation. Some modifications were made in the abbreviated draft which the President had approved. This draft contemplated the establishment of wage boards empowered to fix wages and hours so that gradually an ultimate goal of forty cents an hour and a forty-hour week could be reached. It contained provisions for studies of particular industries with opportunities for hearing and appeal. It seemed to me that the bill contained the bare essentials the administration could support.

This proposal, however, was opposed by the AF of L. The National Association of Manufacturers also opposed the bill, and for the first time in years Congress was treated to the spectacle of the AF of L and the NAM fighting cordially on the same side. The CIO came out in favor of the Ramspeck bill, but its support tended to alienate Southern Democrats, as they were afraid of further CIO organizing campaigns in the South. A canvass of the House revealed that there were not enough votes to carry the Ramspeck bill.

The President sent word to Mrs. Norton through me that he was anxious to say in a scheduled speech in the near future that the Labor Committee had reported out a wage-hour bill. Mrs. Norton decided to present a bill along the lines of the one offered by the AF of L. Her bill set an absolute floor to wages with virtually no procedure for investigation or adjustment of the needs of particular industries. It provided that pay for the first year would be not less than twenty-five cents an hour, with an increase of five cents an hour every year thereafter until a rate of forty cents an hour was reached. It set a maximum work-week of forty-four hours for the first year, with a reduction of two hours each subsequent year until a forty-hour work-week was achieved.

This bill was reported favorably by a vote of 14 to 4, while the recommendations of the Ramspeck subcommittee were rejected, 10 to 8. It was reported to the House on April 21. The Rules Committee, by a vote of 8 to 6, again refused to report a resolution enabling the House to consider the measure. This again necessitated resort to a discharge petition.

Shortly thereafter, however, developments in two Democratic primaries brought about a complete change in the political climate. It had been obvious during the bill's stormy history in the Senate and House that the honeymoon between the President and Congress had come to a rapid close. Most of the congressmen swept into office in 1936 had relied heavily upon the magic of Roosevelt's name, but the clamor against the Court bill and the fact that no one expected him to be a candidate for reelection in 1940—and therefore that his influence and authority over appointments would not be operative—had caused numerous defections. Senator Claude Pepper, then campaigning for renomination in Florida, was bitterly denounced by his opponents in the primaries for his support of the wage-hour bill. This bill also figured in Alabama, for Lister Hill, running for

Senator Black's seat, had been friendly to this labor legislation as a member of the House. When Pepper and Hill were nominated by spectacular majorities, congressmen, especially from the South, were impressed. On the very day the nominations were announced, there was a stampede to sign the discharge petition. In the fall it had taken weeks to get the requisite number of signatures, but on May 6, when the petition was placed upon the Speaker's desk at noon, 218 members signed it within two hours and twenty minutes, and others were waiting in the aisles when the Speaker declared that the necessary number had been obtained.

On May 23, the discharge motion was brought up on the floor. All but the most ultraconservative members of the southern delegation abandoned their opposition, and on that day the bill passed the House by the overwhelming vote of 313 to 97. Amendments brought about the exemption of the fishing industry and the processing of certain agricultural commodities.

There was such a wide divergence of language between the Senate and House bills that Senator Elbert D. Thomas of Utah, who headed the Senate conferees, took the position that the conference had wide latitude. The chief point of contention among the conferees was whether to provide for a differential in minimum wages for different sections of the country. The Southerners favored language which would make it mandatory upon the administrator to set lower rates in regions where the prevailing pattern was below the national standard. It is difficult to understand why so many enlightened men were willing to have low standards permanently in their parts of the country, and the usual reasons have been, to my mind, oversimplified. But the Southerners ultimately yielded, and the conference agreed upon national standards. One conciliatory gesture was a provision requiring the administrator to take into account the cost of living whenever he had under consideration an industry committee's recommendation for a higher rate.

The fashion of the day was against administrative commissions, partly because of a widespread misinterpretation of the Supreme Court's NRA decisions and partly because the National Labor Relations Board was under fire. The conferees decided upon a single administrator, with Congress to set the basic standards, both as to wages and hours. However, the conferees retained in the bill full power of investigation by the administrator with the right to bring action for enforcement in the courts.

As a compromise with Ramspeck and me, they retained the system of industry committees. But, having previously decided upon an escalator clause for the minimum wage, they gave these committees a limited function. They could only recommend that an industry could raise the minimum wage as high as forty cents, the limit fixed by law, in advance of the date set by Congress for that rate to take effect.

Many of the conferees wanted the basic wage at twenty-five cents. The conference finally agreed to that, providing for increases from twenty-five to thirty to forty cents over a period of seven years.

At the same time, the conferees, seeking to placate objectors who held that the legal requirement of forty hours would be devastating if rapidly approved, set maximum hours at forty-four, with the provision that they should go to forty-two and then to forty over a three-year period.

The bill was drafted under a new concept of constitutional power. In addition to covering employees engaged in interstate commerce, it covered persons who "produced goods for interstate commerce." This approach was thought out by Robert Jackson, Ben Cohen, Gerard Reilly, and Rufus Poole—ingenious men who read enormously on the subject. I consulted Joseph Chamberlain, Felix Frankfurter, and other good constitutional lawyers, and they agreed that it might greatly strengthen the constitutional argument for the bill. One lawyer said to me, "Well, if the Supreme Court wants to change its mind, you have at least given them a new point and they can certainly spell out some language to make it appear that while earlier approaches were unconstitutional this bill is clearly within the Constitution."

When the new bill was submitted by the conferees, it was adopted by the House and by the Senate very promptly on June 14. Everybody claimed credit for it. The AF of L said it was

their bill and their contribution. The CIO claimed full credit
for its passage. I cannot remember whether the President and I
claimed credit, but we always thought we had done it. Certainly he gave a sigh of relief as he signed it. "That's that," he
said.

The Wage and Hour Act has been a success, and Roosevelt
took comfort in the fact. Its principal objectives were accepted.
The spread of employment by shorter hours started. The shorter
hours have made a more humane schedule. The fact that excess
hours are penalized by overtime costs has proved sufficient to
keep hours at reasonable levels and yet flexible enough to make
it possible to work more than forty hours when necessary, as it
was during the war.

The Act was a great help in the war industries when the drive
came for new employees and more production. Wage levels for
beginners by this time had been brought up to forty cents by
voluntary action of the industrial boards as provided under
the Act and there was considerable overtime, making take-
home pay sufficient to meet the rise in the cost of living during
the first years of the war.

The Act has retarded migration of industries to cheaper
wage areas and has retarded the tendency toward competition
based on low labor standards.

At this writing the law seems to be a permanent part of the
legal structure and economic pattern of the United States. It
needs amending for clarification and administrative ease, but
there never has been a time when the administration dared to
press seriously for amendments for fear of getting emasculation
instead.

The flat rate of forty cents an hour fixed by Congress has had,
up to the present, reasonably good results. In my testimony and
memoranda, with which the President agreed, recommending
the fixing of minimum wages in different industries by wage
boards, we pointed out the hazards of a flat rate fixed by Congress. We feared political pressure on Congress to raise wage
rates by blanket statute not on a basis of sound change in economic conditions in a particular industry but because a pressure group wanted them raised. A drive was begun in 1945 for

a sixty-five- or seventy-five-cent minimum wage by act of Congress. It may be the correct figure if we have inflation, but this is not the way to establish a sound wage structure. A figure of sixty-five cents may be too high in some industries to permit sufficient gradation between the lowest and highest paid and to allow for a sufficient number of wage levels in between to provide for the promotions, based on experience and skill, which are so dear to the human heart and so productive of stability, order, and responsibility in industry. Minimum wages, determined industry by industry, on the facts, is the better way in the long run.

22.

PUBLIC WORKS

It was characteristic of the early Roosevelt administration that the people on whom he relied for advice and assistance rode their own programs vigorously and never thought of sparing him. Roosevelt apparently did not try to push them off. He was willing to be ridden and harassed. However, he expected his aides to drive ahead and develop their fields. Thus a very energetic set of people were stimulated by their leader to develop programs of reform and action.

My duty in those early troubled times was to present plans providing work for the unemployed and stimulating normal industrial activity which would give further work. When Roosevelt had asked me to become Secretary of Labor I had mentioned an immediate program of public works as one item in a program to overcome the disastrous effects of prolonged unemployment. He had given tentative approval. When we took over in Washington, I set the lawyers in my office to draft such a bill, and in a week or so we had it ready in rough form.

At one of the first cabinet meetings I raised the question of public works, as I thought the bill we were preparing would profit from the ideas of other members of the cabinet and that round-table discussion would help push the plan. In the cabinet I discovered hearty support for public works. Jim Farley, Harold Ickes, Henry Wallace, and George Dern were vigorous in urging that it be done promptly.

I sent the bill to the President for his examination. He talked about it at length. He was anxious to insure that the projects would be practical and worth-while, and he stressed the desirability of constructing sewers and highways on public works money rather than a lot of fancy buildings. I pointed out that a good administrator would be the key to the selection of good projects and that no amount of congressional legislation could provide such insurance.

Although the President had the bill checked by Attorney General Cummings, it did not get introduced. The days were passing and in those early months we counted two days a long time. Finally I discovered that the Director of the Budget, Lewis W. Douglas, had told the President that if money had to be appropriated for public works, the budget could not be balanced, the financial situation of the United States would become desperate, and the crisis would be worsened.

About that time, as I have mentioned, the President decided to ask Douglas to sit with the cabinet occasionally, and that seemed a good idea. If we talked the matter over in cabinet, I thought, we would at least know what Douglas's objections were. We could then offer our arguments to the President.

At the first meeting Douglas attended we brought up the public works bill. He expressed himself very well indeed on the subject. I felt, though, that he was not giving a full expression of his view, but a mild, polite version in terms which he considered suitable for the cabinet. His own philosophy on the subject, however, was completely formed, and he was not open to arguments in any other direction. He was devoted to the principle of the balanced budget, and he saw no way in which the budget could be balanced if government expenditures were to be increased by public works.

Douglas was a man of personal charm, logical and persuasive in argument. He was attractive, well educated, and intelligent. A former Congressman from Arizona, who had served in the House with a good deal of distinction, he had been persuaded to resign in order to take the post of Director of the Budget. He had been introduced to Roosevelt during the campaign by Mrs. Roosevelt's friend, the beautiful Isabella Greenway of Arizona, who succeeded Douglas as Representative. He had been attracted to Roosevelt, partly by his personal integrity and courage and partly by his campaign statements about sound financing and balanced budgets.

I soon realized that good as Douglas might be in handling the budget, he was expressing, in more agreeable and persuasive terms, the very philosophy against which the country had reacted so violently under Hoover: namely, let wages, hours, employment, prices, sales, production drop until natural economic forces begin to restore business and industrial activity. Douglas, however, was humane. He would provide subsistence relief in the cheapest possible terms for citizens out of work and without funds, and this he regarded as the largest expenditure the federal budget could possibly stand.

There is no doubt in my mind that Roosevelt did give him grounds to believe that he wanted a balanced budget and that he was at least doubtful of the wisdom of a public works program if it could not be achieved without throwing the budget out of balance. This was one of the conflicts in Roosevelt's nature and in his thinking. He wanted a balanced budget, but he also wanted to do the right thing by his unemployed fellow citizens. If anyone could have shown him a way to get them back to work in normal, private industrial activities, he would have preferred it to a public works or relief program.

From the way Douglas discussed the matter, I was sure he was seeing the President privately and pressing him to avoid a public works program. I felt that part of his reason for backing away from cabinet discussion was that he could do better in private.

The nearest the cabinet came to hard feeling was over Douglas's ability to postpone action by the President on the public works bill. Douglas adopted a program of delay as a deliberate technique when he saw the President becoming more sympathetic to such a program; and any delay in coming to grips with the subject was clear gain for his side. When Douglas, as I described earlier, gave us our first intimation of the plan that became the NRA, he again delayed consideration of public works.

Neither of the two groups which first developed NRA regarded its schemes for industrial recovery as a substitute for a public works program. Senator Wagner had long favored a large public works program, but the plan on which he and

Jacobstein and others were working included no provision for it. In the Tugwell-Johnson plan, there was a limited reference to the subject. Their idea was to use public works as a method of deliberately stimulating a particular phase of industrial activity at a particular time. If the administrator were permitted to allocate a certain amount of public works money, he could create a demand for the product of a certain lagging industry or give employment in a specific locality. It was a restricted system which, as Tugwell and Johnson explained, would probably never be used or used so meagerly as to make no real demands upon public expenditures. This very limited use of public works attracted Douglas to this program as a substitute for the proposals for a large, nationwide program.

With the President's blessing, I started to transform the meager public works provision in the Tugwell-Johnson plan into a real public works program. It was not too difficult to sell the idea to them. Senator Wagner had no objection. He told me that there was widespread support in Congress for such a measure, and he believed that it would help to carry the other industrial recovery program through if the two were in one bill, since many members of Congress opposed relaxing the anti-trust controls.

By the first of May 1933 it began to leak out in the press that a recovery program was in the making. The news reports were inexact and speculative, but they were correct that the plan to link the recovery with the public works program was dividing the cabinet. The news leak started a barrage of letters and telegrams from people all over the country who wanted a public works program. When the two groups planning recovery programs got together, there was little dispute over the public works section. The only question was whether it should be an integral part of the recovery bill or a separate title.

I always urged a separate title and so did Senator Wagner. Senator Wagner had to take the lead in carrying the program through Congress, and the President tended to accept his advice. That proved to be very fortunate, for when Title I of the NRA was declared unconstitutional, the public works program in Title II survived.

Once more the matter came before the cabinet, and on this occasion the cleavage was clear. Douglas alone, possibly with some support from the Treasury—though my memory on this point is not quite clear and my record does not show—wanted Title II taken out of the bill entirely. The President did not commit himself. He wanted to think it over. My heart sank, for I knew that Douglas saw him morning, noon, and night at the White House. I felt we must fight hard now.

Roosevelt was anxious not to have a split among his advisers so early in his administration. He was also reluctant to rule out any reasonable suggestion that might aid recovery. I sympathized with his dilemma, and I respected his determination to be flexible as others might have respected a "hew to the line, let the chips fall where they may" attitude.

The following Saturday morning the President telephoned members of the cabinet to come to the White House early in the afternoon. He told me, "We are going to have a final discussion with only those present who know and care something about this program. Then I am definitely going to give the answer while you are all still there."

I asked the President if I might bring with me Charles Wyzanski, new solicitor of the Department of Labor, who had prepared the original bill and worked on the final draft of the public works section of NRA. I took him along because I had a feeling that there might be a need to make immediate changes, and I feared that postponement over the week-end would mean another delay.

The President conducted the conference masterfully. He gave each individual an opportunity to make a full statement of his stand. This had not been possible at cabinet meetings where other matters had to be discussed. We had as hot a debate as I ever heard in cabinet. Douglas at last ceased being evasive and polite and came right out with predictions of dire disaster if we moved forward along these lines.

A great deal of what Douglas said had a sound economic basis. One could not but share in his concern that heavy expenditures would create a great deficit in the budget and impair the credit of the government. He feared to spend money that could not be raised by taxation in a period of declining income. The national income, the taxing power of the Federal Government, and the balanced budget all hung together in Douglas's mind. He was persuasive.

Four years later Jesse Jones, head of the Reconstruction Finance Corporation, found the answer when he said at a cabinet meeting, "Mr. President, at the depths of the depression the national income was $42,000,000,000. In 1934 the national income was $49,000,000,000. In 1937 the national income was $71,000,000,000. If we can get the national income up to $90,000,000,000 in the next year or two, and I see no reason why we shouldn't, we don't have to give another thought to the budget. It will balance without the slightest difficulty. Mr. President, what we have discovered is that the national income grows by economic movement. The taxing power of the government applied to those truly economic processes of buying and selling and hiring and manufacturing and paying wages and spending the wages will make for a taxable income sufficient to get us out of this hole without any damage to our program. If nothing unforeseen happens, Mr. President," and he was thinking of the war as a possibility, "we shall be out of the woods."

I wished that Douglas were still in the government to hear these remarks and that we might debate the matter with him once more on the basis of the situation as Jones described it.

After about two hours of discussion at that 1933 meeting, the President made his decision. He decided that Title II should be in the recovery bill. Roosevelt was sufficiently impressed by Douglas's argument to wish to include within the bill a special tax for amortizing expenditures on public works. He decided that the manufacturers' sales tax was the least oppressive way of raising the money needed for such amortization.

The public works program decided upon, Douglas felt defeated and made no bones that he thought the President had let him down. He later had a long interview with the President, who mollified him somewhat and begged him to stay on as Director of the Budget. The President reassured him that he desired to move in the direction of reducing budgetary expen-

ditures once we were out of the woods. Douglas stayed for
another year and finally broke with the President, resigning
with discretion and restraint but with a definite sense of separation from Roosevelt and all his activities. He was a loss to the
Roosevelt administration, for he had talent which would have
been extremely useful if he could have met this difference of
opinion with flexibility.

On May 17, 1933, the President sent his message to Congress
asking for the National Industrial Recovery Act. As Secretary
of Labor, I announced my approval, because the labor group,
determined to have a public works program, needed reassurance that Title II was similar to the separate public works bill
they had previously supported and endorsed.

After the NRA bill was passed, one important problem remained. The decision to make Hugh Johnson the administrator of Title I alone, and to choose a separate administrator for
Title II, the public works section, has been described in an
earlier chapter. At the cabinet meeting at which the decision
had been reached, while Johnson waited outside, the President
had said, "Well, who shall it be? Is there any way we can select
the administrator of public works at once?"

He glanced around the table. We all looked solemn. My
mind ran over a number of people, coming back to Ickes twice.
First, as a cabinet officer, he was closely responsible to the President. Second, he had impressed me, although I had known him
only a short while, as a man of considerable administrative talent. Certainly he was a man with good plain horse sense and
plenty of caution to see that public funds were not wasted. Third,
from brief conversations with him and from information on
what he had stood for in Chicago, I felt he had a good social
point of view. He knew the difference between public works
projects which would add to the people's life and education and
those which would merely serve a few. While the money expended on public works might be the same in either case, one
felt that his choices would surely be in the direction of greater
social usefulness. It also occurred to me to consider the functions of the Department of the Interior. Most of us sitting in

that cabinet meeting that afternoon had made very little study of the internal structure and responsibilities of departments other than our own, but the Department of the Interior surely had to do with the resources, the public parks, the activities of the people inside the country. Where would there be a better administrative unit within the Government than in the Department of the Interior? Moreover, the Department of the Interior had a good set-up with plenty of technical men for supervisory posts.

I hesitantly made the suggestion, "Why not the Secretary of the Interior and keep it all within the present agencies of the government?"

The President responded at once, "I am against so many independent agencies. We ought not to create any more if we can help it. Is there any department or anybody better than the Secretary of the Interior?"

He looked around. Nobody volunteered, and finally the Secretary of the Interior said, "This is so sudden, Mr. President, but I think I have at least the negative and austere qualities which the handling of so much public money requires."

"All right, you are elected," the President said.

The decision to put Ickes in charge of public works turned out to be extremely wise. He established very careful controls over the public money and set up an Advisory Committee that knew the problems. He developed a set of regulations which were thoroughly canvassed by this Committee and were announced to the public before applications for projects were begun. He drew in a competent group of examiners and aides to look over not only the financial character of the projects but their value to the communities. I think, on the whole, the original selections in the first year of public works laid the basis for the sound understanding we now have of the type of public works which will give the most employment per thousand dollars expended and will be of the greatest permanent advantage to the economic and cultural life of the people.

Large housing projects were among the first approved, slum clearance in particular. No type of public works better illustrates the opportunity to put large numbers of people to work, both on the site and in the supply and transportation of materials, and to make, at the same time, proud and worthy contributions to the community. River control projects, having for their purpose prevention of floods, development of irrigation, and prevention of soil erosion, were also among the early undertakings approved. Schools, health and hospital centers, where those facilities were lacking, as well as sound, well-planned highway projects, also received early approval.

Secretary Ickes proved to be an excellent administrator and, above all, a man accustomed to the idea that graft and corruption were likely to follow the spending of public moneys and alert to prevent it. The result was a completely uncorrupted system of public works which brought credit to everyone. Never has there been a breath of scandal about it. This was to be a great help to President Roosevelt in the days to come.

It is well for those who would be critical of the modest scale on which the public works program was launched, to realize the uncertainty of everyone who had responsibility and knowledge of economic factors. This was an entirely new pattern. It was, indeed, a small project in managed economy. It was an attempt to change the direction of economic trends, which were little understood and about which there were no experimental data. After all, members of Congress were afraid of spending too much money. They too needed to be shown.

Roosevelt's decision to proceed with a small appropriation turned out to be wise, because once the method of spending the money was put into operation, there began to be general public approval. As the result of increased income, increased purchasing power was visible within the next year. Then there was agitation for an even larger program of public works.

When things began to get a little better after 1936, there was a disposition on the part of Congress and many others to believe that the time had come to retrench on public works expenditure. A retrenchment policy was put into effect. The recession of 1937 was undoubtedly the result.

It is my opinion that the principal factor in our economic recovery was the expenditure of public funds for public works, work relief, direct relief, and the agricultural adjustment and resettlement programs. Hindsight indicates that the NRA had little to do with recovery in economic terms, but it had an enormous amount to do with recovery in psychological terms.

We have learned enough about the effect of public expenditures when private expenditures fall off during a depression to make the country and the Congress aware of the value of a public works program. If we are to attach our will to a program of maximum employment, as the Congress provided in 1945 by passing the Full Employment bill and making this the policy of the United States, we shall have good use for that knowledge. The experience of the Roosevelt era will be of vast importance to those who, in the next twenty-five years, begin the administration of this new policy.

23.

SOCIAL SECURITY

Before his Inauguration in 1933 Roosevelt had agreed that we should explore at once methods for setting up unemployment and old-age insurance in the United States.

Therefore, early in 1933, the President encouraged Senator Wagner and Representative David J. Lewis, both deeply interested in the subject, to go ahead with their bill on unemployment insurance. The bill, a rough draft, was put in frankly for educational purposes. It was hoped that in the course of hearings the congressional committees and the introducers of the bill would work out a satisfactory and typically American measure.

The President urged me to discuss the matter in as many groups as possible. I began in the cabinet. I made a point of bringing it up, at the least, at every second meeting. Gradually the other cabinet members became sincerely and honestly interested.

Hearings were held before Congress. Effective people were invited to testify. I myself made over a hundred speeches in different parts of the country that year, always stressing social insurance as one of the methods for assisting the unemployed in times of depression and in preventing depressions. We stimulated others to talk and write about the subject.

The Wagner-Lewis bill in the Congress covered only unemployment insurance, but there was a great demand for old-age insurance also. It was easy to add this feature—and politically almost essential. One hardly realizes nowadays how strong was the sentiment in favor of the Townsend Plan and other exotic schemes for giving the aged a weekly income. In some districts the Townsend Plan was the chief political issue, and men sup-

porting it were elected to Congress. The pressure from its advocates was intense. The President began telling people he was
in favor of adding old-age insurance clauses to the bill and putting it through as one program.

A great deal of educational work was done in 1933. The
Rockefeller Foundation brought over two Englishmen who had
worked in social insurance, Sir William Beveridge and Sir Henry
Steel-Maitland. They were invited to speak before Chambers of
Commerce, Rotary Clubs, Church organizations, and their discussions of the practicability of unemployment and old-age insurance did a great deal to allay the fears and doubts of the
business and conservative part of the community.

By June 1934 the Wagner-Lewis bill had not reached committee agreement. There had been divergences of view in the
testimony and recommendations. We began to see that there
must be further study and a more complete plan before it could
be presented to Congress for action.

The President had put the program on the must list. But
the weather grew hot and the Congress was exhausted. Roosevelt was persuaded it might be better to say to Congress that
he would be happy to agree to their adjourning, providing they
understood that he would have a real study made during the
summer and would present a full program on economic security on the first of January when they reconvened. Congress
gladly agreed. Since members of the cabinet had developed
great interest in the social security program, I suggested that it
might be well to have the study made by a cabinet committee.
The President readily acquiesced. He saw at once that a program developed by a committee of the cabinet would be under
his control. It would not be likely to get off into the kind of
political discussion and publicity that might breed doubt and
delay.

One has to admit, in passing, that publicity was a real problem during this phase of the Roosevelt administration. Roosevelt had agreed gladly to keep the press fully informed about
everything that was going on. He saw the press regularly, and
this whetted its appetite. The press wanted news so quickly
and so hot that it was almost impossible for a responsible pub-

lic official to give long, thoughtful consideration to a problem.
The press insisted upon knowing what was to be done almost
before the public official had sat down with the preliminary
papers. If he refused to say what he was thinking about, he was
described in terms such as "Secretary Refuses to Deal with
Unemployment," or "Commissioner Declines to Develop a Program," or "Commission Not Dealing with Question." On the
other hand, if he told the press what he was just beginning to
think about, with the pros and cons not yet even assembled,
much less examined, the tendency was to report something like
"Secretary Planning All-Inclusive Insurance," which alarmed
many readers.

The members of the cabinet Committee on Economic Security appointed by the President were the Secretary of Labor,
chairman; Secretary of Agriculture Wallace, Secretary of the
Treasury Morgenthau, and Attorney General Cummings. Harry
Hopkins was added for his vital experience as administrator of
the relief program.

This turned out to be an admirable technique. It eventually
brought forth an administration program in which all aspects
had been canvassed by men with different lines of responsibility
and different approaches. The inclusion of the Attorney General
made it possible to have an analysis of legal and constitutional
problems before we had become fixed in our views. With the
Treasury Department represented, the most conservative as
well as the most advanced views for financing such a program
were thoroughly examined before final decisions were taken. By
involving the principal relief officer of the government, the Committee got a vivid presentation of the most compelling, immediate needs of the people.

It was evident to us that any system of social insurance would
not relieve the accumulated poverty. Nor would it relieve the
sufferings of the presently old and needy. Nevertheless, it was
also evident that this was the time, above all times, to be fore-
sighted about future problems of unemployment and unpro-
tected old age. It was never, I think, suggested by any reasonable
person that relief should be abandoned in favor of unemployment and old-age insurance, but it was thought that there could
be a blend of the two.

I took pains to make certain that Roosevelt understood and pledged himself to support the program as we worked it out. It must be made clear that this technique of utilizing a cabinet committee to develop the program for him did not mean that he was evading the great issue. I had more than one concrete conference with him about the subjects we would have to consider in Committee.

I asked him if he thought it best for me to be chairman, since the public knew I favored the general idea. Perhaps it would be better, from the point of view of Congress and the public, if the Attorney General were chairman.

He was quick in his response. "No, no. You care about this thing. You believe in it. Therefore I know you will put your back to it more than anyone else, and you will drive it through. You will see that something comes out, and we must not delay. I am convinced. We must have a program by next winter and it must be in operation before many more months have passed."

I indicated to him that there were sound arguments, advanced by many thinkers, that since we were in the midst of deflation the collection of any money for reserves, no matter by what method, would be further deflationary.

"We can't help that," he replied. "We have to get it started or it never will start."

He was aware that 1936 was not too far away, that there might be a change of administration, and that this program, which, in his own mind, was *his* program, would never be accomplished, or at least not for many years, if it were not put through immediately.

To begin with, it was essential to have technical assistance. I got the President's consent, but he said, as he often did, "Be economical. Borrow people around the government from different bureaus. Don't go outside any more than you are obliged to."

We borrowed from every Department; economists, analysts, lawyers, clerical and stenographic workers, statistical experts, and equipment. We had invaluable help from two world experts, made available to us through the International Labor Organization—André Tixier and Oswald Stein, who had studied the operation of every system in the world. But we needed other specialists and we didn't have any money for this.

The Works Progress Administration had money for relief under broad enough terms to provide for employment of unemployed technical people. It could also use funds for research into all subjects relating to the prevention and relief of unemployment. Hopkins was nothing if not broadminded and quick of decision. He made available $125,000 for this research project from WPA funds.

By the time the study was fully launched the President's imaginative mind had begun to play over it. At cabinet meetings and when he talked privately with a group of us, he would say, "You want to make it simple—very simple. So simple that everybody will understand it. And what's more, there is no reason why everybody in the United States should not be covered. I see no reason why every child, from the day he is born, shouldn't be a member of the social security system. When he begins to grow up, he should know he will have old-age benefits direct from the insurance system to which he will belong all his life. If he is out of work, he gets a benefit. If he is sick or crippled, he gets a benefit.

"The system ought to be operated," this country gentleman would go on, "through the post offices. Just simple and natural—nothing elaborate or alarming about it. The rural free delivery carrier ought to bring papers to the door and pick them up after they are filled out. The rural free delivery carrier ought to give each child his social insurance number and his policy or whatever takes the place of a policy. The rural free delivery carrier ought to be the one who picks up the claim of the man who is unemployed, or of the old lady who wants old-age insurance benefits.

"And there is no reason why just the industrial workers should get the benefit of this. Everybody ought to be in on it—the farmer and his wife and his family.

"I don't see why not," he would say, as, across the table, I began to shake my head. "I don't see why not. Cradle to the grave—from the cradle to the grave they ought to be in a social insurance system."

It was not that I did not admire his bold conception of universal coverage, but I felt that it was impractical to try to develop and administer so broad a system before we had some experience and machinery for the preliminary and most pressing steps.

Moreover, I felt sure that the political climate was not right for such a universal approach. I may have been wrong. Having the administrative responsibility, I was more alarmed than he about how we were going to swing it. The question of financing was in the forefront of my mind, and Roosevelt, because he was looking at the broad picture, could skip over that difficult problem.

That phrase, "cradle to the grave" insurance, on which he had sold himself, always remained with him as the desirable objective. It came back to me when the Beveridge Plan was announced in Great Britain in December 1942. With enormous fanfare it was labeled "cradle to the grave" insurance by Beveridge and the newspapers.

When Roosevelt read the reports of the Beveridge Plan he jokingly said to me one day, "Frances, what does this mean? Why does Beveridge get his name on this? Why does he get the credit for this? You know I have been talking about cradle to the grave insurance ever since we first thought of it. It is my idea. It is not the Beveridge Plan. It is the Roosevelt Plan."

He was not jealous of Sir William Beveridge. But in some strange way his intuitive feeling had jumped ahead of the practical, flat-footed first steps we had taken in this country, and he remembered his phrase. He felt a bit as though his own broad outlook on the thing had been chiseled down to a conservative pattern in our plan. No amount of arguing that the British had had twenty years of experience with social insurance before the Beveridge Plan was worked out had any effect upon him. He had approved of our plan and had been glad to recommend it, and in his serious moments realized that it was the only plan that could have been put through Congress. Nevertheless, he regarded himself as associated with "cradle to the grave" insurance and perhaps the inventor of it.

He may very well have been the inventor. He saw Sir William Beveridge here in 1934. Undoubtedly the President talked to him about "cradle to the grave" insurance, the rural free delivery postman, the opportunity of the little man to buy into the system. How much Sir William was inspired and moved by Roosevelt's phraseology and ideas I cannot say.

It was Harry Hopkins who recommended seriously that relief and social insurance be lumped together, that relief payments should be called unemployment and old-age insurance, and that payments should be made as a matter of right and not as a matter of need. This, of course, was a pretty extreme point of view for a country which had not had a social insurance system or a relief program before. When we took it to the President, only Hopkins and I went. Although Hopkins was eloquent, the President at once saw that this would be the very thing he had been saying he was against for years—the dole.

This prejudice served as a guidepost to warn him against unsystematic and unrelated distribution of funds from the Treasury. He insisted that the two systems, however much they might apply to the same people, should be kept separate because relief appropriations should be curtailed and canceled as soon as there was a revival of business and employment opportunities. The systems of unemployment and old-age insurance ought to continue as a permanent part of our economy.

Hopkins fought hard for his point of view. He pointed out that the unemployment insurance payments contemplated in any system then being discussed would not be adequate for the support of families whose breadwinners were long out of work.

This was admitted by all of us. It was pointed out to the President that all that was intended, or hoped for, was to establish a system of unemployment insurance to provide in the future some tide-over income during the early impact of unemployment. We always admitted that, if there should ever again be a major crisis, a cyclical depression, with accompanying unemployment, the unemployment insurance system would not be adequate for all the people. But we also pointed out that in the surveys we had made of the then unemployed, by far the largest number had had intermittent employment. If they had had unemployment insurance to draw upon, even in small weekly amounts, in the early part of the depression, their expenditures would have been sufficient to cushion the decline of business and to make a market for the continuing production and sale of goods and commodities—and thereby to reduce the total amount of unemployment.

Even if the allowance were small—and ten dollars a week for sixteen weeks might be a meager allowance for a family— nevertheless, if it came at the beginning of unemployment, it would sustain savings and credit, it would stave off evictions, it would serve to piece out the intermittent unemployment which members of a family might have during a depression. In short, it would be worth, in peace of mind, and in practical family budgeting, more than its cash value would indicate.

The Committee on Economic Security selected Edwin Witte to be director of its work. He had had long experience as chief of the Legislative Library in Wisconsin and knew how to put his finger on material quickly. We brought in other people who were familiar with social insurance problems and with United States economy; at the President's request we steered clear of people who were too theoretical and who would take months of research before they could make a brief report.

Our instructions to this group were to report upon all the possible alternatives. I recall emphasizing that the President was already in favor of a program of social insurance, but that it remained for them to make it practicable. We expected them to be familiar with every experiment in social insurance in every country. We expected them to make reasonable, practical choices among patterns tried in different countries. We expected them to remember that this was the United States in the years 1934-35. We hoped they would make recommendations based upon a practical knowledge of the needs of our country, the prejudices of our people, and our legislative habits.

Since the President relied on me to drive this program through, I naturally put everything I had into it. The Committee met frequently. As was inevitable, the cabinet officers began send-ing substitutes. Although this is regrettable when long-range policy is involved, in some ways it is a more practical way to operate, since subordinates often know details more completely than heads of Departments, who have multiple duties. Henry

Wallace always came himself. I made it a point to be present in person.

It is difficult now to understand fully the doubts and confusions in which we were planning this great new enterprise in 1934. The problems of constitutional law seemed almost insuperable. I drew courage from a bit of advice I got accidentally from Supreme Court Justice Stone. I had said to him, in the course of a social occasion a few months earlier, that I had great hope of developing a social insurance system for the country, but that I was deeply uncertain of the method since, as I said laughingly, "Your Court tells us what the Constitution permits."

Stone had whispered, "The taxing power of the Federal Government, my dear; the taxing power is sufficient for everything you want and need."

This was a windfall. I told the President but bound him to secrecy as to the source of my sudden superior legal knowledge. I insisted in Committee on the taxing power as the method for building up the fund and determining its expenditure for unemployment and old-age benefits to be paid in the future.

Roosevelt was determined to have a bona fide self-maintaining system—that is, the premiums paid in were to support the benefits paid out. Obviously an insurance program could not begin to pay benefits at once. Obviously it would be confined to those presently employed and paying premiums or having a portion of the premium paid on their behalf by their employers. But the suffering of those now out of work or aged or dependent or sick, for whom no such premiums ever could be paid, challenged our immediate attention.

We agreed that we must bring in a program for unemployment insurance and one for old-age insurance. Without too much debate we agreed that in addition to these two fundamental insurance programs we must recommend what we knew was not insurance but a relief program. It must include old-age assistance, assistance for dependent children, assistance for crippled and handicapped persons, and a continuation of emergency assistance to the unemployed then in operation.

With that much settled, the question was *how*. The Federal

Government had unlimited taxing power, and out of the taxes so raised Congress could either make grants to the states on a matching basis or expend funds direct for the relief of old age, dependency, or the handicapped. Rather early in the considerations, we committed ourselves to support the recommendation of aid to dependent and indigent persons from federal appropriations made available to the states on a matching basis. That did not solve the "how" for unemployment and old-age insurance, which was the next big task. Arthur Altmeyer, Assistant Secretary of the Department of Labor, was assigned to be in charge of this phase.

In the Legal Division of the Department we had a number of young, ardent, and intelligent lawyers. I called a meeting and asked for volunteers. Practically everyone volunteered. Tom Eliot, assistant solicitor, was assigned to give his full time to the job, and he did it well. In fact, we had the development of the social security program as a major project for the whole Department of Labor for the best part of two years. Altmeyer, Eliot, Isador Lubin, chief economic adviser, Katherine Lenroot, head of the Children's Bureau, and several others at subordinate levels gave the principal part of their time for two years to the development of this program, and I did also.

Although the actual work was done by the technical advisory group and the cabinet Committee on Economic Security throughout the long, hot summer, we decided to appoint a citizens' advisory committee and also to call a larger citizens' conference.

A large conference was called for November 1934 at the Mayflower Hotel in Washington, under the auspices of the Committee on Economic Security. More than two hundred experts on social problems and legislation were invited. So great was the interest that those invited not only came but paid their own expenses and bought tickets to a dinner held on the final day of the session.

William Green, president of the AF of L, indicated in his speech that it was perhaps the most important economic conference ever held in America. It had been something of a problem to secure the wholehearted support of the AF of L, which held fast to the old Gompers position that every gain made by working people should be won in collective bargaining. This traditional position was, of course, outmoded in a day of mass production. Organized workers were in the minority in American life. The capacity of a union to bargain with its employer about old-age retirement or unemployment benefits is limited in a country where labor moves freely from one employment to another.

President Roosevelt spoke at a session held in the White House on November 15, 1934. He urged strongly that out of these deliberations a program of economic security to include unemployment and old-age insurance should emerge. He emphasized, however, that recovery of industrial vigor must be placed ahead of any reform.

In the course of his address the President mentioned the three principal items being considered by the Committee: unemployment insurance, about which we had come to definite views; old-age insurance, which looked more difficult; and health insurance. He called health insurance highly desirable. Whether we come to this form of insurance sooner or later, he said, "I am confident we can devise a system which will enhance and not hinder the remarkable progress which has been made in the practice of the profession of medicine and surgery in the United States."

But health insurance was then, as now, a difficult question. Powerful elements of the medical profession were up in arms over the idea of any kind of government-endorsed system.

In that address the President said that unemployment insurance was a must and that it would be included in some form in his message to Congress at the beginning of the next congressional term.

"I am still of the opinion, expressed in my message of June 8," he said, "that this part of social insurance should be a cooperative federal-state undertaking and that it is important that the Federal Government encourage the states which are ready to take this progressive step."

He added that it was no less important that all unemployment insurance reserve funds be held and invested by the Federal Government so that the use of these funds as a means of stabilization might be centrally managed and employed on a national basis.

These remarks of the President had been prepared by and approved in substance by the Committee. The President's statement reflected our view rather than an independent one. The idea that unemployment insurance should be developed on a federal-state basis, rather than national, was at that date the best opinion that we had. But the question was by no means settled, and depended to some extent on the answer to two other pressing questions.

One large school of thought held that unemployment insurance premiums should be assessed only against employers. Another, equally large and vigorous, felt that workers should pay their share of the costs. These were not illiberal or reactionary people either. Those who held, as I did, that only employers should make a contribution to the fund, believed that unemployment should be regarded as a natural risk of industry, just as workmen's compensation for accidental injuries is regarded as part of the cost of doing business. Debate on this point could easily kill the bill in Congress.

Another problem about which there was great divergence of feeling was the question of "merit rating." Should there be a flat contribution from all employers without regard to the particular industry? Or should there be, as had grown up under workmen's compensation procedure in many states, a merit rating, allowing a smaller contribution from firms with a low rate of unemployment and putting a larger tax upon those with a higher rate of unemployment? There was very vigorous feeling on both sides of this question, and again the debate in Congress would have been delaying.

I took a position, which I urged strongly upon the President, that unemployment was a social cost and must be borne by as large an area of the community as possible. I pointed out to him that the workmen's compensation practice of adjusted premiums on the basis of merit rating had had unfortunate results. A badly crippled man might be put back to work on extremely low wages. He would get no compensation, and therefore the accident cost to the employer would go down and with it his rating would go down, while a small employer without the facilities to put an injured man to work would continue to pay the higher rating. The most serious defect of merit rating was the refusal to employ slightly handicapped people on the theory that if such a person had an accident the cost of the disability might be greater than it would be for a healthy man.

Under the federal-state system the Federal Government collects the tax under its taxing powers. It holds the money for allotment to the states for their payment of benefits. The states, in turn, have the right and duty to determine other questions in their own way. Those states that want merit rating can have it. Those that want employee as well as employer contributions can have that. Out of a variety of systems we should get a mature American experience. So we argued.

There was one outstanding, and, in my mind, determining factor, at that time in favor of the federal-state system. Although we thought we were on the right track in using the taxing power of the Federal Government, we were never quite sure whether a federal system of unemployment insurance would be constitutional. The Federal Government could tax; that was clear. But could it distribute its funds on a basis of social benefit? The Attorney General's office, in fact, repeatedly advised us that it was a doubtful constitutional point and that we should be extremely careful.

If the federal aspects of the law were declared unconstitutional, in the federal-state system we would at least have state laws which could be upheld legally under the "police power" of the states. Though state laws might not be uniform, they would be giving unemployed persons some income during a period of unemployment, and that would be an advance. These were the arguments I had presented to the President before he made his November 1934 speech.

The truth is that the Committee could not keep its mind made up on this one point: should it be a federal-state system or a federal system? A few weeks after the President's speech somebody moved that we reconsider the whole matter. Most of us had been under a barrage of letters and opinions from people all over the country. We reconsidered. Henry Wallace argued firmly for a federal system. Josephine Roche, Assistant Secretary of the Treasury, who was sitting in for Morgenthau on this occasion, held with him.

After long discussion we agreed to recommend a federal system. We went back and informed colleagues in our own Departments. Within the day I had telephone calls from members of the Committee saying that perhaps we had better meet again.

There was grave doubt, our latest interviews with members of Congress had shown, that Congress would pass a law for a purely federal system. State jealousies and aspirations were involved. So we met again, and after three or four hours of debate we switched back to a federal-state system.

Four special meetings of the Committee were held between November 15 and January 1 on this one point. Finally, one day during Christmas week, 1934, I issued an ultimatum that the Committee would meet at eight o'clock at my house, that all telephone service would be discontinued at my house for the evening, and that we would sit all night, if necessary, until we had decided the thorny question once and for all. We sat until two in the morning, and at the end we agreed, reluctantly and with mental reservations, that for the present the wisest thing we could do was to recommend a federal-state system.

The President knew of only part of this confusion. He was always sympathetic, but he expected us to find the answer. If we were agreed on a method, then he was for it. The Committee must bear the responsibility for the pattern of unemployment insurance we have in this country today.

With old-age insurance we had an even more difficult time. It became obvious that old-age assistance on the pattern of a federal grant-in-aid for those now aged and needy must be adopted. That was easy to accept. We agreed readily that for old-age insurance the individual as well as the employer should make contributions.

There was greater debate on the size of the benefit to be paid to individuals upon old-age retirement. The easiest way would be to pay the same amount to everyone. But that is contrary to the typical American attitude that a man who works

hard, becomes highly skilled, and earns high wages "deserves"   .
more on retirement than one who had not become a skilled
worker. As one looks back, one can see that there is much to be
said for the flat rate.

We decided on the more complicated system where the benefit rate bears a percentage relationship to previous earnings.

Our next problem was concerned with those who were then
forty-five or fifty years old. Probably they had worked since they
were about nineteen. They were fifteen to twenty years short of
retirement age. When they retired, they and their employers
would have paid less than half the premium required to build
them a decent, normal retirement allowance. The plan finally
recommended paying such people at retirement a benefit larger
than the value of their contributions, otherwise some would receive ridiculously small benefits. However, their benefits would
not be so large as those of people retiring after forty years in the
system.

Even with enlarged benefits to persons reaching retirement
age in the next fifteen to twenty years, there would be ample
funds to meet all immediate payments out of immediate income.
But by any proper actuarial estimate, there would be, in the end,
an accumulated deficit. The reserves would not suffice to pay
benefits when those now twenty became sixty-five and eligible
for retirement.

From an insurance company's point of view this was impossible; but underlying the whole government system was the
credit of the United States. Perhaps in 1980 it would be necessary for the Congress to appropriate money to make up a deficit. After some hesitation and discussion, the Committee decided
to recommend to the President this type of collection and payment, with accumulation of partial reserve and partial deficit
against the future. This, of course, was along the line of what
was later called a pay-as-you-go system. We thought we had
agreement on this approach. A few days before the report was
due, however, Secretary of the Treasury Morgenthau, though
his substitute in the Committee had agreed, indicated his flat
opposition to any system which would require a government
contribution out of general revenues at any time.

The alternative appeared to be contributions in the early stages so large both from workers and employers as to be almost confiscatory.

It was characteristic of the President that when we took this proposal to him, he put his finger at once upon this difficult-to-explain procedure.

"Ah," he said, "but this is the same old dole under another name. It is almost dishonest to build up an accumulated deficit for the Congress of the United States to meet in 1980. We can't do that. We can't sell the United States short in 1980 any more than in 1935." And yet the President had told us that we must develop some kind of old-age insurance benefit.

"We have to have it," he said. "The Congress can't stand the pressure of the Townsend Plan unless we have a real old-age insurance system, nor can I face the country without having devised at this time, when we are studying social security, a solid plan which will give some assurance to old people of systematic assistance upon retirement." The President was in the midst of one of the minor conflicts of logic and feeling which so often beset him but kept him flexible and moving in a practical direction.

Altmeyer, Eliot, a few others, and I immediately went to work on a compromise. The contributions, instead of being so large at the beginning as to paralyze the system and frighten the people and Congress, would remain small for the first year but would be increased more rapidly and to a higher level in subsequent years than originally proposed. Altmeyer was very ingenious about this. He could not understand the President's intellectual conflict on this point, but he said, "You can trust Congress never to require enormous payments as contributions. They will think of some way out."

We finally reached an agreement with the Treasury on this intermediate position: while a full actuarial reserve would not be built up, it would be enough, with the interest added to current contributions, so that future revenues would cover future benefits provided the terms of the act were not changed.

But there was pressure from another direction also. The American Association for Old Age Security, of which Abraham

Epstein was director and Bishop Francis McConnell, president, and which represented many intelligent social thinkers, was convinced that for stability, security, and permanence any old-age insurance schemes must have immediate government contributions. The plan of accumulating a future deficit and expecting that the government would meet it some time in the distant future did not satisfy the association. It set up considerable agitation for a plan requiring immediate annual government contributions in addition to payments by workers and employers.

A group in the Congress was also insistent on this point of view. We must remember, those were the days of the "share-the-wealth" schemes. There was a feeling that, unless the Government made a contribution out of general taxation, the rich who derived their income from investments rather than from business activity would not make a sufficient contribution to the fund. There would not be, these people argued, any sharing of the wealth.

Senator Hugo Black once pointed out to me that the burden on small employers and the poorer paid workers would be too great to allow for the gradual expansion of the coverage and benefits unless the tax resources of the whole United States were involved from the beginning.

Since then a great deal has happened in the field of social security all over the world. Under the new British old-age insurance system everybody will be covered, everybody will make a contribution whether employed or not, and appropriations from the general tax funds are made regularly to cover all forms of social insurance. Most European and Latin-American countries have modified their social security systems to provide for government contributions.

I recall that Epstein predicted that the old-age insurance funds supported without state aid in Germany, Austria, and central Europe would be made an instrument of anti-democratic action encouraging the corporate organization of society. He believed this would be so because the small business concern would find the cost of social insurance more burdensome than the large corporation.

This issue, however, was rather academic in the light of the United States Government's financial condition at that time. Obviously, so long as the Government was operating with a large deficit, any Government "contribution" would be merely a bookkeeping entry crediting the social insurance fund, rather than actual cash. And so no Government contribution was provided in the bill, both for this reason and to satisfy the President's prejudice about the "dole."

The bill embodying the Committee's recommendations was prepared the first week in January, 1935, and we took it to the President to see how it should be introduced. We thought it would be wise to have it referred to a special committee on social security, preferably a joint committee of the Senate and House. Since the measure rested primarily upon the constitutional taxing power of the Federal Government, it would have gone ordinarily to the Ways and Means Committees and not under any circumstances to the Labor Committees. However, Wagner in the Senate and Lewis in the House thought that they ought to introduce the bill.

The news got around that a special committee was being recommended. Representative Robert L. Doughton of North Carolina, chairman of the Ways and Means Committee, went to see the President. He was angry that anyone had thought of by-passing him, though he had never made a speech in the House that had indicated an interest in social security. It was something of a surprise to find that he cared.

As a result the President said to me, "No, no, it will never do. We will have to put it through the Ways and Means Committee. It is the only thing to do. You will hurt Bob Doughton's feelings. You will hurt Pat Harrison's feelings if you don't."

Result—four bills were dropped in the hopper on the opening day of Congress: one by Harrison and one by Wagner in the Senate; one by Doughton and one by Lewis in the House. It was my duty to reconcile Wagner to the idea that the President had said that this was to be a Harrison-Doughton bill. (As a curious sidelight, I recall that years later the President erroneously referred to the Social Security Act as the Wagner-Lewis bill.)

Our Committee had not made a competent, clear report on health and was not prepared to recommend any form of health insurance. Therefore no such measure was included. The bill did include, however, a program for appropriations and grants-in-aid to the states for public health services. The President, in talking with people who came to discuss health insurance with him, spoke in terms of utilizing public money to build hospitals all over the country and to staff them with competent physicians and nurses. He had been impressed with the need for hospital service in many parts of the country and saw this as a substitute for health insurance. I doubt that he was aware at the time of the program, which has become general in the Latin-American countries, of building hospitals, traveling clinics, and centralized medical services in lieu of benefit payments under social security.

Once the social security bill was introduced in the Congress it was our duty to see that the congressional committee hearings were prepared with sufficiently clear and varied testimony. The members of Congress must have a true opportunity to study the bill and to support it intelligently. It is interesting to note that the public educational work in the year and a half preceding the introduction of this bill had been sufficient to insure wide backing from the constituents of the congressmen.

At the first hearing before the House Ways and Means Committee we were startled to have Secretary Morgenthau make an appearance with a carefully prepared formal memorandum in which he apologized to his fellow members of the Committee on Economic Security. He said that the Treasury had decided, and he had concurred, that it would be unwise to give universal coverage under this act. He argued that it would be a difficult problem to collect payments from scattered farm and domestic workers, often one to a household or farm, and from the large numbers of employees working in establishments with only a few employees. He begged to recommend that farm laborers, domestic servants, and establishments employing less than ten people be omitted from the coverage of the act.

This was a blow. The matter had been discussed in the Committee on Economic Security, and universal coverage had been agreed upon almost from the outset. One could concede that it would be difficult for the Treasury to collect these taxes. But the whole administration of the act was going to be difficult.

The Ways and Means Committee members, impressed by the size of the project and the amount of money involved, nodded their heads to Secretary Morgenthau's proposal of limitation. There was nothing for me to do but accept, temporarily at least, though I continued to recommend universal coverage as the best and safest way for the United States.

The fact that in 1946 we still do not have universal coverage, though it had been "must" legislation for a number of years to extend the Social Security Act to all employed persons, is, I think, an indication that it would have been just as well to go ahead with the whole program at that time. But there were enough people afraid of the deflationary effects of this large money collection, enough people afraid of too large a system, and enough people confused about the desirability of social legislation by the Federal Government, to make it a foregone conclusion that if the Secretary of the Treasury recommended limitation, limitation there would be.

The Ways and Means Committee had a number of able men, and they put their minds to this new problem not only of finances but of social and economic policy for the whole United States. It has often been written by the critics of the Roosevelt administration that members of Congress didn't understand the social security bill when it was put before them because it was too complicated. Certainly it was complicated in the wording necessary to put it in bill form. But there were members of that House Committee, notably Fred Vinson, Jere Cooper, and others who fully understood the bill and all its implications and could have given as good an analysis of it as those who had prepared the details.

The House Committee and other members of Congress began to hear from their constituents in favor of the social security bill, and it was soon obvious it was going to be moved along. In August 1935 Republicans as well as Democrats voted for the bill, and there were only a very few who had the temerity to be counted against it.

I remember that when I appeared before the Senate Committee old Senator Gore raised a sarcastic objection. "Isn't this Socialism?" he asked me.

My reply was, "Oh, no."

Then, smiling, leaning forward and talking to me as though I were a child, he said, "Isn't this a teeny-weeny bit of Socialism?"

When the law was signed by the President, we made a little ceremony in his office and he gave out the usual pens. I had brought in not only Senator Harrison and Congressman Doughton, but also Senator Wagner and Congressman Lewis, and one or two other members of Congress, and had provided the pens for them. As he was signing the copies of the bills with pens that would be given to its sponsors, the President looked up at me. "Frances, where is your pen?" he asked.

"I haven't got one," I replied.

"All right," he said to McIntyre, his secretary, "give me a first class pen for Frances." And he insisted on holding me responsible and thanking me personally in very appreciative terms.

After the bill was signed, an appropriation bill came before the House to finance the administration of the Social Security program until the next fiscal year. Huey Long, then a powerful member of the Senate, filibustered until the date for adjournment of Congress. The result was that we passed into the period when Congress was not in session with no appropriation and with an act which was effective immediately.

We were pretty desperate. Conferences with the President about a special session brought a shake of his head. "Oh, that's too terrible," he said. "Not in August and September. We shall have a riot on our hands if we call them back for an appropriation."

Finally he said, "Well, the NRA is being liquidated. There has been an appropriation from Congress to enable them to liquidate. You can take the people laid off there."

That formed a nucleus of workers who could be put to work, especially in the clerical grades, in the Social Security Administration. Then it was agreed that the Department of Labor would present another research project to the WPA for a study of ways and means of administering the social security program. Out of the money we got from the WPA it was possible to employ people who couldn't be lent or financed by other departments of the Government.

The President was always willing to try even a risky technique to accomplish things. But it is indicative of the political skill and underlying caution with which he proceeded that on this occasion he called in Democratic and Republican leaders of the Congress as well as Comptroller General John R. McCarl, a Republican but primarily a disinterested financial officer whose duty it was to see that no moneys were improperly spent. He got their support before agreeing that such a project could be given to the WPA.

We organized the Social Security Board and went ahead. The Board was to be bipartisan, and in discussing available Republicans I recommended strongly John G. Winant, former Governor of New Hampshire, who had done useful work for us on the cotton textile industrial relations problem. Roosevelt liked Winant. He felt him to be a man of good will, consistent, reliable, and wholly trustworthy in his general purpose and direction. He named him chairman. The President cautioned me to find a Southerner, and we appointed Vincent Myles, an Arkansas lawyer. I suggested Altmeyer, and he was named to be sure that someone who had worked on the planning and was close to the Department of Labor would have a hand in setting up the original policies.

It had been anticipated that the Social Security Board and its operation would be in the Department of Labor. That indeed would have been logical. But as soon as the matter got into Congress it became obvious that it was the same old story.

Neither the Congress nor state legislators wanted money to go to the Labor Department. There is always the feeling that a Department of Labor will be soft on workers, that it will be too much influenced by working people and their point of view.

Rather than have any delay, I readily agreed to an independent agency. I talked it over with the President and we agreed that the matter of the place was not a major one on which to make a fight. It would be better to give way and have an independent agency, even though in the long run that might be awkward, than to run the slightest risk of retarding the passage of the bill.

Several years later a move got under way for a modification of the Social Security Act, particularly the old-age insurance system, to have what was euphemistically called the pay-as-you-go system. The President didn't like it, but he was interested in extending social security. He wanted it to protect more people. He wanted the benefits raised when the time came. The pay-as-you-go policy was a secondary consideration and all right if the Congress wanted it. I don't think he ever realized that that was the exact system which he had rejected in at least a modified form when the Committee on Economic Security had reported it to him in 1934.

He always regarded the Social Security Act as the cornerstone of his administration and, I think, took greater satisfaction from it than from anything else he achieved on the domestic front.

24.

LABOR RELATIONS

Almost the entire period of the Roosevelt administration was marked by difficulties in normal relationships between workers and employers. It must be remembered that from 1933 to 1945 we were always in a crisis. First there was mass unemployment and falling wages and labor standards, accompanied by real exploitation of workers by some employers. Next came the excitement of NRA with the accompanying drive of labor to organize. The recession of 1937 brought uncertainties and confusions. Then came the splits in the labor movement with the consequent factionalism and conflict. Then the defense emergency period with its desperate demand for goods and supplies, and finally the war with its need for unity, uninterrupted production, and, above all, speed.

These crises were bound to create tensions between employers and workers. They were bound to involve the Government more than ever in the tasks of resolving tensions and settling disputes. In earlier, more normal times these would have been merely disputes between a group of workers and an employer. Nothing stronger than conciliation was used except during World War I and during the coal strike in Theodore Roosevelt's day. Earlier the intervention of the Government to protect the United States mails in the Pullman strike of the 1890's had played an effective part but had not involved the Government in the negotiations or realities of collective bargaining. There again it was crisis that moved the Government to take action in a field which had always been regarded as a private affair between employers and workers.

Contrary to public belief, Roosevelt took almost no part in

the labor disputes, strikes, and settlement of strikes that went on during his administration. He was not a good negotiator in a labor dispute. He was too imaginative. He had too many ideas, and they sometimes were not in harmony with ancient policies, prejudices, and habits of the union or industry he was dealing with. That made them think him impractical. Also, he was in too much of a hurry. It takes unlimited patience to wait for the slow process of negotiation in collective bargaining. Roosevelt, or any other President, would have too many other things on his mind to sit patiently through long, tiring discussions and wait while the play and interplay of suggestions and counter-suggestions—the game, as it is called among experienced negotiators—went on. The fact that many moves were made merely for dramatic effect on the public or the members of unions back home or business rivals, was lost on him. He always felt that they ought to come to their conclusions more quickly and concisely. But this is not the way of collective bargaining, as the most experienced negotiators, employers, and workers will agree.

No President of the United States ought to take part in the detailed negotiation for settlement of labor disputes. Every Government agency that advises a President ought to make that a clear matter of policy. Although in times of emergency the presidential powers may have to be invoked to appoint a mediation board, that ought to be routine—his signature on the advice of the responsible agency, with his full assent, of course. But he ought not to be asked to deal with the details of the problem. The presidential office in our system is far too complex and has far too many responsibilities. It leaves no man free to give his whole mind for days to controversies, sometimes important and sometimes not.

In 1933 General Johnson attempted to deal with a group of automobile workers who had come to Washington to protest conditions under the NRA codes and to threaten a strike. He also conferred with Walter Chrysler and one or two other automobile manufacturers. The workers represented few men. There was not as yet a real labor organization. This was part of the first move for organization and the men had no officers.

Johnson properly called in William Green, president of the AF of L, and asked him to act as their consultant and make a systematic statement out of their complaints. The men stayed around for two or three days, harassing Johnson. Then he pressed the White House to let him bring them to see the President, who, he felt sure, could solve all their problems with a few kind words.

I was in the West that day and could not advise the President that I thought he ought not to see them. He good-humoredly agreed to let them come. They took up most of the day and most of the next, and he made no headway. The problem grew more confused. Finally Roosevelt got it out of the White House by proposing a board and asking them then and there whom they wanted on it. The employers hastily got together and nominated their lawyer, Nicholas Kelley. The workers in the room scarcely knew one another; they had little basis for selection since they had no officers and no representative committee. They said they would take Richard Byrd, a good-looking man who was present that day with the delegation but whose background and previous experience were almost unknown. The President agreed to appoint a public member later and with a sigh of relief sent them on their way. He eventually named Leo Wolman, and this became the Automobile Board, which sat in Detroit for well over a year attempting to adjust complaints.

The President told me about this episode in detail when I returned, "I must never again do a thing like that," he said.

I agreed.

He chuckled. "How much do you pay your conciliators?"

"Mr. President," I said, "you were attempting to practice a trade for which experienced conciliators in the Bureau of Conciliation get $3,600 a year."

"So you don't think I am worth $3,600?" he demanded.

"You would be worth a lot more if you would learn the trade," I said, "but it will take you five years."

Thereafter he never willingly got himself into the details of any labor disputes until the war, when it was necessary to have his assent and signature on any order to seize a plant. After Pearl Harbor, when production for the war effort had top priority, every effort was made to secure the co-operation of labor, with or without unity. Roosevelt, stimulated by the reports of administrative officers of difficulties in dealing with labor on boards which had to include AF of L and CIO, which often were in opposition to each other, made another effort to bring them together. Roosevelt's idea was to create a new committee of three from each organization and to let them confer with him about the war effort, hoping that out of this there would grow a new movement for co-operation. Finally such a committee was named. The Victory Committee, as it was called, was composed of labor leaders of both the AF of L and the CIO, who met occasionally with the President to stimulate labor co-operation in the war effort. Lewis by this time, however, had begun his split with Murray, and although the Victory Committee met once in a while, there was no way by which it could make substantial progress toward reunion in the labor movement.

The coal strikes which became so critical during the war were not handled direct by Roosevelt after the failure of his radio appeal, made on the advice of Hopkins and Byrnes, to the miners to go back to work.

When the coal mines had to be seized, those who knew the coal situation dreaded an attempt by the Army to occupy and work the mines. Nor did the Army's plans reassure those who knew the explosive character of the miners' situation. Roosevelt was glad of the suggestion I made at the last moment that control of the mines be given to the Administrator of Hard Fuels, Harold Ickes. It was a great surprise even to Ickes, whom I had told only that morning what I planned to recommend. He thought well of it, however, for he feared that Army control would stop or reduce the output of coal which he was responsible for delivering. Control by the Fuel Administrator worked out all right. Ickes had a hard time and a lively exchange with other Government officials. The President was spared the dangers of Army occupation and operation of the coal mines, since the miners went to work.

Eventually, by permission of the War Labor Board, Ickes made a contract with the miners for a wage increase with complicated applications. The operators later signed the same contract and it was approved by the War Labor Board, whose jurisdiction to approve Lewis admitted only after the Smith-Connally Act was made law.

Altogether the history of the dispute in the coal industry in 1943 is a picture of irregularity, with extension of the contract followed by certification of the case to the War Labor Board with Lewis's refusal to appear, a walkout on the date of the termination of the extended contract in spite of the President's request to miners to stay on the job, the seizure of the coal mines, the miners' return to work under Government contracts, an extended truce for a month, another strike, a reopening of the mines, a difficult conflict between the War Labor Board and the Administrator, with the miners attempting to evade the handling of their case in any form by the War Labor Board. The whole matter was not settled—the Northern field, the Southern field, the anthracite, and the captive mines, until May 1944. This matter was very trying to those involved. It ought never to have happened. Although there was a falling off in the production of coal, the industrial furnaces did not stop, the trains did not stop, and we got enough coal for war needs, although not enough for peace of mind. It was a picture of conflicting ideas and Government agencies insisting on authority. The truth is that a year earlier, on the first of April 1943, the case could have been settled for $1.25 a day without a fuss. In wartime, with the seizure powers the only means of enforcing a no-strike order, it was almost impossible for the President to escape a part in labor disputes. The Army and the Navy never lost an opportunity to impress upon him how disastrous were strikes. The labor division of the OPM and later the War Production Board continued to present a picture of excitement and pressure in labor-employer relationships. The Office of Price Administration and other agencies concerned with economic factors were in a constant turmoil over the changes in prices that might follow a change in labor costs. However much advice the President had to give, he did not become involved directly in negotiations until the railroad difficulties early in 1944 after his return from Teheran.

He attempted to handle the situation in a meeting called immediately upon his return. His mind was full of everything else. A railroad strike which, he was told, had been threatened was unthinkable. Upon the advice of James Byrnes, who then headed the Office of War Mobilization, he announced what wage changes would be allowed and said no other program could be contemplated. Railroad labor people were deeply offended. Certain brotherhoods went so far as to threaten a strike in his presence, I believe. Days later they accepted the decision and forgave him, saying that they knew he didn't understand the situation. They realized that they themselves were partly responsible for playing their cards so that he was brought in.

In many ways it is a pity that so many labor disturbances had to come in the administration of a President so well disposed to trade unions as Roosevelt. He believed in trade unions. He had no fear of them, and he saw no reason why employers should fear them. He recognized that there had been an occasional crook in the trade union movement, but so had there been in every other human activity. He recognized that the labor unions had usually rid themselves of crooks, just as the directors of a business got rid of the occasional scoundrel they had unwittingly entertained.

Roosevelt thought he understood why men went on strike. He could hardly believe that more than the stated reason lay back of a strike call. He knew that workers had often been exploited and that their recourse to a strike or a threat of strike had been at times the only way they could bring any influence to bear upon their employers.

I heard him explain to people, "You don't need to be afraid about unions. They only want to be in a position to arrange their own affairs, to agree to their own terms and conditions of work, and not be pushed around by their bosses. They really have no other objects in mind. You shouldn't be afraid to have them organize in your factory. They don't want to run the business. You will probably get a lot better production and a lot more peace and happiness if you have a good union organization and a good contract."

When someone once argued that unions might get too pow-

erful, he said, "Too powerful for what? It might be a good
democratic antidote for the power of big business, which certainly tries to dominate in many cases."

It must always be remembered that Roosevelt had no hatred
of business; in fact, he had considerable admiration for what he
called the good businessmen, those who made a contribution
not only to the goods of the country but to the social advance-
ment of their employees, customers, and community. While he
had no dislike for businessmen as such, he was always in strong
opposition to the idea that business should dominate the life of
the country; he felt keenly that it was unhealthy for our economy and contrary to decent principles of human development
and culture. Productive business that did not dominate he considered a blessing to the community.

Internal politics in the labor unions did not interest him
much. He was hardly aware of the tensions and quarrels among
unions within the AF of L. When the Amalgamated Clothing
Workers returned in 1934-35 to the AF of L after several years
as an independent union, he was pleased. Anything that made
for unity, he felt, was a good thing.

The beginnings of the split in the labor movement were a
surprise to the President. He thought personal animosities were
responsible, as indeed they were in part.

The differences in vertical and horizontal unions, so much
talked about at the time, probably had slight meaning. General
Johnson was the inventor of the phrase "vertical and horizontal unions" and he gave lectures in the evenings of the hectic
days of the NRA to all and sundry about the differences.
The vertical union, according to General Johnson, was a general union which embraced all of the workers in a particular
plant. Horizontal unions were a series of labor organizations
which offered membership to and represented the ancient and
well-established crafts such as carpenters, plumbers, steam
fitters, machinists, metal polishers, etc. The term "vertical
union," before General Johnson's day, was usually expressed as
"industrial union"; that is, a union in which all the workers of
a particular plant or even a particular industry were involved.
There was never a real ideological difference of conception be-

tween the two, since the form and structure of the membership
were always subject to the practical consideration of the moment. The AF of L, when it organized in the mass production
industries, would almost surely have followed an industrial
union pattern. Many employers thought industrial unions pref-
erable and encouraged the idea. Gerard Swope often said that
in the General Electric Company they would have no objection to a trade union if they could have one trade union. But
the company simply could not deal with twenty different craft
unions and have jurisdictional disputes between them. It could
not have twenty different contracts with attendant restrictions
and differences in wage levels.

Roosevelt was impressed by Swope's arguments, and at least
on one occasion when he was Governor of New York had
talked to John Sullivan of the State Federation of Labor in New
York about the possibility of industrial unions being organized
in plants like General Electric. Sullivan, a conservative fellow,
gave no encouragement, and the matter was dropped. But there
was no disposition on Roosevelt's part to feel that there was
anything necessarily wrong about an industrial union or out of
date about a craft union.

The drive for organization by the Committee on Industrial
Organization after it had formed itself within the AF of L led to
the split. There were some in the AF of L who felt that the drive
was merely a method of self-aggrandizement for the unions involved and that just as good results could have been had by the
slower, more traditional process of organization to which the
AF of L had been accustomed. But the drive was successful and
a new strong group emerged.

Roosevelt gave no special attention to the split and no special
aid to those who broke away, although from time to time different elements in the labor movement would claim he was on their
side or complain that he was on the other. The split, however,
was a serious difficulty. It prevented free, comfortable consulta-
tion with labor by the Department of Labor. It prevented agreements on labor policies. It prevented agreements even on labor
legislation. The hard feeling ran through the whole country at
one time and threatened to interfere with the orderly develop-

ment even of state labor legislation. That was happily overcome by practical approaches to problems by state labor leaders. Although at one time both the CIO and the AF of L issued orders to their state organizations not to co-operate, the fact is that most of them, without regard to orders, did co-operate at the state level. There was a time when actual bloodshed was threatened in the fight, but most local labor men had too much common sense to go to such lengths.

Roosevelt sincerely wished the breach healed if for no other reason than to ease the difficulties of the Government in dealing and consulting with labor. He gave his blessing to any effort to heal the breach. On his authority I used many approaches, some of which seemed likely to be fruitful at times. But they were always upset by some untoward event, which I think was usually willful. Many labor leaders did not and do not now want the breach healed.

Beginning in 1938 every message the President sent to the annual AF of L convention contained a formal but sincere request that a way be found to make peace. But, since I drafted the message, I know that, although Roosevelt was earnest about it, the problem was not a matter of first concern to him.

There were indications at one time that a personal request from the President might be regarded seriously by both parties.

These suggestions came to me confidentially and it seemed worth trying. I recommended to Roosevelt that he formally ask William Green and John Lewis as heads of the AF of L and the CIO to appoint committees to negotiate a peace. Harry Bates, Matthew Woll, and Dan Tobin served for the AF of L, while Philip Murray, Sidney Hillman, and John Lewis served for the CIO. In some quarters it was thought that Lewis, by naming himself, intended to make agreement impossible. Lewis told me, however, that by putting himself on the committee he had indicated his intention to press for settlement to the limit. By this time we had secured resolutions from the AF of L and the CIO locals in two hundred different communities urging that there be peace. The rank and file never have liked the split.

At the first meeting Lewis proposed his overambitious plan for creating an entirely new labor body to supersede the AF of

L and the CIO, to include the four big Railroad Brotherhoods, and to name a president from the Railroad Brotherhoods with Lewis and Green not eligible for office. The plan was not realistic but it sounded well in editorial rooms. The AF of L, anxious to make a good impression, promised to study the plan. Harry Bates, a very sincere but diplomatic man, privately pointed out how impractical it was and how unlikely it was that any such coalition could be arrived at. The Railway Brotherhoods were entirely content with their status and did not wish to be involved too closely with the rest of the labor movement.

Roosevelt's 1939 letter to the AF of L convention again appealed for peace. Again, following a confidential report that the prestige of the President's office might move the negotiations forward, the President invited Green and Lewis personally to come and see him. The words on the surface were pleasant, but the President remarked to me after they went, "I don't think they had the slightest intention of making peace, do you?"

Politics were now entering into the situation. Roosevelt had not made up his mind whether he would run for a third term, but he was being urged to do so. He was anxious for a unified labor movement and the voting support of the working people, if he should decide to run. As I related in an earlier chapter, Lewis had suggested to the President that he might well be chosen as running mate for Roosevelt on the 1940 Democratic slate. If he got approval, Lewis's plan, I suppose, was to agree to the AF of L proposal for reunion.

After the Democratic convention Lewis did not immediately make the expected attack on Roosevelt. I understand that Willkie's agents spent considerable time wooing him. In the end, about a week before election, Lewis appealed in a much advertised radio address to the workers of America, particularly the workers of the CIO, to vote against Roosevelt, saying dramatically that if Roosevelt were re-elected, he, John L. Lewis, would know that that meant a vote of no confidence in him and he would at once resign from the leadership of the CIO.

Roosevelt was astonished at Lewis's action—not at his going over to Willkie, for he had been a lifelong Republican and had been sparring with the administration since 1937, but at his notion that his threat to resign would make the CIO membership follow his advice in voting for President. We know that communities in which organized labor was strong voted for Roosevelt in 1940. He even carried mining towns and counties all over the country. Lewis's estimate of his own power and leadership even in his own union, in strictly political matters, had to be revised.

Later, when Roosevelt once asked the striking mine workers to go back to work, and they did not do so until Lewis told them to, the President said, "I have learned one thing. The mine workers won't vote for President of the United States as John L. Lewis tells them, but they won't do what I tell them on matters that have to do with their union activities. That is something to know, at any rate."

There were industrial disputes in 1933 and 1934 which were a considerable problem to all of us. The longshoremen's strike on the West Coast was a ticklish one to handle and settle. Roosevelt took no hand in it beyond letting me make representations to people on the Pacific Coast that he wanted it settled and that he saw no reason for ship owners to hold back from making a contract with the longshoremen and seamen.

The strike, which had barely begun in San Francisco, spread at the outset to other unions which appeared to have no natural relationship to the waterfront workers. The waterfront workers' protest was a reaction to sixteen years without a union, the union having been crushed by the employers at that time. San Francisco had become almost an anti-union town, and more than one small and only partly accepted union had felt the restriction of the employer attitude against unions.

I had pretty good information on what was going on, not only from official but from private sources. These small sympathetic strikes of milk wagon drivers, building trades workers, and other unions conservative by tradition appeared to be a spontaneous movement to get recognition. A government board had been appointed by the Secretary of Labor to look into conditions along the waterfront, and the other unions hoped to attract attention to the fact that San Francisco was an open-shop town and thus perhaps get some remedies for themselves. For a few days there was quite a tie-up in San Francisco but it never had a generalized purpose, plan, or leadership and could not, therefore, be regarded as a general strike.

There was a great deal of solemn editorializing, particularly in the West. The alarm apparently reached Attorney General Cummings and Secretary of State Hull, who was Acting President. Roosevelt had gone to sea on the U.S.S. *Houston* for a rest and a naval inspection during the early part of the strike, but the matter had been discussed in cabinet meeting before he went, and the President had said that the Secretary of Labor was in charge of the problem and that he had perfect confidence we would be able to handle it during his absence. If he were needed, he said, Howe could get a message to him on the *Houston.*

One morning Secretary Hull called and asked me to come to his office at once. I arrived and found the Attorney General and the Secretary of State surrounded by law books and looking very solemn indeed. It was their opinion, based on a definition in the *Encyclopedia Britannica*—in the article written some thirty years earlier by P. Tecumseh Sherman, an elderly gentleman who had once been Commissioner of Labor Statistics in the State of New York—that the situation in San Francisco was legally a "general strike." Under the laws of the United States and the State of California, drastic action could be taken in case of a general strike.

A "general strike," I protested, was a strike of a large body of workers planned and co-ordinated in advance to force the Government to take a position on some matter of interest to them. Secretary Hull and Mr. Cummings appeared to think that the National Guard and Army should be called and the "general strike" put down. I pleaded that this was in no way an alarming situation and that the likelihood of anything more than a brief strike of delivery and transportation services was remote, and I thought it unwise to begin the Roosevelt administration by shooting it out with working people who were only exercising their rights, under our Constitution and laws, to organize and demand collective bargaining. At any rate, I insisted that before any action was taken we must communicate with Roosevelt, and I sent a message to him through Howe.

His reply thanked me for my "estimate of the situation." He suggested an offer of arbitration to all employers and unions involved, with work to be resumed immediately. If I thought it advisable, he said, I could state that the offer of arbitration came from the President. He suggested that we make a clear statement to the press explaining the issues. "Confidentially please consult with Hull and Cummings as to our authority to maintain food supply and traffic in the affected areas," he ended. "I am inclined to think that after Howe's radio it is at present best for me not to consider change in my itinerary."

We did not have to make the offer of arbitration or use the President's name. Sensible labor leaders advised the men to get back to work, that this was no time for an unconsidered sympathetic strike, even if it was also in their own interest.

It was characteristic of the President, though, that he saved everybody's feelings by advising me to appoint an arbitration board and to consult Secretary Hull and Mr. Cummings as to our authority to maintain a food supply, which, when read together, was a delicate hint that we use peaceful, persuasive methods rather than the drastic, violent approach suggested.

It is difficult to say whether the problem of the deportation of Harry Bridges was a problem in industrial relations or a plain problem of justice. Before he became an effective leader in the longshoremen's strike on the Pacific Coast in 1934, Bridges was an unimpressive fellow. He first received public attention when he appeared before the Mediation Board which was trying to make a connected story out of the confused, conflicting statements of workers and employers. The Board, appointed by the Secretary of Labor with the President's assent, consisted of Archbishop Hanna, Roman Catholic Archbishop of San Francisco, Otto Cushing, a leading liberal citizen of San Francisco, and Edward J. McGrady, Assistant Secretary of Labor. Bridges and a small group came before the Board to represent the workers on one pier of the Moore-McCormack Lines. They were not aggressive, they appeared to be quite intelligent, and were asked to come back the next day with more information and a better worked-out plan for the settlement of the strike. Eventually Bridges became the leader of the striking San Francisco longshoremen and the strike was finally settled by negotiations between his committee and the employers. It rested partly on a vote (one of the early ones) conducted by the Department of Labor whereby the workers indicated their choice with regard to being represented by the union.

During the early negotiations I was in San Francisco for the convention of the American Federation of Labor. Bridges sent word through a subordinate of a subordinate in the Department of Labor that he would like to see me. I had heard his name and the report of his constructive suggestions for settlement of the strike from McGrady and Tom Eliot, assistant solicitor of the Department of Labor, who had been assigned to this difficult case. I suggested that he come to the back of the platform of the Convention Hall immediately after I made my address. I have a clear memory of him. He was a small, thin, somewhat haggard man in a much-worn overcoat, the collar turned up and pinned around his throat, and with a cap in his hand. He was polite, deferential, hardly finding the voice to make demands for the striking longshoremen. His suggestions seemed practical and reasonable. I recall putting down in my mind that he was a typical British worker.

In the course of the next six months Bridges became an important and dominating factor in the West Coast industrial picture. As he established himself as a leader of the longshoremen, there began to be violent protest against him locally and nationally.

The cry against him in San Francisco was that he was a "Communist." The Immigration Service made an investigation of his status. The FBI and the San Francisco Police Department, not at my suggestion, but on their own initiative, conducted elaborate investigations of Bridges and his background.

They discovered that he was an Australian, the son of a well-to-do Australian family, whose father was an estates manager, and whose family lived in what the report said was a fine villa outside of Melbourne. The report said that the family bore a fine reputation in the community, that they were devout Roman Catholics, that there were several brothers, and that one brother, Harry, had mooned around the docks and run away to sea when he was fifteen. Harry Bridges, according to the police report, became a seaman, turned up in South American ports, in Texas, eventually in California, and settled down in San Francisco as a longshoreman. He worked for eleven years steadily with the Moore-McCormack Lines; he had a good reputation; he was regular in his attendance, a steady, competent workman. The police probed into his private life. They found he had lived in a boarding-house. The landlady told the police that he was a quiet, orderly tenant; that he worked every day; that he paid his board promptly. As for his evenings, she didn't know much, but he rarely went out; mostly he went to his room after supper and played the mandolin until bedtime.

Such was the man, or at least what we knew about him, when the agitation for his deportation began. Until he became an effective labor leader, no one thought of demanding his deportation as a subversive or dangerous alien. In the summer of 1937, suddenly and without preliminary information, there came a report from an immigration officer in the State of Washington that there was evidence showing that Bridges was a Communist. It was in the form of affidavits and information which had been put before the Commissioner of Immigration in the Port of Seattle. The persons making the affidavits were otherwise unknown. The evidence as it stood was not sufficient to prove that this man was indeed a member of an organization which sought to overthrow the Government of the United States by force and violence. Under the immigration law an alien is deportable if he attempts to overthrow the Government of the United States by force and violence or if he is a member of an organization with that program.

The evidence forwarded to me from Seattle was mostly hearsay, vague and indefinite. A principal witness was a man who had been known before for his anti-labor activities and who, moreover, had given perjured testimony in at least one other case. I was considerably surprised to receive this information.

The conflict of interest within the Department was clear. On the one hand, we must enforce the immigration laws without fear or favor. On the other hand, in the effort to settle strikes and industrial disputes, we must deal with anyone who appeared to be effective and to represent the workers.

Because I recognized that this was no ordinary deportation case, since the man was an important labor leader with whom settlements and bargains were being carried on constantly, I decided to inform the President and to get his view. I asked for an opportunity to see him at length and alone. I was told that he would be at Hyde Park on a Saturday, and that if I could come up, there would be a good opportunity to talk. I got there in time for lunch with the family. After lunch the President said, "You want to talk about something. Come on in my little car. I'll show you my trees and we can talk."

We got into his little car. Secret Service men followed in their heavier one. He took me over roads and paths where they could scarcely follow except at a distance, and finally he parked on a little promontory which accommodated only one car.

"What's the problem?" he began.

I told him briefly that Bridges, a conspicuous and successful labor leader, had been charged with being a Communist by witnesses whose veracity and competence remained to be proved, and I wanted his advice as to how to proceed.

His first reaction was that of the ordinary American liberal.

"What's the idea?" he asked. "Has he done anything to overthrow the Government?"

"No," I admitted.

"Then why in the world," asked the President, "should a man be punished for what he thinks, for what he believes? That's against the Constitution."

I had to explain to him that the statutes and court interpretations had set up limitations on what an alien could believe or think. I told him all we knew about Bridges. He laughed heartily over the picture of this dangerous fellow, playing the mandolin in his San Francisco boarding-house in the evenings.

His advice was entirely correct, of course: to carry out the law, if indeed the evidence supported a finding that made deportation necessary, but not to let our imagination run away with us.

The case dragged on for years. Occasionally Roosevelt would say, when some aspect of the case had been in the newspapers, "How's your mandolin player getting on?"

Eventually the case became a *cause célèbre*. The preliminaries of an impeachment were brought against me by Representative J. Parnell Thomas of New Jersey for failing to deport Bridges. They were dismissed by the House Judiciary Committee as having no merit.

Roosevelt made light of these proceedings. "It's all nonsense. Who is this fellow J. Parnell Thomas? I hear his real name is Feeney. Why did he change his name? Who bothers about him? Don't pay any attention to him. You've done the right thing."

I didn't like the idea of being impeached and was considerably disturbed by the episode, but Roosevelt, with his complete confidence that if you do the thing that seems right to you, you'll come out all right, patted me on the back in a brotherly way and said, "Don't worry."

I decided the Bridges case on the report of James Landis, dean of the Harvard Law School, who found after exhaustive hearings that there was no evidence to support a finding on which Bridges could be deported.

A few years later the case was reopened after the Immigration Service had been transferred to the Department of Justice and was referred by the Attorney General, Robert Jackson, to Judge Charles Sears. Judge Sears found that in the light of new legislation Bridges was deportable. The Board of Review in the Immigration Service reversed Judge Sears on the ground of no valid evidence. Francis Biddle, by this time Attorney General, decided to review the case himself. It was unnecessary. At any rate, he set aside the verdict of his Department's Board of Review and found Bridges deportable. Bridges appealed to the Supreme Court, which found there was no valid evidence to support the Attorney General's findings, and therefore set aside the deportation order. Bridges then applied for naturalization and became a citizen of the United States in September 1945.

Whether President Roosevelt was even consulted about these later actions I do not know. I took pains not to ask.

When the sit-down strikes started, Roosevelt was as much surprised and bewildered by the new technique as anyone else.

The first such strike I heard of occurred in Akron, Ohio, in 1935, a year before its use at General Motors. My impression has always been that the sit-down strike in the rubber works at Akron was spontaneous. It was the idea of a few men, old-fashioned, stubborn Americans, who were determined to be heard. They had a real grievance. The company had changed its system of figuring wages. The men didn't understand it; the foremen didn't understand it; the floor superintendent didn't understand it; and when they finally reached the superintendent, he scratched his head and said he didn't understand it. It had been worked out by accountants in New York, the superintendent said, and he didn't know what it meant but it would have to be followed. This was extremely irritating to the men. They couldn't keep track of their own work records and daily earnings under this system. They took the position that they just wouldn't go home until they had an explanation or satisfaction of their demand for a return to the old system of figuring wages. Whatever other demands or grievances they had were thought up later. They just folded their arms and sat by their machines. I heard of no statement by them that a man has property rights in his job.

This strike attracted almost no attention in the country and hardly anyone knew about it except those of us in the Department of Labor attempting to settle it. The company executives did not lose their heads. They were surprised but not too irritated that the men would not leave the factory. They said they knew them to be good honest fellows who had worked there a long time and nothing unfortunate could possibly happen. If they wanted to sit there all night, that was their business. They refused to get excited or take theoretical positions about interference with property. The matter settled itself in a few days. Adjustments in the method of figuring wages were made, and the strike was over.

One remembered it because it was an unusual, disturbing, and dangerous technique. One wondered about it when it was used in Paris the following spring (1936) in department stores and some service industries.

When the sit-down strikes broke out in Flint, Michigan, and spread to other General Motors plants and then to industries all over the area and finally to different parts of the country, the situation was different.

The automobile companies were outraged by this method, which, of course, put them at a disadvantage. They proclaimed from the housetops that such a procedure was illegal, immoral, unconstitutional, and anything else that might damn it. But the men remained in the plant. The sheriff's order to get out did not move them; it resulted in hoots and jeers. The sheriff asked the Governor of Michigan to call out the National Guard and put the men forcibly out of the plant.

Certainly the sit-down technique is unwise and demoralizing. It has been agreed by nearly all sensible labor leaders that it is a method of excess and should never be used. It imperils the stability of the union, the safety of the plant, and the peace and order of the community. The opposition of the public to the sit-down strikes was great, and they undoubtedly did a great deal to set public opinion against the automobile workers and the CIO. But the employers took a very intransigent attitude. They would not talk with a workers' committee until the strikers were out of the factory, and they continued to hold that position. No matter what happened, they would not give way on that. I never could see why employers should be so stuffy about it—and Roosevelt agreed with me.

These workingmen, he said privately, are doing something quite wrong and hazardous and they ought not to do it in a country like this where, although their employers have been difficult to deal with, the men now have certain rights under the law, and eventually the government will get around to seeing that those rights are recognized and that the employers deal with them in collective bargaining.

In another discussion of the sit-down strikes Roosevelt said, "Well, it is illegal, but what law are they breaking? The law of trespass, and that is about the only law that could be invoked. And what do you do when a man trespasses on your property? Sure you order him off. You get the sheriff to order him off if he tries to pitch a tent in your field without your permission. If he comes on your place to steal, why, you have him for theft, of course. But shooting it out and killing a lot of people because they have violated the law of trespass somehow offends me. I just don't see that as the answer. The punishment doesn't fit the crime. There must be another way. Why can't these fellows in General Motors meet with the committee of workers? Talk it all out. They would get a settlement. It wouldn't be so terrible."

The situation, of course, grew very tense because no one could persuade the General Motors people to meet with the men. The General Motors people took quite a lofty, even self-righteous attitude, implying that among their duties as automobile makers and sellers was the duty to define and enforce certain aspects of public morals. Yes, perhaps it is their duty, but a little more flexibility and sense of the common errors of all mankind would perhaps have made them more influential in correcting the obvious bad behavior and certainly would have helped to end the strike more quickly and constructively. The CIO came to the support of the automobile workers, although I know for a fact that John Lewis and Sidney Hillman and Lee Pressman, CIO counsel, made great efforts to get the men to leave the plant as a matter of public duty. But they would not publicly desert them, such is the sense of union solidarity.

Lewis said, "The men will leave—I can assure you of that—when the company begins to bargain with them or even with me, in good faith."

Those were the days when Lewis was called a labor statesman and was much thought of by businessmen as a "better type" of labor leader.

Frank Murphy, then Governor of Michigan, motivated by a humane conscience, refused to shoot it out with the strikers. Roosevelt made no official or unofficial recommendation. He was in touch with me almost every day no matter where he was, and I was in daily touch with Governor Murphy. We were working constantly at different plans and schemes to get a conference between the workers and the employers and to give the workers an excuse that would save face for getting out of the factories. Murphy was alarmed, and so was I, that people who did not work in the industry were filtering into the factories. On a pass from the union, the employee went out, ostensibly to get a change of clothes and see his family. He would not return; a substitute would slip back on his pass and sit down for him. This was extremely hazardous and, as Governor Murphy said, morally repulsive.

The breakdown in industry was serious. I talked with the officers of General Motors, Chrysler, and other companies many times. Jim Farley and Jesse Jones both took a hand at it and were persuasive and reasonable. Myron Taylor, greatly disturbed by the interference with production and the deep cleavage being established, talked with the employers and with Lewis, and played an important role in getting agreement. Finally, Walter Chrysler, seeing that the situation was getting worse rather than better, decided to take the credit for being the first to make peace with the automobile workers, and, as he said to me with a chuckle, "leave General Motors guessing again."

I had been told that General Motors and other employers would take it better if they could say that the President had asked them to relent. The President picked up the telephone at my suggestion late one afternoon and called William Knudsen, president of General Motors. Roosevelt had a bad cold and hated further exertion. But he took the memorandum of facts which I had given him, not more than five or six typewritten lines.

I warned him, "Don't discuss the issues with Knudsen. Just tell him that you want them to agree to go into conference and that you have reason to believe that if they go into conference there will be an evacuation of the factory and that a reasonable settlement of the dispute will be reached."

He sighed and rubbed his head, which ached, as he sat up in bed, read the memorandum, picked up the telephone, and called Knudsen. He had not met Knudsen but had liked what he had heard about him. As the operator said, "Mr. Knudsen is on the telephone," Roosevelt said to him in a pleasant voice which did not reveal that he was aching and uncomfortable, "Is that you, Bill? I know you have been through a lot, Bill, and I want to tell you that I feel sorry for you, but Miss Perkins has told me about the situation and what you are discussing and I have just called up to say I hope very much indeed that you go through with this and that your people will meet a committee."

It was characteristic of the President to think of and speak warmly to people he did not know personally. It was a part of his sense of community of interest. He did it to many others.

Knudsen was as agreeable as the President. They exchanged a few words of mutual admiration. I heard the President say, "Fine, fine, Bill. Thank you very much, Bill. That's good."

Then he put the telephone down with a sigh. "Well, I hope that's over."

It was over. At least his part was. It took a long time to make an agreement, and the end is not yet. But the companies did meet with Lewis and a committee of the workers. The factories were evacuated, the sit-down strikes were over, and the road to peace in the automobile industry had been opened to the rule of reason and collective bargaining.

Members of the cabinet and friends and political associates gave me great help in opening the minds of the employer groups all over the country to the pressing necessities of the labor dispute situation and to the wisdom of a liberal and co-operative attitude in dealing with their employees. Jim Farley never hesitated to telephone long distance and give his advice and suggestions to employers who were having difficulties. Jesse Jones was also helpful. It may be surprising to some people to realize that men looked upon as the conservative branch of the Roosevelt administration were co-operative in bringing about a new, more modern, and more reasonable attitude on the part of employers toward collective bargaining agreements. Averell Harriman of the Union Pacific Railroad, Carl Gray of the same railroad, Daniel Willard of the Baltimore & Ohio, Walter Teagle of the Standard Oil Company, Thomas Lamont of J. P.

Morgan and Company, Myron Taylor of U. S. Steel, Gerard Swope of General Electric, and Robert Amory, a textile manufacturer, were among those whom I asked for help from time to time in difficult situations, where the problem was to get employers to start collective bargaining negotiations. Roosevelt knew that these people had helped and was always very grateful to them. I think he sometimes took occasion to express his feeling to them.

There were many things about trade unions that Roosevelt never fully understood. I doubt that he understood what solidarity really means in the trade union movement. He tended to think of trade unions as voluntary associations of citizens to promote their own interests in the field of wages, hours, and working conditions. He did not altogether grasp that sense of their being a solid bloc of people united to one another by unbreakable bonds which gave them power and status to deal with their employers on equal terms.

When labor moved into the national political field, he did not appear to realize that they might have any political interest other than in two contending candidates and parties. The two-party system seemed to him settled policy. He thought working people would choose one candidate or the other; one party or the other, depending upon local circumstances or the platforms and needs of the particular times. The fact that John L. Lewis, for instance, had been head of the labor committee of the Hoover presidential campaign committee had not left any sting. When I had brought a delegation of labor leaders to the White House shortly after the 1933 inauguration, Lewis had been among them. I am not sure whether Roosevelt had met Lewis before—I had not, before that conference—but he always thought that Lewis, just like John Frey, Matthew Woll, William Hutcheson, and other trade union Republicans, was entitled to his private views on politics. When labor people endorsed him, Roosevelt considered them a "Labor for Roosevelt Committee," and it was, in many respects. As he saw it, labor's effectiveness in political questions would put working people in a better position to participate in the civic and cultural life of the United States and would give them a better status in American life. He never doubted that such status and influence would tend to make individuals and unions more responsible, more public spirited, more willing to co-operate with others for the benefit of all the people in the United States. If labor, or some individual labor leader, had other ideas—ideas of using the political power acquired by an organization formed to elect Roosevelt to establish political controls for themselves—that was unknown to Roosevelt.

He made few pronouncements about specific labor-employer situations, but he came out clearly about the limitation of collective bargaining in the case of government employees. He said, "A strike of public employees manifests nothing less than an intent on their part to obstruct the operations of government until their demands are satisfied. Such action by those who have sworn to support the government is intolerable."

He pointed out that the government as an employer is the whole people and that administrative heads of departments cannot bargain collectively with employees since their action on personnel is governed by laws enacted by the representatives of the whole people in Congress.

Although Roosevelt practically never took part in labor negotiations and followed the trend of labor relations only superficially, he always stood ready to put his name to a call for a conference or a recommendation for a meeting or to appoint a board as recommended by his aides in the labor field, or even to seize a factory when recommended by the War Labor Board and the Labor Department.

The President's name in appointing a board, or making a recommendation for the acceptance of a decision made by a board or committee, was effective and saved face. He regarded this as a part of the natural executive function of backing up his subordinates and utilizing the prestige of the presidency to persuade employers and workers both to do what those directly responsible for handling the negotiations had recommended. In this way he took action in several of the coal disputes from 1933 on, where the statement that the President wanted this matter settled or this point arbitrated was often effective with both workers and employers and was deliberately planned for by both sides in the negotiations as the dramatic climax of their circuitous and complicated route to a settlement.

The officers of the mine workers and the officers of the coal operators liked to be photographed coming out of the White House. It made a better picture back home for whatever they had agreed to. As a matter of fact, the President rarely knew more about the situation when he made a proposal to the two sides in this formal way than what could be put down on half a sheet of paper by the Secretary of Labor or others having the jurisdiction. He also had the assurance that both sides would accept, and had agreed to, what he was about to ask of them.

I don't think he bothered much about the economics of coal, but even after he had been the subject of considerable abuse by John L. Lewis, he was still well poised enough to say, "Well, you have to admit Lewis has done a lot for the miners." He could remember that, even though he thought an intransigent attitude intolerable, particularly in war time.

25.

A LITTLE LEFT OF CENTER

I knew Roosevelt long enough and under enough circumstances to be quite sure that he was no political or economic radical. I take it that the essence of economic radicalism is to believe that the best system is the one in which private ownership of the means of production is abolished in favor of public owner-ship. But Roosevelt took the status quo in our economic system as much for granted as his family. They were part of his life, and so was our system; he was content with it. He felt that it ought to be humane, fair, and honest, and that adjustments ought to be made so that the people would not suffer from poverty and neglect, and so that all would share.

He thought business could be a fine art and could be con-ducted on moral principles. He thought the test ought to be whether or not business is conducted partly for the welfare of the community. He could not accept the idea that the sole pur-pose of business was to make more and more money. He thought business should make and distribute goods with enough profit to give the owners a comfortable living and enable them to save something to invest in other productive enterprises. Yes, he felt that stockholders had a place and right and that a business ought to be conducted so that they would earn modest interest, while the workers got good wages and the community profited by low prices and steady work.

But he couldn't see why a man making enough money should want to go on scheming and plotting, sacrificing and living under nervous tension, just to make more money. That, of course, made him unable to sympathize with the ambitions and drive of much of the American business fraternity. But he liked and got along well with those businessmen who shared, as many did, the point of view that business is conducted partly for the welfare of the country as well as to make money. They liked and trusted him and understood his objectives. Gerard Swope of the General Electric Company, Thomas J. Watson of the International Business Machines Company, Ernest Draper of the Hills Brothers Company, Donald and Hugh Comer, southern textile manufacturers, who had a humane if not a trade union conception of the rights of their workers and of the employers' duty in relation to them, were all comprehensible to the President. He liked Walter Chrysler, although I am not sure that Chrysler fully embraced the idea that enough is enough, particularly if his rivals were making more. But he did have some of the attitude that there was nothing remarkable in itself about making money.

It is true that Roosevelt never met a payroll, and many businessmen took it into their heads that he could not possibly comprehend business unless he had had that experience. This, of course, is part of the limitation of the business fraternity itself.

Roosevelt was entirely willing to try experiments. He had no theoretical or ideological objections to public ownership when that was necessary, but it was his belief that it would greatly complicate the administrative system if we had too much. He recognized, however, that certain enterprises could best be carried on under public control. He recognized that we probably would never have enough cheap electric power to supply the needs of the people if the Government did not undertake vast programs in the Tennessee and Missouri valleys, and he believed that plenty of power at low rates was necessary for the development of a high standard of living and for business progress. Just as the need for production in wartime is so great that the government must take a hand in it, so he was able to accept the idea that in peacetime too the Government must sometimes carry on enterprises because of the enormous amount of capital expenditure required or the preponderance of the experimental element. He was willing to concede that there were some fields in which such Government participation might be required permanently. But he always resisted the frequent suggestion of the Government's taking over railroads, mines, etc., on the ground that it was unnecessary and would be a clumsy way to get the service needed.

A superficial young reporter once said to Roosevelt in my presence, "Mr. President, are you a Communist?"

"No."

"Are you a capitalist?"

"No."

"Are you a Socialist?"

"No," he said, with a look of surprise as if he were wondering what he was being cross examined about.

The young man said, "Well, what is your philosophy then?"

"Philosophy?" asked the President, puzzled. "Philosophy? I am a Christian and a Democrat—that's all."

Those two words expressed, I think, just about what he was. They expressed the extent of his political and economic radicalism. He was willing to do experimentally whatever was necessary to promote the Golden Rule and other ideals he considered to be Christian, and whatever could be done under the Constitution of the United States and under the principles which have guided the Democratic party.

The young reporter, or his editor, did not think the answer had any news value, and nothing was printed about it. I suppose if the President had answered that he thought there was something remarkable in Communism or capitalism, it would have been a headline story.

I am certain that he had no dream of great changes in the economic or political patterns of our life. I never heard him express any preference for any form of government other than the representative republic and state-federal system which have become the pattern of political organization in the United States under the Constitution. At the beginning of his administration, and also, I think, at the end, he would have said that the states and their administrative systems should be strengthened and maintained. Nevertheless, federal legislation and administration must occur in some fields. If there could be greater co-operation among the states, that would be fine. But they should permit federal intervention on behalf of certain things that could not be done by them alone.

He believed in leadership from the office of the President, a leadership based upon the immense sources of information and analysis which the Executive Department had and which were available to the President. He fully recognized, however, the importance of Congress and the desirability of maintaining the strength of our congressional system. For that reason he wished at times that the people of the country would be more careful about whom they sent to Congress, to be sure that the congressman elected would not only represent his constituents but take part, intelligently and constructively, in making laws for all the people.

When he came to Washington, he had no idea whatever of reforming, changing, or modifying the Supreme Court. He believed strongly that Congress and its law-making powers should be seriously regarded by the Court, and that all the courts ought to exercise extreme care not to interfere with the development of law and procedures as times changed. As witness his casual reference that EPIC, even if it won in California, would "make no difference in Dutchess County, New York"—or other states or counties. He believed that Congress, suitably advised by its own legal committees, should be permitted to decide what was best for the country, and that the will of the people as expressed by an act of Congress should not be frustrated by overmeticulous decisions on abstract constitutional lines.

Roosevelt was not very familiar with economic theory. He thought of wealth in terms of the basic wealth in agriculture, transportation, and services which were the familiar pattern of his youth. He recognized or took for granted the changes that had come about in our economy in his own lifetime: the shift in emphasis from agriculture to industry and distribution, the importance of the financial elements. Honorable methods in all business matters seemed to him imperative and to be insisted upon, by changes in the law if necessary. And under

"honorable" he instinctively included wages and working conditions of the best, together with friendly, fair industrial relations. But, he had, I am sure, no thought or desire to impose
any overall economic or political change on the United States.
Some of the high-strung people who advised him from time to
time did, I think, have ideas of this sort, but he always laughed
them off and used their brilliant analyses for some project that
would do some immediate good to people in distress.

It was his way to be concerned about the concrete situations.
One recalls his ideas for salvaging and preserving the fertility
of the soil where this was needed, his plans to develop and preserve the forests for their value not only as timber but as aids
to the soil and the water supply. He had ideas for developing
water power all over the country by great dams and irrigation
systems and for distributing electric power and light to remote
areas at low prices. He had plans for a transcontinental through
highway with a network of feeders to serve farmers and city
folk. He had plans for a chain of small hospitals all over the
country with medical services available as the people needed
them.

The objective of all these plans was to make human life on
this planet in this generation more decent. "Decent" was the
word he often used to express what he meant by a proper, adequate, and intelligent way of living.

If the application of these and similar ideas constitute revolution, then the phrase "Roosevelt revolution," used half in jest,
may be correct. If such it was, it was a social revolution—a
revolution in living—not an economic or a political revolution.

Radicals were always getting angry at Roosevelt for not
being interested in overall economic and political changes. For
him, the economic and political measures were not the end but
the means. He was not even a vigorous anti-monopolist. Big
enterprises, if morally and socially responsible, seemed entirely
all right. Efficiency interested him only as it produced more
comforts for more people and a better standard of living. Big-
ness did not frighten him as it did many people. He would insist on moral and social responsibility for all the institutions of
human life; for the school, for the family, for business and in-

dustry, for labor, for professional services, for money management, for government—yes, even for the Church. He would
insist in his way of thinking that all of these institutions should
accept and practice a moral responsibility for making the life
of the individuals who make up the life of the common people
"more decent," and in the common people he included the rich
and the poor alike. I remember that he wanted to find a way
for well-to-do boys, as well as relief boys, to go to CCC camps
(to get the advantages of the training and democratic living).

What he cared about was improvement in people's lives. If
economic changes were necessary, he would make them, but
only to do a specific task. When he said of himself that he was
"a little to the left of center" he described accurately his thinking and feeling in political and economic matters.

PART FOUR

THE WORLD

26.

APPROACHES TO
WORLD ORDER

Early in the Roosevelt administration, an episode occurred which I include here not so much for its own importance as because it revealed an aspect of Roosevelt's mind which became of increasing significance as his activities widened to the international scene.

In 1933 we faced the problem of whether the United States should apply for membership in the International Labor Organization. The ILO was affiliated with the League of Nations but not totally integrated into the League. Some nations were members of the League without being members of the ILO, and some were members of the ILO without being members of the League.

The ILO had existed before the League of Nations. To be sure, it had been a small, not very strong organization, but it had existed as an international body and had held meetings and conferences on the Continent. Its purpose was expressed in such terms as these: to set up minimum standards to which all civilized nations would adhere with regard to hours, minimum wages, safety and sanitary conditions, and to establish the rights of individuals in industrial employment.

When the heads of States met at Versailles to draw up the treaty and the charter for the future League, it was natural that the ILO should ask for recognition and inclusion. Samuel Gompers of the American Federation of Labor, the British labor representatives, and many others had been insistent upon this. It was eventually affiliated with the League but remained independent in its organization and programs.

In 1946 some people are bewildered that this should have been considered important in the treaty negotiations. But one must remember that there had never been recognition of the working people as a group in society with separate, yet interlocking, problems. There had never been any declaration by any great power that the promotion of the welfare of the working people was a high objective of the nation and its legislative policy. It was therefore a major victory for Gompers and the British trade union leaders that at Versailles, President Wilson, Clemenceau, Lloyd George, and others gave the ILO official status.

The fact that there was an agreement among the powers to give attention to the recommendations of an agency made up of representatives of the organized workers, of the organized employers, and of governments was in itself a great step forward. So too was the conception that the approach of this agency to the governments would be through Ministries of Labor rather than through Departments of Foreign Affairs. This implied that there should be a Minister or a Department of Labor in every country, which was a new idea for some countries. It was also a recognition of the idea that the world's competitive production system, as a matter of principle, ought to rest upon fair and humane competitive practices and not upon the exploitation of labor. Previously it had been usual for prices to be based upon the cost of labor.

It is easy for Americans to understand that good labor conditions and good wages do not necessarily increase competitive prices seriously, because efficiency and high production have in this country been offsets. But efficiency in other countries had not been so intensively developed. It was not easy for Americans to realize how important to the world was this enterprise of International Labor Organization. Wilson and his principal advisers recognized it. Franklin Roosevelt, though not too much involved at Versailles, heard about the ILO. He sat in on conferences and subcommittee meetings long enough to realize that the working people of the world had a special problem. If the human race, as he often said, was to keep the peace, there must be an understanding that human beings would not be exploited.

He met Gompers, the British labor leaders, labor leaders from the Continent—working people struggling to establish their rights for a chance to live well and to express themselves politically and economically. He became aware of the importance of this international agreement on labor standards, and saw that it was vital to the new world.

The ILO had its first meeting as a universally recognized organization in Washington, in 1919. Many of us who were engaged in the improvement of labor conditions in the United States attended those meetings and felt that at last we had an international agency which would set standards and hold up ideals of sound, humane labor conditions throughout the world. How much Roosevelt followed those meetings I do not know. He knew of them and was in favor of this kind of association. In his strange way of being familiar with and an adherent of enterprises about which he was not technically well informed, he was "all for" the ILO. That became clear to me from later conversations.

I had not talked with him about the ILO in February 1933 when I had had my interview with him about proposed labor policies of the Roosevelt administration. I had passed over this item since the evening was short and there seemed to be many other programs of more immediate significance to talk about. But in the summer of 1933 I had a letter from Harold Butler, director of the ILO, urging me to take up at once the question of the adherence of the United States to the ILO.

The more I thought about it, the more important it seemed to me that the United States should become a part of the ILO. I took the matter up tentatively with Roosevelt. I said that many serious people interested in international affairs thought that the United States ought to join immediately and that we might make some contribution in that field even though we didn't belong to the League of Nations.

At once he said, "Fine, I agree, a good idea."

We talked a bit about general policies and then I said, "Mr. President, have I your permission to go ahead and prepare the way for the United States to join the ILO?"

He thought a minute and said, "Yes, certainly, *but* remember a few things. Don't try to do this without the full assent and

understanding of the members of Congress primarily responsible for foreign policy."

"But," I countered, "this is hardly foreign policy. It is just an
agreement to participate in an organization which attempts to
set labor standards on the international level. The standards it
has set thus far are actually well below what progressive states
in this country have written into their statute books."

"Remember how Wilson lost the League of Nations," he replied, "lost the opportunity for the United States to take part
in the most important international undertaking ever conceived.
He lost it by not getting Congress to participate. They have a
sense of their responsibility, and they can't have sincere convictions unless they are given a chance to examine the situation at
close range. Make sure that the men on the Senate Foreign
Relations Committee have information and convictions about
this idea of our going into the ILO."

He went on, "You know we stayed out of the ILO only because there was such terrible opposition to the League of Nations." He advised me not to get into that tangle again, not to
let the old prejudice be an obstacle to this one small aspect of
international co-operation.

"First," he said, "be sure to see Cordell Hull. Go over it all
with him and ask his advice and assistance. Remember, the
Democratic and Republican members of the Senate Foreign Relations Committee will have to come to a belief that this is a
good thing. That is something I can't do. I may be President of
the United States, I may be in favor of the ILO, but I can't do
it alone. That is a function of the Senate, and you must prepare
the way systematically and carefully. Take plenty of time about
it. Don't be discouraged. Give them ample opportunity to examine all the facts."

Then he added, with one of his pleasant, courageous smiles,
"You know you can always do this kind of thing if you only
give people time to think about it. Don't rush them. Don't press
them to do it before they are ready. Give them time to think.
The facts justify the action."

I said, "Then I have your blessing, I can go ahead?"

"We'll go in if you can win the support of the Senate Foreign
Relations Committee."

I went to see Secretary of State Hull. I had written him a memorandum in advance, stating what I wanted to see him about and giving him a brief digest of the arguments in favor of our joining.

Hull was different from Roosevelt—more deliberate, more thoughtful perhaps, more cautious. For years he had been in Congress. He was aware of all the complications that stood between the United States and international co-operation. He knew it on the political side. As a member of the Congress when it had defeated overwhelmingly Wilson's noble idea, he had seen the breakdown of human reason and aspiration in the face of bitterness, pique, and personal desire for aggrandizement.

He told me that he would like to see the United States a member of the ILO. It would be a good experience, he said, for the United States to join in a movement based on the idea of international co-operation.

I told him I had heard that there was in the files of the Department of State a report on the ILO from Prentiss Gilbert, United States Consul at Geneva. It was a careful, legalistic analysis of the difference between adherence to the ILO and to the League of Nations. Gilbert had been in close touch with the League and the ILO for many years. He had told me, when I was in Geneva in 1931, that the differences in the constitution and qualifications for membership between the two were not fully appreciated in the United States.

He had pointed out that the ILO had great strength because its membership involved not only the official representatives of the member governments but also direct representatives of the people themselves, the people affected by its decisions. In other words, it had a democratic feature which had not been established in the League. Under the constitution of the ILO, representatives from organized labor and from employers act and vote as full delegates, just as the government representatives do.

I asked Secretary Hull to look up the Gilbert report and let me know what he thought. He read it and was impressed. I had previously seen a copy, but he lent it to me and I read it again. We discussed it for several weeks.

"How shall we proceed?" I asked Secretary Hull.

He gave me one of the best pieces of advice I have ever

had. "If I were you," he said, "I would personally take a copy of this Gilbert report, confidentially, of course, to the principal members of the Senate Committee on Foreign Relations, and I would ask each of them to examine it and let me have an opinion. I feel sure that if they read it and have your recommendation, based upon this report, that the adherence of the United States to the ILO is logical and practical, they will agree."

I asked him if I might also say to such members that the Secretary of State was of the opinion that it would be a sound policy. He agreed that I might do so.

I proceeded to see principal members of the Foreign Affairs Committee: Key Pittman, Joseph Robinson, Pat Harrison, Hiram Johnson, William Borah, and J. Hamilton Lewis. I had a pleasant talk with each of these gentlemen. I left them the State Department documents and my own brief memorandum of recommendations. I left each under seal of confidence, remembering the advice of the President and the canny, shrewd ideas of Secretary Hull.

I telephoned each one from time to time to be sure that a little progress was being made. I felt quite certain that none of them were yet reading the report, but the fact that they answered with good will indicated that they would eventually read it and come to a decision.

After about three or four months I raised the question again with the President. "I think now is the time for you to press and ask them to come to a conclusion," he said.

I went to see the senators again. Republicans and Democrats agreed that it was wise for us to act at this time. They agreed to discuss it among themselves a little, and one by one I heard from them.

Senator Johnson called up and said, "I have read the report of the Consul at Geneva and I have read your memorandum. I have looked up the debates in Congress, I have analyzed the proposals, and I believe that it is perfectly possible—in fact, a good idea—for the United States to adhere to this *one* organization. It is quite clear to me that in adhering to the International Labor Organization the United States does not commit itself to the League of Nations in any way and that the two are quite separate institutions."

Senator Borah said almost the same thing. One by one the members of the Committee agreed that it would be an appropriate action for the United States.

When I reported this to Roosevelt, he said, "Fine." And with his sure sense of the right time to act, he said quickly, "Do it right now. Don't let any grass grow under your feet. Get a resolution prepared. Get Pat Harrison to introduce it and go ahead."

Senator Harrison introduced a resolution, which he knew had the President's approval, authorizing the President to apply for membership in the ILO. This resolution went through without opposition.

Roosevelt remarked later, "This is a lesson in patience. You have to give men an opportunity to understand for themselves in their own way. You can't rush them. Not in a democracy."

With the resolution passed by the Senate, it was a simple matter for the President to make formal application for membership.

The excitement in the Assembly of the ILO when it became known that the United States had taken this action was illuminating. It indicated to Roosevelt and to many other Americans how much the people of the civilized world desired our participation in every effort at international understanding and co-operation. This was heartening to Roosevelt. Moreover, because of the ease with which the Senate had passed the resolution when the influential Committee members understood the whole matter, his belief was strengthened that there was a desire on the part of the people for us to take a more active role in world affairs. This became basic in his thinking about further international co-operation.

His warm regard for the ILO remained strong, and he took time from his burdens to devote himself enthusiastically to the ILO delegates when later, in the autumn of 1941, they came to a meeting in the United States.

His willingness to sponsor this meeting was an aspect of his courage, imagination, and foresight. The world was at war.

The ILO office had been evacuated from Switzerland by John G. Winant, who was then the director. Winant had cabled me that it was essential that they get out and asked if they could come to the United States. I talked with the President. He thought it would be unwise for them to come to the United States since we had agreed to harbor the League of Nations in Princeton.

"We mustn't press the members of Congress too hard," he said. "They may think we are trying to take over an international program. The League of Nations may be all they can stand. Why can't they go somewhere else? Why not Canada?"

I arranged with McGill University in Montreal to give hospitality to the staff and headquarters of the ILO for the duration of the war. After the office was established in Montreal one began to realize how terrible was the black curtain which had fallen over Europe and how inadequate was the direction of the staff in Montreal without a conference of all the delegates.

When, in 1941, I suggested that the United States invite and sponsor a meeting of delegates, Roosevelt said at once, "I think it is a good idea. I'll tell you why. These people need to be in a free country. They need to see one another. Some of these former delegates to the ILO are hiding underground. But they will get out. There are the governments-in-exile, of course, and there are neutrals who are members of your ILO?"

I nodded.

"The Latin Americans—there are many members, aren't there?"

I nodded again.

"Well," he said, "it gives an opportunity for the people in this country and in Latin America who really have not experienced the war firsthand to learn from the delegates of countries at war what war means physically to them, and how it has interfered with all civilized standards. It will also be good for these delegates from Europe and China and India. It will start them going again to feel that even now, in the midst of war, they can plan for peace, security, and continuation of their program for improving labor conditions. Go ahead. Do the best you can."

We invited the ILO to meet under the auspices of the Government of the United States in New York City. Roosevelt could not come to these meetings, which were very successful, but agreed that we might hold the last session in the White House. This was a great experience for the delegates. To sit in the East Room and hear the President of the United States declare himself in favor of their policies and principles and promise his support and the support of the United States in the achievement of better labor conditions was a tremendous gain for them.

I remember the warmth of his personality on that occasion. After his address I introduced each member of the official delegation of each country to him by name. As he stood there leaning on the rostrum from which he had made his address, he shook hands with each one of them, repeated the name after me, smiled warmly and personally, and said, "I'm glad you came. Hope you come again. I am glad to see you."

The delegates responded to his humanity. Some regarded this meeting with Roosevelt as a high point in their lives.

Sir John Forbes Watson, an employers' representative from Great Britain, said, "I have never met a man whom I liked so much so quickly. It was a great experience. It was like a breath of fresh air to come here and meet Roosevelt when we in England have been under this constant terror and bombing and blackness."

The workers' delegate from Poland and his counterparts from Norway and from Greece, who had all literally "escaped" to get here, expressed themselves as heartened and inspired to know Roosevelt—that he cared deeply about what became of them and their people.

The remarks Roosevelt made on that occasion were so important that they were broadcast all over the world and were transmitted by the underground radios. I was later told they were heard by former ILO delegates in hiding in Belgium, France, Norway, Hungary, and Spain.

One young woman later told me how she, her brothers, parents, and neighbors heard that speech, like others, in a stable, their radio hidden under a pile of hay.

"I felt when he spoke," she told me, "that he was thinking of me, my family, and all our troubles. We truly loved him, and the United States."

The skill with which the President handled our membership in the ILO indicated the breadth of his understanding of why the United States had not joined the League of Nations after President Wilson had so completely sold the idea, not only to the people of the world, but to the rank and file of the United States. As early as 1934 it was clear that Roosevelt had thought out the necessity of involving the opposition, as well as his own party, in any ideas for participation in international affairs. The success with the ILO was to bear fruit in a broader sphere.

27.

THE WAR YEARS

For Roosevelt the war years began in September 1939 when the Germans opened their offensive against Poland, but the war problem had begun long before that for him. With the outbreak of actual fighting he never forgot that it was a world war. He hoped the United States would be a mediator; he hoped we could limit the spread of the war. But he was fully conscious of the moral responsibilities of the people of the United States. Having seen the defeat of Wilson's hope for building a structure that would prevent war, Roosevelt realized that the United States had evaded responsibility for the peace and order of the world.

Long before 1939 reports of our ambassadors and of competent, informed travelers who had had opportunities for more than superficial observation had convinced him that a war was in the making. Like many others, he felt at first that Hitler's violent statements were evidence of an hysterical attitude which would probably not end in war. But that was early. Soon, ahead of most people, I think, he became fearful of the worst.

The aggressions against the Jewish people in Germany filled him with horror. They seemed to him almost unbelievable. He was inclined to think they were the work of gangsters, like the fanatical organizations in the United States which took, in times past, a violent attitude toward one minority group or another. But continued reports from our ambassadors and from occasional refugees convinced him that this was an approved program of the German government itself. He saw that it might grow rather than decline. He saw that it was Evil rampant.

He saw some of the refugees and found that many were cul-

tured, educated people who had had social and intellectual
position in Germany. They were college professors, writers,
social workers, scientists. Because of Jewish background, possibly only one Jewish grandparent, they were persecuted and
driven out of home, job, and country. He felt great sympathy
for them. There was fierce indignation in him at the forces
perpetrating these horrors upon orderly, useful, well-behaved
human beings.

The United States was prevailingly isolationist. There had
been a long period of propaganda against being involved in
outside affairs. The picture of Evil stalking across the world
had made thousands of Americans retreat further behind the
supposed shelter of the flanking oceans. Isolationism was accompanied by a feeling against further immigration. That feeling was accentuated by the depression and the belief that we
had too many mouths to feed.

Jane Addams of Hull House in a White House visit once
said an illuminating thing to Roosevelt. She pointed out that
we had millions too many bushels of wheat, the prices had
fallen, and that the farmers on that account were poverty-
stricken. "Those bushels of wheat," she said in her gentle voice,
"I figured it out the other day, Mr. President. It is just about
what a million immigrants a year would have eaten up. I think
it is active population that is needed."

The President made a mental note of that, and he said to me
several years later, "You know, population never made a country unprosperous. Not so long as our farmers can grow enough
for that population. We may have to think of our immigration
policy in those terms some day."

This was in a conversation about permitting some immigration to relieve the strain on terrorized people in Germany. An
Executive Order against immigration handed down during the
Hoover administration was still in force. The Government had
thought then to halt additions to our unemployed population.
Roosevelt moved to make it possible to bring over people who
had relatives here to guarantee their support. He endorsed a
program to bring over orphaned and handicapped children
who had no relatives. They were to be brought with guarantees

of support, training, and upbringing by the Council of Jewish Women and also by the Hebrew Immigrant Aid and Shelter Society. This move was not too popular in some quarters, but he insisted on this clear gesture of human sympathy for the sufferings of persecuted people.

Roosevelt was avid for light on European countries that might be storm centers. In 1936, when I returned from Switzerland and Austria, I reported to the President on Geneva and the ILO meetings. The Central European delegates had painted a picture of confusion, doubt, and fear in their areas. The President questioned me closely about Austria. He wanted to know the degree of poverty, and how widely Nazi ideas were in circulation.

I told him that the simple, poor people I had seen were not Nazis, but they were so worried that they might be easy prey. They were good, religious people, but I didn't see how they would be able to resist Nazi propaganda. The Jews in Austria had seemed to be in no danger. There was no trouble with their neighbors; they were well treated in the villages; if they kept a shop, there seemed to be no boycott. Yet when the Nazis marched into Austria in the spring of 1938, some of these nice, simple Austrian village people had behaved with Nazi-like beastliness toward the local Jews.

All through the years when we were developing a program of social and economic reform on the domestic front, the specter of war and the suffering and confusion of the people of Europe were in Roosevelt's mind. I don't think he consciously said to himself that these reforms at home would make us a more united people if we had war. Yet the fact is that, quite subconsciously, he was getting us ready for grave tests.

He was developing our water power.

He was improving our highway systems.

With rural electrification carried out for the benefit of living standards in remote farm areas he made it possible to put war factories in remote rural communities.

He developed a free public employment service, and this network of three thousand offices was ready to register volunteers for various projects in time of war, and to help recruit and place the millions of industrial workers needed for war production.

The CCC camps gave reserve officers experience and hundreds of thousands of young Americans training in group cooperation and orderly living—a first step in military training.

The National Youth Administration helped young people squeezed by depression to get an education by providing work and study for them, and saved many colleges and universities from the ravages of the depression. Thus a whole generation of young people who would have missed that training because of poverty were educated. They were the core of the new officers—the industrial lead men of the war period.

With NRA he habituated American business to know and deal with the Government and to think in terms of large national policy. When we needed men in the war years, he knew, and the rest of us knew, where to get them: out of former NRA business and labor aides.

Above all, his constant insistence upon legislation for the protection of the working people won loyalty and confidence. When he asked them to step up production and to permit the stretch-out, the upgrading or dilution of labor, the unskilled to work direct with the skilled on jobs that had always been reserved for the highly skilled, the answer was yes, and the results were astonishing.

He brought about the recognition of Soviet Russia in the early days of his administration when there was no thought of war and no idea that Russia would be our ally in war. It was recognition based upon the promotion of American interests. Yet the fact that we had diplomatic relations with Russia made it possible for us, without delaying formalities, to become allies when necessary.

He began to educate his cabinet about the possibilities of war. By the time of the Spanish Civil War and the Japanese aggression in China, he had begun to inform us of trends that showed war was a possibility which must be borne in mind.

He began the education of the American people too in those years by telling them about internal political conditions in Europe and Asia.

These items, which had nothing whatever to do with preparedness for war in his mind, turned out to be an amazing preparation. I doubt that he ever realized this relationship, but it was obvious to one who looked back after we were deep in the war. His administrative officers found they had tremendous equipment to work with.

Roosevelt's diplomatic activities in attempting to prevent and limit the war can be described by others with much more competence, since I was merely a bystander and observer in this activity. But I was aware that he was deeply involved intellectually in all that was happening. There were months when his first question at every cabinet meeting was to the Secretary of State, "What's the latest on Spain? What happened in Austria?"

His Good Neighbor policy was sincerely felt, not just an affair of State. He liked the Latin-American people he had met. He always asked for the reactions of officials who went to conferences in the Latin-American countries.

When he visited Brazil, he was delighted with the atmosphere of enthusiasm and hope. On his return, he said that Brazil was firmly democratic, although the Vargas government had not been so pictured. He was impressed by the fact that people stood in the streets and shouted "Viva Democracia! Viva Democracia!"

When someone in the cabinet teased him about the revolutionary techniques so often used in Latin-American countries, he said quite naïvely, as though he had just thought of it, "Well, you know there is more than one way of establishing democratic governments. Some do it by elections the way we do, others by revolutions. It means much the same thing down there. A revolution is like an election."

After the ILO meeting in Geneva in the summer of 1938, I made a brief, solitary, and intensive trip through industrial areas in France. I talked with working people, shopkeepers, manufacturers, industrial superintendents, and petty government officials. I hesitated to draw conclusions because I was not an informed political observer; I was only an experienced social investigator. When I came home I told the President and the Secretary of State that my impression was that France would fall to pieces quickly if any enemy gave it a big punch. There was no unity. Every Frenchman hated some other Frenchman so intensely that power to act was paralyzed and capacity for right feeling atrophied. I saw no possibility of any government they could devise holding them together.

The Secretary of State, much better informed than I, nodded politely and said, "That's very interesting, but our information is quite contrary."

The President's reaction was different.

"You might be right," he said. "I know what the State Department thinks. You know, official channels of communication and information are often pretty rigid. They are bound to be based upon official sources of information. People making such studies rarely get near the common people. I don't know how it can be done. But there might be something in what you say. At least it is worth thinking about."

When the French collapsed in 1940, he said to me, "You know, I remember what you said in 1938. I don't know that I altogether agreed with you at the time. But I remembered it. Queer thing about hunches, isn't it? Sometimes they are right, and sometimes they are awful. You have to be careful how you rely on them."

With German aggression against Poland, the European war was on with a vengeance. The invasion of Denmark and Norway in the spring of 1940, followed by the blitzkrieg on the Low Countries, removed all hope of practical limitation of the war. The horrible stories of refugees fleeing before the invading armies in Belgium, Holland, and France began to pour in. Then came the tragedy and heroism of Dunkerque. The bombing of English cities began. The enormous unity of the British people was demonstrated.

Roosevelt was profoundly stirred by British courage and integrity. One saw him quickly take the position, which all right-thinking Americans were coming to, that the preservation of the British spirit as a factor in the affairs of the world was essential and that you could not let these decent people down.

Roosevelt took a personal interest in aid to the English. He told us to be sure to find old hunting guns, pistols, anything that would shoot, and see that they were shipped to England. He also suggested binoculars and opera glasses for their home guard. He felt that if the British Isles were invaded the slaughter would be so terrible that Americans would not be able to endure it, and public opinion might rush us into war long before we were adequately prepared.

I don't know just when he began to think of Lend-Lease. Others who know and helped him with it will write about that. But he saw early that economic assistance should and could be given at once to the British for the defense of European civilization.

After 1939, and particularly after the fall of France in 1940, Roosevelt was acutely aware of the necessity of preparing ourselves for the possible onslaught of war. He asked us to evaluate our departmental activities, programs, and personnel as they might bear upon a possible emergency situation.

The President had been impressed by the universal call-up in England. There every man and woman over eighteen, and in some cases younger, was called up and assigned to the job where, in the judgment of the Minister of Labor and National Service or his assistants, that individual was most needed. Military recruiting was carried on in the same way at the same time. National Service even included taking care of babies of women who had skills needed for government or industrial activity. But Roosevelt and many others forgot how small the British population was, how immediate and pressing was their problem, and how relatively short were the distances.

Many people in our Government thought in terms of universal service and a call-up. We finally registered all males from eighteen to sixty-five, and then there began a clamor from women's organizations who felt that they had been slighted. It would have been almost impossible to register them too. As a matter of fact, male registration never meant anything. No facilities or funds were made available for an analysis of the registration. The Employment Service, together with the unemployment compensation people in some districts, volunteered to do night work without pay to run some of these registrations through an analysis system and make the notations which would make the cards useful. But only a few thousand were ever tabulated or used.

On the whole, men didn't fuss that they were not immediately called up. Most of them used their wits and got the war jobs they wanted. Or they recognized that they would be called into the Army and got as good a job as they could in the meantime. But the question of registering the women continued. I felt sure that women who did not work ordinarily would be irritated if, after having gone through the patriotic, emotional crisis of registering and telling the Government all their accomplishments (and age), they were not called for special work promptly. I knew that the likelihood of their being called was very, very remote, for we had a large labor supply in this country not touched in the first years of war. In spite of the excited wringing of hands about the lack of labor, the industrial labor supply was never really depleted. The talk was part of the propaganda to urge people from non-essential work to essential work.

The women who wanted and knew how to work went out and got jobs because good jobs were available. The women who wanted to volunteer their services worked in the American Red Cross, the American Women's Voluntary Services, the Friends' Service Committee, the USO, and a variety of other activities. Those who didn't really want to do anything, didn't do anything. They were not numerous. The greatest needs for women workers were for nurses, and in the service trades— hotel and restaurant workers, laundry workers, and other uninteresting jobs. It was hard to attract and keep people in these dull but necessary occupations. As a matter of fact, five and a half million women were added to the labor force and without any actual compulsions were moved into the essential activities as needed.

One of the earliest acts indicating that the President foresaw the likelihood of war was his revival of the National Defense Council. By an Executive Order in May 1940 he declared that an emergency existed and revived this council provided for under law.

The idea of reviving the National Defense Council seemed wise to all of us. A lot of planning and thinking would be necessary. The President's ingenuity led him to make the National Defense Council the effective core. The cabinet officers who were, under the law, members of the Council, were to be on it, he said, but the Advisory Commission to the Council was to advise us and we were to do whatever they requested.

When he announced the members of the Advisory Commission, there was a mild protest from cabinet officers who thought he might have done a great deal better.

One cabinet officer spoke up to say that William Knudsen was a mighty fine manufacturer of automobiles but as an organizer of the resources of the country there were a lot of better people. The President, however, liked Bill Knudsen. He had confidence in him. The fact that he had a following and a certain amount of affection in American business life was not lost on the President. There was bound to be a willingness by business to do whatever good old Bill Knudsen asked it to do. That was the important factor in Roosevelt's decision, and he gauged it correctly.

I commented upon the President's selection of Sidney Hillman as the labor member. Hillman was an old and valued friend of mine. However, there was the split between the AF of L and the CIO, and Hillman was in the CIO, which made his name anathema in AF of L circles, which were inclined to blame him rather than John L. Lewis for the whole CIO. There was also a split brewing inside the CIO which, although not known to the public, was perfectly clear to those of us who knew the inside story. Moreover, Hillman was an officer of a rather small union not engaged in heavy industry. I strongly recommended that the President appoint two labor men, one from the CIO and one from the AF of L.

The President replied he had thought of all that and wasn't going to have two labor men; too much trouble to have two. This sounded a lot like Harry Hopkins to me.

"Anyhow," said the President, "in times like these people can't bother about their private quarrels, they just have to work together. We know Hillman to be a good man. He knows about labor development in the United States. We know he is honest and trustworthy. I am not going to bother with two labor men, and besides I haven't a place for two labor men."

I pointed out that he didn't need an economist on the Advisory Commission. He had listed Leon Henderson in that role. I said he could get Leon Henderson on loan as an adviser.

No, he had made up his mind about having an economist.

"Well," I said, "you don't absolutely need Miss Elliott."

"No, we have to have a woman," he said. "Got to pacify the women. If there is a woman, you won't have women's protests against actions that are too military, against giving too much help to the allies. The presence of a woman on the Commission will stop all that."

He was adamant. I never knew him to be so stubborn. It has always been my thought that somebody prepared the plan, sold it to him in toto, and even selected the personnel. At any rate, he went through with it and the rest of us did our part. Labor was angry but as usual came around in the end, because they loved and had confidence in the President and because the times were serious.

The appointment of the Advisory Commission of the Defense Council was the beginning of the administrative confusion which has been pointed out so often by critics of Roosevelt and his administration.

The President was drawing on the experience of the NRA. He was drawing on his knowledge that you can attract people to come temporarily into the Government and to work hard and enthusiastically for a cause, but that these people would not work for the Government in routine jobs, and they will not obey rules. He was aware that the burden of the world's work is done by the people with routine jobs, and he often said so. But he pointed out that you had to get the nation enthusiastic to bring it to top effectiveness, and in this way, with an Advisory Commission with a lot of freedom, he thought the enthusiasm could be spread. There was a lot of truth in it.

A more systematic administrator, I think, would have made fuller use first of the great resources of the Government's permanent staff. He would have made the Advisory Commission members policy consultants. Instead, as administrative officers, they invented their own jobs as they went along and had, at least in the first year, only the vaguest conception of the resources of the Government agencies which might have been made available to them if they had but asked.

The President asked me to help Hillman, and I made all of the Labor Department's resources available. In my first interview with Hillman, I suggested that, if he thought well of it, I would like to lend him Daniel Tracy, Assistant Secretary of Labor, to assure complete liaison between the Department of Labor and the Advisory Commission. I had talked to Tracy, a member of the AF of L, and had secured from him a promise that he would do his utmost, and his utmost was considerable, to get the AF of L to co-operate with Hillman.

Hillman was quick to appreciate the advantage of having Tracy as his assistant. So they proceeded, and, on the whole, a very good job was done. Tracy persuaded the AF of L to send representatives to a weekly conference with Hillman and to assist him in every possible way. The CIO also appointed its group. AF of L and CIO representatives met together, although there was so much antagonism that they used to have separate meetings as well.

Hillman began to have great influence in the Government. In addition to Tracy, I lent him Isador Lubin, head of the Bureau of Labor Statistics, a man of vast comprehension of economics and ingenuity in finding ways to do things. Hillman built up a large staff, as was almost inevitable, and some were people with their own ideas and ambitions, which, I think, was not anticipated by the President. Some made confusion and conflict within Hillman's own organization. Others developed secretive habits and tried to cut corners around old-line Government establishments, even when they were operating in the same field.

Conciliators from the Department of Labor going about their customary duties ran into bright young men sent to settle a strike from Hillman's office—often self-assigned. Often Hillman knew nothing about it. The "troubleshooters," as they called themselves, kept turning up in the most unexpected places. It wouldn't have mattered, except that we were short of people to do this work, and the customers sometimes got angry and confused over multiple advice.

Into the melee sprang the Army and Navy. The armed services appointed labor advisers and labor relations adjusters. These young men, most of them out of industry or law offices and suddenly clapped into uniform, were well meaning, and many were good. But they too would turn up, without notice, to adjust a complaint or threatened dispute. Sometimes three or four adjusters would meet in the same place. First they would glower at each other. Then it took persuasion to get them to settle things among themselves as well as with the firm. Finally, the fellow who could handle it best took over.

It was almost impossible to work out an orderly system of operation. We met again and again and signed compacts of co-operation and co-ordination, but still energetic and enthusiastic men would start off under the sole guidance of their own consciences.

Speed was so essential that people acted without sufficient reflection. Units which had jobs to perform thought to perform them without reference to any other agency of government on the theory that it would slow them down if they waited to consult. Conference does slow people down. But in the end we had to confer anyhow, just to prevent slow-downs due to misunderstanding.

A good many agencies in Washington equipped themselves with labor advisers. This was in no way the fault of the President. A well-intentioned man with a particular job to do would think of all the problems he would have to deal with and get someone to assist him on each. He thought of labor as one of the problems and tended to get himself a labor adviser. There weren't enough good labor advisers to go around. Competent labor leaders were taken away from important work in the field with their unions and brought to Washington, and as labor advisers outside their own industry and sphere of experience they often were not particularly good. There is no magic formula.

No one asked the President's advice, nor should the President have had to give advice on the details of a job someone had been asked to do. But when these labor advisers began to get into conflict and to give conflicting advice which brought the heads of their units into conflict, there was a snarl. In such cases the agency heads often would come to me. Sometimes they went to the President. Always astonished at such conflict, he would say, "Go straighten it out. See the Secretary of Labor. Confer with Hillman. Come to an agreement. That is your job, not mine."

He had a serene belief that his whole administration should work like a team and that his associates should find ways of adjusting their problems. When I once talked with him about these conflicts, about which complaints were reaching the public ear, he gave me a little philosophical dissertation.

"This is the way I have always looked at it," he said. "We have new and complex problems. We don't really know what they are. Why not establish a new agency to take over the new duty rather than saddle it on an old institution? Of course, a great many mistakes are going to be made. They are bound to be made in anything so new and enormous as supplying our allies, training our Army and Navy, and recruiting the necessary industrial reserve. Mistakes in military strategy are made. They just absorb them. There will be mistakes in domestic and supply strategy. We have to be prepared to absorb and correct them quickly. We have to be prepared to abandon bad practices that grow up out of ignorance. It seems to me it is easier to use a new agency which is not a permanent part of the structure of government. If it is not permanent, we don't get bad precedents that will carry over into the days of peace. We can do anything that needs to be done and then discard the agency when the emergency is over.

"I think that there is something to be said for this," he went on. "There is something to be said too for having a little conflict between agencies. A little rivalry is stimulating, you know. It keeps everybody going to prove that he is a better fellow than the next man. It keeps them honest too. An awful lot of money is being handled. The fact that there is somebody else in the field who knows what you are doing is a strong incentive to strict honesty.

"You take the lead," he wound up, "in getting them together and keeping them together."

That became my principal wartime job. At his direction I sat in on so many interdepartmental committees and held so many conferences that the Department of Labor had the air of a service agency for the war activities.

But the Department of Labor was not weakened during the war. It was strengthened. It got larger appropriations. Special technical duties of all sorts were assigned to it by the Congress and the President. At the President's constant insistence, all projects of investigation, inspection, and statistical analysis of labor supply and needs were carried out by the Department. At first there was a tendency on the part of the war agencies to plunge ahead on their own. Once they accepted the facilities of the older agency, however, they admitted they got good service.

I had been recommending for five years that the Immigration Service be taken out of the Department of Labor and put in some more appropriate place. During the war the opportunity came to do this. Because the main problems of immigration during the war period were the recognition and apprehension of spies and foreign agents, it seemed appropriate to move it to the Department of Justice near the FBI. The Immigration Service had for many years swamped the Labor Department. Immigration problems usually have to be decided in a few days. They involve human lives. There can be no delaying. In almost every administration the Secretary and his principal assistants had functioned chiefly in the immigration field. That is, I think, one of the reasons there had been, until the New Deal, so much neglect of the true function of the Labor Department.

The President decided to transfer the Immigration Service to Justice at least for the duration of the war. Whether that is the appropriate place for it in years to come has not been decided. I doubt that it is. It deals with human affairs and, I should say, is more properly related to the Federal Security Agency or the Department of the Interior. It should not be a permanent function of the Labor Department or the Department of Justice, and certainly not of the FBI.

As the defense industries got going in a big way in 1940 and

1941, there was an increase in strikes. One cannot even now assess any general reasons for them. They had particular causes in particular cases.

For the first time in years the supply of jobs equaled the labor supply. Fear of unemployment was not always before the workers. They were less disposed to accept conditions that did not meet their ideas of a good standard. There were also many new plants, with no body of experienced employees to provide a nucleus of wisdom and conciliation. Employers in many industries put great emphasis on young workers. This was especially true in automotive and aircraft industries. Youths just out of high school, even in high school, were hired. The presence of so many young, reckless, and inexperienced people was an invitation to disorder and irresponsible action. Such strikes proved difficult to handle. They came so quickly that experienced labor leaders often could not get to a plant in time to head them off. The Consolidated Aircraft strike was a case in point.

There were other reasons. The organization drives of the CIO and the AF of L were being waged without let-up. A great many new men were being taken into the unions, plants never touched before were being organized, and some of the strikes were for the purpose of organizing.

The irritation of the American public was growing, and it was reflected in Congress. A number of bills were introduced to box up labor unions or prohibit their right to strike or take independent economic action.

We decided that one of the best things that could be done was to set up a Board of Mediation for the defense industries, to have that Board surrounded with presidential sanction, and to give it all power possible under the law. We knew it was not possible to create a Board with authority to settle a strike by fiat. But the prestige of such a Board, which could not be reached easily and to which petitioners could come only after going through the mill of the conciliation service, might do the trick.

The President readily agreed, with this proviso—"For heaven's sake, get everybody who has any interest in it to be in agreement. The Army, Navy, Maritime Commission, everybody who ever kicks about conflicting jurisdiction. Get them all together, please, and get agreement."

I took pains to sell the idea to labor. Leaders of the AF of L and the CIO agreed that it was a good idea and that they would stand by provided they had equal membership. That meant we had to have employer membership. We were launched on a tripartite scheme for settling labor disputes, with public members as the third party.

On March 19, 1941, the President created an eleven-man National Defense Mediation Board.

Clarence Dykstra, who had been head of Selective Service and had made a considerable reputation for himself—although the Army claims it did all the work—was the President's choice for chairman. I made out a list of people for him, and it was characteristic of Roosevelt that he went over it and checked with his own pen, one, two, three, four. As the public members he picked Dykstra, William H. Davis, a New York lawyer, and Frank P. Graham, president of the University of North Carolina. The employee members were George Meany, George Harrison of the AF of L, Philip Murray, and Thomas Kennedy of the CIO. The employer members were Walter Teagle of Standard Oil, Eugene Meyer of the Washington *Post*, Cyrus Ching of the United States Rubber Company, and Roger Lapham of the Hawaiian-American Steamship Company.

With the exception of Dykstra and Lapham, they were old NRA people who knew government business and the differences between what a government officer and a private individual or institution can do. They were men whose character and ability we had had ample opportunity to observe. The fact that Roosevelt had known or heard about them when they had worked in the Government made possible a quick, safe, and easy decision.

We decided, and I agreed, that the Board had better be set up within the Office of Production Management, since it was to be a part of the defense set-up.

The Office of Production Management had emerged as the result of a reorganization of the Advisory Board of the

National Defense Council in January 1941, with William
Knudsen as Director General and Sidney Hillman as Associate
Director. Rather soon conflicts and cross purposes began
between these two and particularly between their aides and
associates. Hillman, more dynamic, more subtle, and more
radical than Knudsen, attempted to do by indirection and over-
the-telephone agreements what never would have been accomplished by direct public approaches. At one point Hillman was
trying to cancel or deny contracts for war supplies to firms
which had been found to be in violation of the National Labor
Relations Act or the Walsh-Healey Act in the past. He used
considerable pressure (perhaps justified) to impress upon particular employers the necessity of accepting his solution, issued
as a directive or advice for their labor relations problems if they
were to continue to receive government contracts.

Knudsen, who was not over-alert, acquiesced in many of
these suggestions and opposed others by indirection. Hillman
encroached gradually upon Knudsen's field, exercising great
influence with regard to the awarding and cancellation of contracts. Over-the-telephone agreements that contracts would be
continued if labor disputes were settled along the lines recommended by Hillman's organization in the OPM did develop a
certain speed in the settlement of many disputes but raised
many questions.

The tension and friction between Hillman and Knudsen developed almost from the first. The reorganization of January
1941, in which the OPM was set up within the Office of Emergency Management in the hope that Lowell Mellett would
be able to keep the peace, was succeeded in January 1942 by
another reorganization in which the War Production Board
emerged. In this case Donald Nelson was made Director of the
War Production Board and recognized as top man in that
field. Hillman was made a subordinate. Knudsen was made a
General and taken out of the management of the war program.
Hillman was made Director of the Labor Division of the War
Production Board in 1942 but soon resigned, as he had no authority. He became seriously ill of the first of a series of heart
attacks. He was a highly emotional, imaginative, driving per-

son who could hardly endure the curbs on his personal decisions which were imposed by controls of the Civil Service, the Congress, and even the President. Hillman's interests were more political than had been contemplated and his later extreme irritation and even condemnation of President Roosevelt probably began with the emotional conflict generated at this time.

He threw his energies into building up labor's political strength and political organization. He became a very astute politician, as his early training in techniques of trade union politics, which are intense, had prepared him for this kind of action and judgment.

His status had been greatly improved in the labor movement and in the community generally by Roosevelt's recognition of him. Roosevelt believed, and it certainly appeared, that his enthusiasm, and labor's enthusiasm and politics, although newly found, was an enthusiasm for Roosevelt. All the strength of the political activities which Hillman organized was thrown to the support of Roosevelt and to the Democratic ticket and to getting out the vote, but the organizations had generated considerable power. The degree to which the PAC and other political activities in the labor movement could have been relied on as a permanent support for Roosevelt is open to question. This was one of Roosevelt's personal political problems. He was sufficiently simple so that the defection of anyone always surprised him. The harshest comment that I ever heard him make about a man who "fell away" was: "He got a lot of attention from us down here. I guess his head swelled—that's all."

The war years were full not only of the war but of inner conflicts bound to arise in a situation so dynamic.

The barrage of proposed legislation to prevent strikes continued. Most proposed bills would have been absolutely impossible to administer and would have had no effect whatever. The President was shrewd enough to see this and was not taken in by the fine-sounding phrases. It was Knudsen of the Office of Production Management who first urged that the Selective Service Act be amended so that the Government could seize plants which failed to deliver goods on time. Thus, he argued, strikes could be stopped. The usefulness of such a measure was very doubtful. But the idea that the Government should have the right to seize plants if things did not go right was strong, and it continued to appear in congressional bills until, finally, it was enacted in the Smith-Connally bill.

Dykstra could not stand the pressure for legislation in and out of Congress, since his attendance was required constantly at hearings. Nor could he stand the incessant strain of sparring for position between the labor and employer members. He couldn't take the bitter denunciation and tangled problems presented to the Board by some industrial disputes. It troubled him. He resigned on June 19, and the President appointed William H. Davis as his successor. As the President said to me, "We know that Davis can take it."

The Board was useful but not long lived. The question of the closed shop raised its head at an early meeting and split the Board. By the end of July the Board was involved in the question as a principal item.

It managed to avoid definite and therefore disruptive action until October-November 1941, when the question arose in the United Mine Workers' dispute with the steel companies, in particular with United States Steel, over the captive mines, which are coal mines owned by and producing coal only for a steel company. As a matter of principle, the officers of the steel corporation said, they would not under any circumstances agree to a closed shop.

An ideological wrangle developed. Members of the Board joined in the battle with strong feeling. The final decision of the Board was no closed shop.

This roused the ire of John L. Lewis, who was not accustomed to submitting disputes to mediation and who believed that, with labor representation on the Board, he would get whatever he asked for. After only a day's consideration Murray, Kennedy, and the five CIO alternates resigned in a body, crippling the Board. Without labor membership it could not function, and labor membership was useless if it did not include CIO representatives, since many of the strikes were CIO strikes.

On November 27 the President rejected the resignation of the

CIO bloc, but it was of no avail. The Board never met again except for purely administrative duties.

The President asked me to think of something else. I racked my brain and proposed that we hold a conference of labor and employer representatives and that after the amenities we should lay before them a brief agenda and try to get agreement on principles of labor relations for the emergency period.

The President thought well of the idea. I proceeded to select the people to be asked and prepared the agenda. Then came Pearl Harbor. Fortunately, the preliminary plan for the conference had been made. We modified it a little to meet the new situation, and the President called an industry-labor conference on December 10.

The President agreed when I suggested that I should not be the presiding officer. Labor would resent it if I did not rule in their favor, and the employers certainly would resent it if I did. It occurred to us that it might be a good idea to have someone from Congress involved in this conference to take some responsibility for decisions and to be able to defend them as a method of preventing strikes. We accordingly asked Senator Thomas of Utah, chairman of the Senate Committee on Labor, to be the presiding officer.

John Lewis was sobered by the reality and horror of the sudden war and all it meant to the country. I had a preliminary talk with him and felt sure that he would agree to the establishment of a labor board to have certain functions in settling strikes during the war only. The other labor delegates felt as he did.

The employer delegates were chosen from names suggested to me by the heads of the United States Chamber of Commerce and the National Association of Manufacturers. Both the President and I were a little sensitive on this point. Some of the employers who had worked for the Government under Roosevelt's leadership had been accused by other employers of being "stooges," for the President, traitors to the employers, and "easy touches" for the Secretary of Labor. We knew, of course, that neither the Chamber of Commerce nor the National Association of Manufacturers had authority over its members and that persons they recommended could not bind any member. But we hoped that by having these people recommended by the organizations themselves, the prestige of the agreement would be such that employers would be persuaded to go along as a patriotic duty.

The conference opened in the Federal Reserve Bank's magnificent conference room, and developed into one of the most interesting ever held in Washington. Ample opportunity was given every individual present to express his opinion. Problems of labor and industry were canvassed freely. Groups were invited to lunch and dinner, and an effort was made to bring together employers and labor leaders on social, human terms so that understanding and confidence might be increased.

The conferees were invited to the White House to meet the President. John Lewis had not been in the White House for a long time, and his breaking up of the Defense Mediation Board had not endeared him there. Among the employers were, the President knew, some real Roosevelt haters. He was warm, confident, buoyant, serious, and met each delegate personally. He made an excellent speech (even though I did prepare some of it), in which he used with great effectiveness the prayer of a Chinese Christian, "Lord, reform Thy world beginning with me."

He was moving in his expression of his willingness to submerge his own hopes, ambitions, and plans in the large and desperate duty of saving our country. He persuaded them that he did not "hate" business or businessmen and he did not denounce labor for trying to win better conditions. To the businessmen, who were being asked to agree to accept the orders of a government board, a thing he knew they dreaded, he managed to convey that he would not be hard on them. They actually needed that assurance, for many believed he had been deliberately trying to "ruin" business. He asked them to give up divisive action and submerge their private interests and separate judgment to the end of our working together.

His manner was sober, sincere, frank, simple, and touched with humility. It was leadership of the highest kind, arising from common danger and a sense of human decency. It was an appeal to work together in a common cause and cancel old scores. It was such a contrast to the screaming, arrogant, aggressive leadership of the dictators who were our enemies that its effect was immediate. Everyone was obviously moved, determined to do the right thing. Many spoke to me later, agreeing that he was a changed, more potent, and dedicated personality.

I thought myself as I watched and listened to him that he *was* different. The terrible shock of Pearl Harbor, the destruction of his precious ships, the unknown hazards which war might bring to the people, the death to his hope of being the peacemaker and mediator of the world had acted like a spiritual purge and left him cleaner, simpler, more single-minded. This became his prevailing mood for the war period in which he worked so hard and made such difficult decisions. He gave himself to the need of the people for defense and victory against evil, and he asked these men of business and labor to do the same. "Lord, reform Thy world beginning with me."

The Conference labored and brought forth this action: Labor and employers pledged that there would be no strikes and no lockouts for the duration. They agreed to settle disputes by negotiation and collective bargaining and agreed to accept the aid of conciliation. They agreed that all unsettled matters on which they could not agree should be referred to a board to be appointed by the President and they agreed to be bound by its decisions.

The employer group, having met separately, insisted that no matter involving a closed shop should be referred to the new board. The labor leaders were equally determined that no such limitation should be applied.

The conference had been long—five days. Christmas was at hand. The conferees insisted that they could not agree on this one point and asked me to let them go home. We had worked nights and argued and persuaded to the point of fatigue. I remembered then that they had been told to report back to the President. I arranged for them to go to the White House in mid-afternoon.

I preceded them to tell the President about the dispute over the closed shop and to prepare him for disappointment.

"Oh, well," he said, "I can handle that. We can't expect perfection. I'll accept the three important points they *have* agreed on with thanks. I'll promise to appoint the board promptly." His right eyebrow lifted quizzically. "We'll let the board make its own rules and regulations and determine its jurisdiction."

That was exactly what he did after he heard the report of each group. He did it with such skill and so good humoredly that some did not appreciate that he had taken only the constructive part of this report and had acted on it. He had not taken sides at all but passed on to the new Board the question of whether it would consider cases involving the closed shop.

The agreement led to a War Labor Board which would work.

Be it said for the employers of America that, with few glaring exceptions, they followed this proxy promise and accepted rulings on all questions, including closed shop and union security.

I urged that the Board be an independent agency, so that it might be a court of appeals. However, we located it physically in the Department of Labor for ease of co-operation. There was always good co-operation, and although the inevitable jealousies arose among subordinates, no damage was done.

The union leaders undoubtedly took advantage of the existence of a Board to hold out for items in their contracts which they could not have won through collective bargaining. As is always the case when a Government board sits, a series of precedents was bound to develop. There gradually grew up among industry, labor, and public members of the Board a knowledge and understanding of labor relations problems that had not previously existed in American life on so broad a scale.

One can say the War Labor Board was a success. It was an emergency agency and was so regarded. It would probably be folly to attempt to operate a Board with such duties except in a war or postwar emergency. Trade unionism would be badly weakened if settlement by boards rather than by collective bargaining were to become the rule. But President Roosevelt anticipated keeping the Board alive for a while after the fighting on the battlefronts ended and during the adjustment period.

The War Labor Board cut down the number of strikes. The fact that there continued to be strikes made many commentators critical of the method. But the only way to measure the extent of the strikes is to estimate the number of man-hours lost in proportion to the man-hours worked. This proportion ran throughout the war period at something like two-tenths to four-tenths of one per cent, and we regarded it as a bad month when it rose to six-tenths of one per cent.

The pledges were kept, if imperfectly. Strikes tended to be of very brief duration and small in extent. Occasionally employers refused to obey orders or to submit cases, but these were not the rule. The Congress later backed up the Board with legislation authorizing the President to seize a plant in which there was a stoppage of work in a dispute which the board could not resolve. This was effective with employers and it became effective with workers, because the Board refused to consider their complaints in a seized shop until they had gone back to work.

For the most part, unions, after long and trying hearings— during which, it must be remembered, they continued at work— accepted and obeyed the rulings of the Board. Toward the end there were cases in which the unions defied the Board. This generated new problems which had not been resolved when the Board was abolished after the war.

The seizure of a plant as a method of enforcement is not a good technique. On the whole, it is embarrassing to the Government, and there is no way of operating such a plant except to ask those who have operated it before to continue to work under the American flag with some officer of the Government theoretically in control. Roosevelt was never perfectly satisfied with the device, but it was good enough for the moment and enabled us to get on with the war. His advice to the Army or other agents of the Government taking over a plant or a business was to be moderate.

A long-range program of legislation covering industrial rights and obligations for labor and employers may be worked out in the future. It must rely on free negotiation followed by conciliation, then by the use of special mediation boards, and finally by emergency boards. But such legislation cannot come about until after prolonged conferences between responsible groups of workers and employers, and probably can be effective in certain industries by special agreements even if not in all industries.

Once, when I laid such a systematic program before Roosevelt, he asked how long it would take to carry out.

"A couple of years," I said.

He laughed. "It's a fine idea but obviously we have to make shift during the war."

I think he was right. The labor situation worked itself out despite exaggerated headlines which kept people nervous, particularly Army and Navy procurement officers who just could not endure arguments and conversation on the subject. We delivered the goods. The situation never really got out of hand. When, in a case of desperate necessity on secret work, there was a request from Washington, which could be said to have the sanction of the President even though he did not make it himself, there was a vigorous effort on the part of the labor leaders, and the men went back to work promptly. It was the response of full confidence in Roosevelt even in a moment of disappointment. He would not ask the unnecessary sacrifice of labor.

One bill finally was passed in Congress, the Smith-Connally Act, which had for its main objective the prevention and reduction of strikes. The officers of government who would have to enforce such an act opposed it on the ground of its impracticability. It was one of the bills that required a "cooling off" period. There is a totally erroneous conception in many minds, including newspaper editors' and congressmen's, that men go out on strike because they are angry about something, "mad" at the boss or in a temper about their wages. The truth is that the number of walkouts caused by men who are in a temper is infinitesimal. If that is the reason for a walkout, as it sometimes is in small plants where social relations between the foreman and the workmen get tense, it is the easiest strike in the world to settle.

The modern strike is not based on anger, and no amount of "cooling off" does the least bit of good. Often it can properly be referred to as a heating-up period. Between the date of notice of strike and the date of walkout, leaders have the opportunity to organize and make speeches, to stir up resentments, to fortify determination, and to create enthusiasm for the walkout.

Roosevelt was not the least bit excited when this bill was denounced by labor leaders and others. His reply to a protest always was, "If it isn't any good, as you say, it will be abandoned. Congress is entitled to make an experiment. Do the best you can to carry on."

Soon after 1941 many in Washington began to worry about the inequity of men being called up for military service under a compulsory draft act while others were not called up for industrial service. There began to be talk of a universal call-up like the English system. The flow of labor supply was unequal. There were complaints of high labor turnover and of unregulated migration of labor into districts where there were unemployed people who could have been used on the war jobs and where the housing shortage made it undesirable for new workers to come in. There were also complaints of racial discrimination and complaints of unfortunate hiring practices.

This talk resolved itself into pressure on the President to create, by Executive Order, what was called the War Manpower Commission. Most of labor was opposed to it. It seemed like conscription of labor, at least in the conversation of its more extreme advocates. Harold Smith, Director of the Budget, came to the conclusion that inter-agency conflicts could best be smoothed out if a War Manpower Commission were set up. He saw in it a centralized function and thought that the Government thereby could get rid of a lot of excess personnel and activities. Paul McNutt, head of the Federal Security Agency, was in favor, provided it was established in his office, where he felt the Employment Service was just beginning to do a good job. The Army and Navy were for it in the hope that it would solve the problems of their contractors for a steady, competent, regulated, docile labor supply.

I was opposed on the ground that it was bound to create an enormous institution of government, many of whose functions would be in competition with activities of existing agencies; that it was unnecessary, and that it established a foolish and dangerous control over human beings; that the regulations would probably be more confusing than helpful; and that all we needed to do to handle the free flow of manpower into the war industries was to revive and release the Employment Service, giving it an independent status or attaching it either to the Labor Department or the War Production Board, which in January 1942 succeeded the Office of Production Management. Many others objected to a War Manpower Commission on a variety of grounds.

The President undoubtedly was confused and disturbed by this conflict of opinion among his advisers. Sam Rosenman was appointed to examine the matter and make a recommendation. Rosenman heard everybody. The ayes had it, however, and in April 1942 the War Manpower Commission was set up with Mr. McNutt as Director. On this Commission every agency of the Government with any interest in the matter was represented: War Production Board, Labor Department, Army, Navy, Social Security Board, Civil Service, Selective Service, and many others.

The War Manpower Commission served its purpose. If too much paper was distributed in the effort to cover the small things of life under specific instructions, it did not particularly matter in the long run, since the major task was done without resort to conscription of labor. Roosevelt more than once told me he was glad "we didn't have to resort to that."

The maintenance of labor standards during the war was important and difficult. The Army-Navy procurement offices were harassed by contractors who constantly claimed inability to operate with speed and efficiency under state and federal labor laws. The contractors wanted the rules taken off entirely. Unfortunately, many Army and Navy officers agreed with them, and there was an outcry to repeal all labor laws, or, if not that, to suspend them for the duration.

Some governors, anxious to show their patriotism and not always counting the costs, introduced legislation to repeal part or all of their state labor laws. There is no doubt that some sections of the Army and Navy were encouraging this trend.

Roosevelt saw the peril as soon as it was called to his attention and agreed that labor legislation, either of the states or of the Federal Government, must not be repealed. If any act interfered with a particular program in a particular factory, he agreed that we should suspend the operation of that act or limit its application temporarily, with provisions to protect the basic needs of the workers.

"We must," he said, "accept the principle which has been established for years, that the eight-hour day is the most efficient productive day for the worker. Three eight-hour shifts are the most productive scheme for machinery and the plant. Protection of workers against accidents, illness, and fatigue are vital for efficiency. Children under sixteen, certainly under fourteen, are not productive workers."

The result of his stand was that we were able eventually to stem the tide for repeal of labor legislation. We worked out a temporary scheme of variations under the wartime powers of the governors or the President. We came through the war with basic labor legislation intact. Moreover, it was proved clearly by the record that the standards for labor protection make for efficiency.

During the war Roosevelt was cut off from people more than usual. He was too busy to see them. Most people knew this and did not press him. Most of all he missed the labor people whom he had been accustomed to seeing from time to time in groups to discuss legislation or politics. It was obvious that their pleasure in his companionship was one of the elements that gave them confidence in him and kept them co-operative. John Lewis once characterized these conversations as "chit-chat." Possibly they were, but they were the basis of mutual understanding.

With his acute political mind, Roosevelt saw the importance of labor's support in the 1944 election if the war should not by that time be won. He recognized that the democratic forces in working for liberty and "decency" would need the full support of the trade unions in the postwar world. He decided to set up a consulting Labor Advisory Committee for himself. That was the Victory Committee. He enjoyed it. He had a good time talking with the labor leaders. But eventually they began to make demands which he had neither time nor energy nor full enough information to cope with. He wanted to keep it alive and did so by less frequent meetings. But the presence of so many rivals for leadership of the labor movement and their sparring for the prestige of Roosevelt's friendship were a strain. He said to me once, "We ought to keep this going in some form, for it will be a valuable instrument for straightening out things when the situation gets bad, as it may after the war."

He suffered actively from separation from the life of the people during the war. Occasionally he managed to get out among people in spite of the Secret Service's inhibiting regulations. He went to see some of the achievements of American war industry and was enormously enthusiastic about the efficiency and skill of industry. He was even more enthusiastic about the speed, skill, and precision of the workers of America. He was delighted and heartened by the warmth and affection of their spontaneous welcome to him when, unannounced and unexpected, the President of the United States turned up in the middle of the factory and said, "Hello, what are you doing?" to John Jones or Sally Smith.

The President's enlarged "war cabinet," I think, became a problem to him eventually. He began by asking to cabinet meetings various people who had undertaken special war tasks and whose presence, he thought, would bring about a spirit of co-operation. It did this to a certain extent, but there was great jealousy and maneuvering among persons not members of the official cabinet, who felt that they were doing as important war service as anyone else. One of the great Washington games for prestige is always to be seen going in and out of the White House, preferably in important company. Plenty of people have provided themselves with a passport to importance by being photographed on the steps of the entrance to the Executive Office.

The war cabinet not only became large but was made up of people not well known to one another. A strange reserve came over meetings. Less and less were confidential or important matters discussed. There had been a good many leaks. What a cabinet officer said in meeting might meet his eye in the public press the next morning, and that did not encourage him to further frank expressions of opinion. The President realized this and occasionally sent word that he wanted a meeting of just the "regular cabinet."

Henry Stimson, in his prepared statement to a Senate Investigating Committee, told of the occasion of the President's canvass of every member of his cabinet for an opinion of what ought to be done if the Japanese attacked Singapore or some other British or French base in the Pacific. He recalled that every member of the cabinet advised the President that he believed the people would regard it as an act of aggression and would expect the United States to take military action. Stimson said that this was one of the best cabinet meetings we ever had. He is quite correct. But in the early days, there had been many cabinet meetings with just that flavor of full cabinet discussion and expression on matters of policy. But as the years went on, Roosevelt's cabinet administration came to be like most previous ones—a direct relationship between a particular cabinet officer and the President in regard to his special field, with little or no participation or even information from other cabinet members. Certainly almost no "cabinet agreements" were reached. Something about our governmental form and the tensions between the legislative and executive functions seems to make fully responsible cabinet action unlikely.

The strangest cabinet meeting was the one held at eight-thirty in the evening in the President's upstairs study in the White House on December 7, 1941. Most members of the cabinet had been out of town. They had been traced by the White House telephone operators and summoned hastily. Some of them had hardly heard of Pearl Harbor and knew little of what had happened. I myself had been locked up in a room in my club in New York with my secretary, writing an important report, and had seen no one and had heard no radio when the telephone call came from the White House to tell me to be at a cabinet meeting "at eight o'clock tonight."

"What's the matter, Hacky," I asked the telephone operator, "why the cabinet meeting tonight?"

"Just the war, what's in the paper," she said and hung up.

I hastily telephoned for a plane reservation. No one at the offices of the club had heard any unusual news. The taxicab driver, taking me to the plane, said, "They said on the radio there was shooting somewhere." By the time I got to the airport there were others hurrying to get to Washington. The company was putting on extra planes. Henry Wallace and Frank Walker were there, and they did not know much more than I. Walker, I recall, had been at a Sunday School concert hearing his children perform.

We speculated quietly, out of the hearing of other passengers. We knew, the President had discussed it at the last two cabinet meetings, that a large Japanese fleet was at sea, but its destination was a matter of speculation and American intelligence incomplete. The Navy Department, speaking through Frank Knox, had seemed to believe that it might be headed for Singapore and other Malay ports. The Army had been cautious about the possibility that it might be headed for the Philippines.

Roosevelt had said, "They might be going north. That's always a possibility. To cut the Russian supply lines now would hurt the European war. Perhaps they'll entrench themselves further in the northern waters."

He had often been worried about the Japanese appearing in the Bering Straits.

Cordell Hull had contributed, with drawn face and with widespread fingers meeting in a characteristic gesture, "You can count on them to do something unexpected."

We went directly to the White House and were shown at once to the President's study, where several cabinet officers had already arrived. Knox and Stimson, tense, were studying dispatches, as was the President. New information kept coming in every few minutes.

The President nodded as we came in, but there was none of the usual cordial, personal greeting. This was one of the few occasions he couldn't muster a smile. However, he was calm, not agitated. He was concentrated; all of his mind and all of his faculties were on the one task of trying to find out what had really happened. His voice, as he told Naval aides what to reply to dispatches, was low. He wasn't wasting any energy.

After we had all come in he began to speak, without the

usual preliminaries of good fellowship. He looked down at the dispatches as he talked.

He began in a low voice, "You all know what's happened. The attack began at one o'clock [our time]. We don't know very much yet."

Someone, I think it was Francis Biddle, spoke. "Mr. President, several of us have just arrived by plane. We don't know anything except a scare headline, 'Japs Attack Pearl Harbor.' Could you tell us?"

The President asked Frank Knox to tell the story, and he told it with interpolations by Stimson, Hull, and the President.

A great change had come over the President since we had seen him on Friday. Then he had been tense, worried, trying to be optimistic as usual, but it was evident that he was carrying an awful burden of decision. The Navy on Friday had thought it likely it would be Singapore and the English ports if the Japanese fleet meant business. What should the United States do in that case? I don't know whether he had decided in his own mind; he never told us; he didn't need to. But one was conscious that night of December 7, 1941, that in spite of the terrible blow to his pride, to his faith in the Navy and its ships, and to his confidence in the American Intelligence Service, and in spite of the horror that war had actually been brought to us, he had, nevertheless, a much calmer air. His terrible moral problem had been resolved by the event.

As we went out Frank Walker said to me, "I think the Boss really feels more relief than he has had for weeks."

Roosevelt gave every evidence that he knew what to do. He refused to be panicked by public reactions and reactions in the Army and Navy.

Frank Knox told him he had decided to fly the next morning to Pearl Harbor to see for himself. The President gave his endorsement.

Then he called in the congressional leaders from both parties and told them the story briefly and simply. It was agreed that night that Congress should be asked to declare war on Japan at once. It was clear in everyone's mind that night that this was not an isolated incident of aggression but part of the Axis pattern of evil seeking to assert itself by force.

During the war years his transcending preoccupation was with the war itself. He spent more time with Army and Navy officials, as was proper, than he did with the civilian officers of government. We saw him less and tried to carry out our activities in conformity with the over-all plans and necessities of the war, as its needs were described for us from time to time in cabinet conference.

It was here that his peculiar method of administration showed itself creative. He administered by the technique of friendship, encouragement, and trust. This method of not giving direct and specific orders to his subordinates released the creative energy of many men. They looked to him for courage, for strength, for nobility of purpose, for the leadership that a democracy must have for its full effectiveness. His four-track mind proved invaluable. Without revealing war secrets from one group to another, he could keep many activities operating at top efficiency. His free system involved trust in his colleagues and a recognition of the value and capacity of every individual. I am told that this is more or less the system of combat which the American Army has encouraged. There is agreement on purpose, plan, and objectives. Then there is reliance on individual and group initiative, co-operation between units, and mutual helpfulness. To some old-fashioned European military minds it looked disorderly, but it got there.

I used to think often as I watched Roosevelt's operations with so many different elements that not only was this method effective in an emergency, when people knew they couldn't stop to quarrel over prestige, but that this American technique does not breed the corroding power out of which dictatorships are born. Many people had fragments of power which could be brought together only by mutual respect and recognition of leadership based upon a moral purpose rooted deep in the common life of our free society. The only intellectual enthusiasm which might mislead Americans into accepting a dictatorship would be an enthusiasm for efficiency itself.

Although I took no part in the planning of the war itself, I was an observer and heard in cabinet meetings Roosevelt's comments on many episodes. One thing was clear: he never lost sight of the peace throughout the war years, and at every point in the war his concern was how each victory could be woven into a pattern of permanent peace and world organization.

More than once, in discussing world organization, he pointed out that he liked the International Labor Office structure of representation, which had in its membership not only representatives of government, but also representatives of the people concerned.

I once said to him, "Isn't it possible in the new international organization to have a people's delegate from each country?"

His reply was interesting. "I don't believe it practical now. We have to work with what we have, with existing prejudices and experiences, but I hope some day that kind of thing will grow. Certainly the people as distinct from the governments ought to be drawn into every kind of international organization."

When Americans began catching up with German armies and taking prisoners, Secretary of War Stimson once said to him in cabinet meeting, "It won't be long now, Mr. President, before we shall be capturing some very important Germans, High Command generals, and any day we may run into civilians who have been the very brains of this aggression. It will be a problem, Mr. President."

Roosevelt remarked without much meditation, "Of course, there's got to be severe treatment, but I wouldn't make too much out of it. It's pretty obnoxious. Just a few drumhead trials in the field and have it over quick."

Once when a report was being made of the extremely rapid advance of General Patton's army, it was accompanied by comment that Montgomery was pretty slow in getting under way on his end of the front.

Roosevelt replied, "Well, I understand Monty never starts until he's got all the guns and all the men he needs. He never gets going until he is positive of victory. Of course, that has its good points. Patton is just the opposite, reckless, quick."

"He gets his victories without being sure in advance," put in Stimson.

"That's right," said the President. "You know I think these two are a good combination, but they will never admit it. I think it works out well to have one cautious and one reckless fellow operating on the same objective."

In view of the postwar tensions about spheres of influence and ports, it is worth recalling what he once said after his return from Teheran, "You know, I really think the Russians will go along with me about having no spheres of influence and about agreements for free ports all over the world. That is, ports which can be used freely at all times by all the allies. I think that is going to be the solution."

He felt himself on very good personal terms with Marshal Stalin. He liked him and found him extremely interesting. He regretted the language barrier, but he sent communications and cables to Stalin from time to time. I saw the exchange of cables with regard to the American desire that the Russians should join the International Labor Organization. The tone was friendly and personal. When Marshal Stalin indicated in a cable that he wished to postpone action, I suggested to Roosevelt that he press for further consideration and a definite answer.

"No, I don't want to appear to press him," Roosevelt said. "I like this man and I want to keep on good terms with him. We can talk it over later."

Commenting on the brilliance and success of the Normandy landings, Roosevelt spoke of the indispensable part played by Omaha Beach and Utah Beach, artificial harbors formed by sinking old ships filled with concrete, one on top of the other, until breakwater and protection of a rough coast were established. Without this device the landing of supplies and reinforcements would have been almost impossible.

"You know," he said, "that was Churchill's idea. Just one of those brilliant ideas that he has. He has a hundred a day and about four of them are good.

"Yes," he went on, "when he was up visiting me in Hyde Park he saw all those boats from the last war tied up in the Hudson River and in one of his great bursts of imagination he said, 'By George, we could take those ships and others like them that are good for nothing and sink them offshore to protect the landings.' I thought well of it myself and we talked about it all afternoon. The military and naval authorities were startled out of a year's growth. But Winnie is right. Great fellow, that Churchill, if you can keep up with him."

All through the war he worried about food supply to Europe

and Asia. We began to get food to England early under the Lend-Lease program, but the black curtain shrouded Europe, and we had little information about how people were faring. Shortly before the landings, through underground contacts, we began to get a good idea. Roosevelt knew, and Secretary of Agriculture Wickard frequently told him in cabinet meeting, of the imminence of famine. He foresaw the shortage of fats and cereals once the war was over and directed more than once that a reserve of fats and cereals be built up. He anticipated continuance of rationing in this country for a time after the war. "The first cargoes we send overseas must be food, and to our allies first," he would say.

He thought a good deal about the plight of the people in occupied countries and never failed to mention his concern for them and his pleasure at the reports that the American armies, at least in the beginning, tried to help them out. The Americans seemed to him the best of all possible people; not necessarily the smartest or the most powerful, although he recognized their cleverness, but the ones with more goodness per thousand of population than in other countries. By goodness, I think, he meant good-heartedness, kindliness. He hoped very much that our soldiers in liberated countries would behave in such a way as to show our best qualities.

To sum up Roosevelt's role in the war, I would say that he was the catalytic agent through whose efforts chaotic forces were brought to a point where they could be harnessed creatively. He was a creative and energizing agent rather than a careful, direct-line administrator. He trusted people to whom he gave a job to do it. If they couldn't or wouldn't or didn't, he appointed someone else or gave part of it to someone else. If he had taken the time and the energy to straighten out major and minor administrative difficulties, if he had heard judicially the complaints and arguments of all the men who thought their duties were in conflict, he would have done little else, and he would not have been able to get on with the war.

I myself spent hundreds of hours straightening out such tangles—some of them artificially created—and if the President had been doing that we should have had no leadership, no drive, no victory. His was a magnificent performance at home and abroad. His political astuteness and know-how and his courage steered relations between us, the allies, and the rest of the world into channels likely to make for permanent peace. This was his contribution, and in some strange way he had insight and genius enough to know it.

In retrospect, one wonders if the American people want to pay the price of having an extremely competent, straight-line administrator as President. It is not an administrative job, nor should it be. It is a post of political and spiritual leadership, an office through which all the people speak and make their bid for attention. A strong straight-line administrator endowed with special powers might be tempted to get the right thing done promptly and expeditiously by removing obstacles in the most efficient fashion and thus overlooking the will and true welfare of the people, since in his own mind he would be sure he was doing the right thing and the best thing for the people.

All Americans will eventually be grateful, as most of them are now, that Franklin Roosevelt, by the nature of his temperament and mentality, brought in a lot of people with differing views, ideas, and objectives; that he had no interest in generating an internally powerful administration; that he had an instinct for loose, self-directed activity on the part of many groups; and that he had the spiritual, emotional, and intellectual capacity which made it possible for him to give leadership and strength to those who had to work out the details and make the machine go.

His capacity to inspire and encourage those who had to do tough, confused, and practically impossible jobs was beyond dispute. I, and everyone else, came away from an interview with the President feeling better. It was not that he had solved my problem or given me a clear direction which I could follow blindly, but that he had made me more cheerful, stronger, more determined to do what, while I talked with him, I had clearly seen was my job and not his. It wasn't so much what he said as the spirit he conveyed. This is very important in the leadership of a democracy, where the life, freedom, and independent judgment of each unit in the land is precious and must be preserved and cultivated.

General Eisenhower, speaking in Congress at a special meeting in his honor after the European victory, used almost the perfect phrase in describing this quality in Roosevelt: "From his strength and indomitable spirit I drew constant support and confidence in the solution of my own problems."

In retrospect one is amazed at the enormous scope of the program Roosevelt led; amazed that such a prodigious amount of the war supplies should have been produced with such speed, accuracy, and high quality. That they should have been delivered with such promptness and precision in the exact places where they were needed. That a civilian Army and Navy of twelve million should have been raised, trained, outfitted; and millions of men shipped overseas ready for combat of the most difficult and unknown kind. That the patriots in occupied countries should have been contacted, equipped, and prepared to assist in the liberation of their own countries, in one of the most imaginative and statesmanlike operations in history. That the people of the United States should have been educated in their responsibilities in world affairs, not only for war but for peace. That the preparations for peacemaking should have been developed and advanced so far that preliminary international conferences for peace were held while the war was on. That the political opposition in the country was invited and prepared to participate. That without labor conscription huge battalions of workers were raised and sent to do the most hazardous work in remote and unlikely places when their services were needed. That the threat of inflation was recognized early and held back within reasonable proportions by a variety of devices acceptable to a democratic society. That an equitable system of rationing was devised and the people persuaded to accept it for the good of all. That the humanitarian instincts of the American people were harnessed for relief to people of war-devastated countries.

As one looks back on the period, one realizes that we who were administrative officers and advisers were absorbed in the administration of the details of some of these large objectives and that the confusion of having so much going on in so short a period of time led plenty of people to frantic complaints of administrative confusion. But none of us saw the whole picture, nor do we see it clearly today. It is too soon. We are too close to evaluate the details. That which seemed of first importance in December 1943 sometimes looks inconsequential today, and trifles to which we gave little attention now loom as key operations or decisions.

The miracle is that Roosevelt kept his head above the welter of administrative problems and technical adjustments and kept his eye on the objectives of highest importance. The miracle is that he managed to keep the whole machine moving in the direction which made victory possible and laid the foundation for peace.

As Quentin Reynolds once said in a brilliant address: "This enormous program must have been thought out and planned by someone. Could it have been the President?"

28.

LAST MONTHS

The 1944 campaign may have been a strain on Roosevelt, but he came back ten pounds heavier, cheerful and rested. Those of us who were close to him have often been asked whether we thought his health had begun to decline when he accepted the nomination. For myself, and I think for most of his colleagues, the answer is definitely no. No one in the cabinet had any fears for the President's health other than the natural concern for a man who was working too hard and getting too little exercise, too little rest, and too little recreation. His were the terrible, unceasing strains of wartime demands and the constant need to make decisions which would be far reaching and have favorable or disastrous consequences.

During the years he was President, Roosevelt grew older. We had all seen that. We had all grown older. His hair had grown thinner and whiter. Lines had come into his face. The difference between a sculptured portrait made of him in 1933 and one made in 1940 was striking. The face was thicker; he looked more like the Delano family, more like his uncle and his mother. He had lost that look of a slender young man which had been so becoming as late as '33 and '34. This was partly because of the sedentary life, partly because of age coming on, partly because, just as he worked hard, he ate heartily.

His appetite was vigorous. He hardly knew what he ate, but it all tasted pleasant to him and he would eat a large meal without much thought. His doctors were always trying to get him to reduce a little because his weight made it harder for him to use his braces. Every pound he could lose was clear gain.

He was subject to colds, and Washington has a very bad

climate. But everybody in the cabinet circle had colds, and most of them got put to bed for some such minor ailment from time to time. It was one of the President's little jokes that I, a "delicate woman," was never ill.

Roosevelt's health in the years of his presidency seemed to me to be definitely improved. He seemed more robust. He was always ready for fun. He seemed to have more endurance than he had when I knew him earlier and he never complained of fatigue. He was always ready for something more and he looked well and strong. He paid no attention to his handicap. He was so unconscious of it, so above it, that everybody else was unconscious of it, and it never was a source of concern. If he found his braces tiresome, nobody noticed in the least that he used a little wheel chair to move around in. He always wore his braces for formal occasions, but frequently did not wear them in the office or at cabinet meetings.

When he had a serious cold in the winter of 1944, we all knew that it was not just an ordinary cold. We knew too that he had had a touch of laryngitis a day or two before. But colds were going the round in Washington, and no one thought much about it. The illness lasted. When a week went by, then another week, and then a third week, without a cabinet meeting, we became concerned. Some of us were told that he had a really bad cold. I knew he had been for a short time in the Naval Hospital for treatment of sinus, but there had been no danger. We were greatly relieved when he reappeared, looking as though he had had a little illness but was all right again. He had had a complicated cold with bronchitis and possibly a touch of pneumonia, although one was not told and did not ask. Anyway, it was all over.

But for the first time since I had known him he did not get his strength back. He was tired, and he couldn't bear to be tired because he had important things to do. He looked paler and a trifle thinner. We all thought that would pass. When he told us he was going down to South Carolina to sit in the sun for several weeks, since the doctor said it was the only way he would get his strength back, we were all pleased; we felt he needed it.

He came back sunburnt, tanned, with better color and tone, with vigor and buoyancy restored. But he was thin. He called our attention to it with a note of pride.

"Doctor McIntire," he said, "wants me to get thin, and look, I'm a young man again. Look how flat my stomach is."

He slapped himself with a sense of glee, as many a middle-aged man does when he finds he has that boyish figure again. This was all to the good, and I confess I did not have another moment's concern about him until very near the end.

Yes, I saw the picture taken in a railroad car when he made his speech of acceptance by radio to the Democratic national convention in Chicago. I thought it was a horrible picture which exaggerated his new leanness. I thought it had been taken with a long-range lens and had been selected for publication by his enemies in newspaper offices to give the impression that he was not well. I had seen him only a few days earlier and knew he did not look like that. I still think that was photography rather than illness, for the shadows in the photograph gave an exaggerated hollowness to his cheeks.

He came through the campaign well, as I said, and looked better at its end than at its beginning. But the weeks between election and inauguration were hectic. They were weeks of great decisions in the war, with the Battle of the Bulge adding to the terrible strain and uncertainty. They were weeks in which he had to prepare himself on an infinite number of details for the Big Three meeting to which he was going. He was studying and working hard, going over a great mass of material with experts who were trying to prime him. He was trying to learn all that he would have to know so he could have it at his fingertips at the conference.

One or two cabinet meetings were omitted. It was understood that the President was very much occupied. Then we came to the cabinet meeting on the Friday afternoon before Inauguration, which was on a Saturday. When he came in I thought he looked badly, and this was the first time that I had ever thought so. I had never been alarmed by the whispering campaign that he wasn't well, and I still think that he had been well until that time. His clothes looked much too big for him. His face looked thin, his color was gray, and his eyes were dull. I think everyone in the room privately had a feeling that we must not tire him, that we must end the meeting quickly, if possible, for he still had so much to do. He was, however, gay and happy. He told us his Inauguration Day speech was going to be the shortest on record. He said it was wise to follow the advice of the Secret Service and hold the Inauguration on the south portico of the White House.

He mentioned that he would be away for some time. He never told even his cabinet on these occasions where or when he was going. If we knew individually, as a group we never knew officially.

The meeting lasted less than the usual two hours. I had a very important matter to take up with him. He had agreed, after the election, to accept my resignation. I had suggested, and we had agreed, that Inauguration Day would be a good time for it to take effect. A new appointment could then be made for the new term. I had raised the question once or twice as to when he wanted to make the announcement. He had asked me to make no announcement since he preferred to do so himself when he was ready to announce the appointment of my successor. Several times I had tried to discuss the matter of my successor. He had put me off.

"Take it up another day, will you?" he had said. "I haven't time to think about it now."

I would say, "Well, why not so and so?"

"I just don't think I want him around. I don't feel easy about him. I think there would be trouble over that man."

He talked about John G. Winant once or twice. Did I think Winant would be a good man?

I thought Winant would be fine. But would he want to take Winant away from his post as ambassador to Great Britain?

He wasn't sure, but there was somebody who wanted that post very much indeed. "Jimmy Byrnes," he said, "you know, ought to be an ambassador. I don't know, but don't you think Winant would be good?"

I repeated, "Winant would be fine if you want to take him away from Great Britain."

He did and he didn't. I kept suggesting people to him—good

people. I felt it very important that he appoint a labor person as my successor. I thought it would make for peace of mind for him. A labor man dealing in 1945 with the rising pressure of labor might take the edge off the pressure on the President. I kept recommending Daniel Tracy, Assistant Secretary. He had been extremely useful. He had developed a great deal, knew the administrative duties and problems thoroughly, and had been tried out enough so that I knew he was absolutely trustworthy. He could sit in cabinet meetings, hear State secrets and not tell, which, of course, is one of the qualifications which has to be considered in appointing cabinet officers. Dan Tracy was well liked by the CIO and AF of L. Of course, the CIO would make an objection to the appointment of an AF of L man. The President knew that and would always raise the point.

"Yes," I said, "they will make an objection, but they will accept the situation after they have made the objection."

He was doubtful, would shake his head and say, "Let's talk about it another day."

In the meantime I had told the people immediately around me in the Department of Labor so that they could be making their own plans. I packed my books and papers. Carpets were cleaned and chairs reupholstered. Everything was in readiness for a successor.

Here it was the eve of Inauguration Day. I felt something must be done, because we had agreed upon that date. I had sent him a note in the morning to remind him to tell the other members of the cabinet that this was my last meeting. It was a little courtesy he had observed when other cabinet officers retired. I felt he would make a nice little speech, the other members of the cabinet would comment on our long association, all the amenities would be observed and we would part in friendly fashion. He did nothing of the kind, so I asked to see him after cabinet. Several of us wanted to see him. Since we always waited in order of our rank, I was last, for the Secretary of Labor is the lowest ranking officer of the cabinet, not because of his subject matter but because the office was created last.

We had been in session almost two hours. It was four o'clock. The change in his appearance was marked. As I sat down beside him I had a sense of his enormous fatigue. He had the pallor, the deep gray color, of a man who had been long ill. He looked like an invalid who has been allowed to see guests for the first time and the guests had stayed too long. In a hospital a nurse would have put her arm behind him and lowered him down onto his pillow. But he was sitting in an office chair. He supported his head with his hand as though it were too much to hold it up. His lips were blue. His hand shook. I hated to press him, but I had to.

"Don't you think," I said, "I had better get Early [his press secretary] to announce my resignation right now? I'll go in and write out the announcement."

"No," he said. "Frances, you can't go now. You mustn't put this on me now. I just can't be bothered now. I can't think of anybody else, and I can't get used to anybody else. Not now! Do stay there and don't say anything. You are all right."

Then he said beautiful words which I shall always think of as our parting; he said them in a voice filled with exhaustion, and I knew that it was an effort for him to speak and that he was saying something that he felt.

"Frances, you have done awfully well. I know what you have been through. I know what you have accomplished. Thank you."

He put his hand over mine and gripped it. There were tears in our eyes.

It was all the reward that I could ever have asked—to know that he had recognized the storms and trials I had faced in developing our program, to know that he appreciated the program and thought well of it, and that he was grateful.

I could not say more, although I felt, intellectually and logically, that I ought to have insisted that the resignation go through. I could not insist. I felt I must stand by until this pressure and strain were over. I felt it would pass. When he came back, and if the war load lightened a little, the question could be opened again.

I rang for Mr. Simmons, the guard, who came and pushed the President's wheel chair into his office. I whispered to him, "See that he lies down. He is tired." I said the same thing to Grace Tully, who had also noticed that he was not looking well.

I was frightened. I had never seen him like that. When I reached my office, my face was grave. My secretary, who had known me for years, asked what was the matter. I closed the door and said, "Don't tell a soul. I must tell you, I can't stand it. The President looks terrible. I am afraid he is ill."

The next day was Inauguration Day. I dreaded it for him. But he braced up. He looked much better than he had the previous afternoon. He made his speech in a clear, ringing, forceful voice. It was short but good. It was in the Roosevelt style.

The only difference between this and other Inaugurations was that, instead of meeting all the people who came to lunch, he sat in the Red Room and saw only a few intimate friends who had come a long distance. Earlier in the morning he had attended a service of intercession and thanksgiving led by the Rector of St. John's Church in the East Room of the White House. I felt a bit easier that day. He still had recuperative powers.

On Sunday morning I had breakfast with the Wallaces. When Henry left the room, Ilo, his wife, said, "Did you take a good look at the President yesterday?"

I nodded.

"You know," she said, "I haven't seen him for several months. I was frightened. He looked so badly. Are you sure he is well?"

I put my finger to my lips, and she put her finger to her lips. We knew we must not talk about it.

He went to Yalta, a hard trip although he had his usual rest on the ship, which he liked so much. He visited Malta. He went through the experience of having his beloved "Pa" Watson, his secretary and aide, suffer a stroke at Yalta, and he had to look after him and see that he was taken to the best place for care. On the way home Watson died on shipboard.

The President paused in the Mediterranean and met the Kings of the Middle East and discussed their problems with them. There seemed to be no load too great for him to bear, and he enjoyed life at sea at all times. Anna Boettiger, his daughter, was with him. She had gone expressly as a kind of authoritative secretary who could reduce the number and length of exhausting conversations. He returned from that cruise looking fit and fine. When he came into the Speaker's room at the Capitol the day after attending funeral services for "Pa" Watson, the cabinet was gathered to greet him. His face was gay, his eyes were bright, his skin was a good color again. He looked as though he had put on a little weight. He was not apparently exhausted and thin, as we remembered him before his trip. I remember saying to myself, "That Roosevelt man is a wonder. He gets tired, but just give him a little rest and a sea voyage and he comes right up again."

He asked Congress's permission to sit, so that he would not fatigue himself by standing on his braces. This was the first time he had ever mentioned his affliction or asked any quarter on account of it. He did it with such a casual, debonair manner, without self-pity or strain, that the episode lost any grim quality and left everybody quite comfortable. It was one more spiritual inner victory for him in his long adjustment. His speech was good. His delivery and appearance were those of a man in good health. All of us, I think, felt that whatever unspoken fears we might have had were dissipated.

We saw him a number of times before he went to Warm Springs. I saw him, as a matter of fact, the day before he went to Warm Springs, where he was going to prepare both his Jefferson Day speech and his opening address for the United Nations conference in San Francisco. He talked to every member of the cabinet briefly, to check up on business matters and give his opinion or approval of various projects. I saw him for fifteen or twenty minutes to go over a list of small matters.

Among other things, I asked him if, in the middle of May, I could bring in a delegation of people who would be conferring in Washington on matters having to do with the extension of labor legislation at the next session of Congress. It always helped them to have his blessing. I promised the meeting would be very short.

"I can't do that," he said. "I am going out to San Francisco to open the meeting, make my speech, and receive the delegates in a social and personal way.

"Then," he said in a whisper, "we are going to England. Eleanor and I are going to make a State visit."

I expressed some astonishment.

"Yes, it is planned." He spoke with a sense of pleasure and anticipation. "I have long wanted to do it. I want to see the British people myself. Eleanor's visit in wartime was a great success. I mean a success for her and for me so that we understood more about their problems. I think they liked her too. But I want to go. We owe it as a return visit, and this seems to be the best time to go. It is going to be all right. I told Eleanor to order her clothes and get some fine ones so that she will make a really handsome appearance."

I made a mild protest. "But the war! I don't think you ought to go. It is dangerous. The Germans will get after you."

Although we were alone in the room, he put his hand to the side of his mouth and whispered, "The war in Europe will be over by the end of May."

It comforts me to know that he was so sure, two weeks before his death, that the end of the war was at hand.

Index

National Labor Relations Board
      (NLRB), 167–68, 228–34,
      252
   genesis of, 223, 228
   personnel of, 232–33
   upheld by Supreme Court,
      245
National Recovery
      Administration (NRA),
      117, 166, 167, 189–203,
      204–6, 212, 221–23,
      224–31, 237–46, 258,
      259, 260, 262, 336, 342
   administrative difficulties,
      201
   advisory committees, 197–98
   constitutional problems,
      237–43
   educational value of,
      200–201, 246, 336
   enforcement of, 200
   experiments in social
      adjustment under,
      199–200
   genesis of, 189–91
   Labor Advisory Board, 204,
      206, 222, 225, 236
   personnel of, 198–99
   procedures under, 199
   stimulus to collective
      bargaining, 243–44
   structure of, 196, 202
National Re-employment
      Service, 171
National registration, 339–40
National Service, British, 339
National unity, 113, 114
National Youth Administration,
      336
Navy Department, 363
Nazis, 335
   philosophy of, 140, 141, 335

Nelson, Donald, 84, 349
Newcombe, Josiah, 13
New Deal, 109, 115, 117, 124,
      129, 131, 150, 158–68, 235
   agencies of. *See* U.S.
      Government, New Deal
      agencies
   development of program, 165
   genesis of, 158, 165–66
   legislation, 144–45, 167–68,
      170, 191, 228–32,
      242–54, 261–62, 286
"New Freedom" program, 15
New York State Conservation
      Department, 160
New York State Department of
      Education, 160
New York State Department of
      Labor, 54, 56, 58, 92
New York State Department of
      Public Welfare, 160
New York State Employment
      Service, 89, 160
New York State Health
      Department, 160
New York State Industrial
      Board, 54, 57
New York State Industrial
      Commissioner, 54–58,
      144
New York State relief program,
      177–78
New York State Temporary
      Emergency Relief
      Administration, 175
New York Times, 92
Niles, David K., 178
NLRB. *See* National Labor
      Relations Board
Norton, Mary, 247, 248–51
NRA. *See* National Recovery
      Administration